# AN INTRODUCTION TO MEANING AND PURPOSE IN ANALYTICAL PSYCHOLOGY

The question of meaning is a central one in Analytical Psychology. Human suffering can result from meaning disorders both at an individual and a cultural level, and people often fail to find meaning through religion or philosophy. How can analytical psychology help us to find individual meaning and social purpose?

*An Introduction to Meaning and Purpose in Analytical Psychology* is a highly original take on the fundamentalist theories of psychoanalysis, and encompasses other disciplines such as cognitive psychology, developmental theory, ecology, linguistics, literature, politics and religion. Dale Mathers presents the basic insights of analytical psychology as a set of useful tools to examine answers to fundamental questions of meaning, using a wide range of clinical examples. By achieving a sense of individual meaning, it can become possible for people to find their own creative purposes.

*An Introduction to Meaning and Purpose in Analytical Psychology* will be useful for those in professions such as therapy, counselling, psychiatry or those involved with religious explorations or society and social change.

**Dale Mathers** is a psychiatrist, humanistic psychotherapist and analytical psychologist in private practice in London. He teaches at several analytic schools in the UK and Europe. He directed the Student Counselling Service, London School of Economics, and did research on addiction.

# AN INTRODUCTION TO MEANING AND PURPOSE IN ANALYTICAL PSYCHOLOGY

*Dale Mathers*

First published 2001
by Brunner-Routledge
27 Church Road, Hove, East Sussex BN3 2FA

Simultaneously published in the USA and Canada
by Taylor & Francis Inc
325 Chestnut Street, Philadelphia PA 19106

*Brunner-Routledge is an imprint of the Taylor & Francis Group*

Typeset in Times by RefineCatch Limited, Bungay, Suffolk
Printed and bound in Great Britain by
TJ International Ltd, Padstow, Cornwall

*British Library Cataloguing in Publication Data*
A catalogue record for this book is available from the British Library

*Library of Congress Cataloging-in-Publication Data*
Mathers, Dale, 1955–
An introduction to meaning and purpose in analytical psychology /
Dale Mathers.
p. cm.
Includes bibliographical references and index.
ISBN 0–415–20768–1 – ISBN 0–415–20769–X (pbk.)
1. Psychoanalysis. 2. Meaning (Psychology) I. Title.
BF173.M35686 2001
1510.19′5 – dc21

00–069664

ISBN 0–415–20768–1 (hbk)
ISBN 0–415–20769–X (pbk)

TO CAROLA

# CONTENTS

# CONTENTS

# SPECIFICALLY HUMAN
# MEANING

*A Foreword by Polly Young-Eisendrath, Ph.D.*

> Your worst enemy cannot harm you
> As much as your own thoughts,
> Unguarded.
> (The Dhammapada, Byrom 1993: 13)

We now seem to have all but forgotten one of the key concepts from the foundations of developmental psychology: that we humans are capable of understanding and imagining experiences that we have not had. This is called 'decentering' from our ego perspective. We are also able to communicate what we imagine even to someone who did not have that image ever before. In this way, we are different from other animals. Many other species may have symbols and languages for communication among themselves, but only humans have the ability to see, think about, and theorize actual places and events they have never encountered, to imagine themselves into worlds that are too small to be examined by even the most technically enhanced human eye, or so alien or infinite as to be literally unreachable.

This form of specifically *human* intelligence is both our greatest gift and our saddest curse. It is a gift because it allows us to imagine ourselves into other people, places, and beings that can bring us expansive compassion or extraordinary achievement. Most functional adults are capable of some empathic connection with the ill, the insane, the bizarre and the virtuous. We also travel to outer space, investigate black holes and superstrings, describe science fiction worlds that are the opposite of ours, fly over the ocean, and explore the bottom of the sea. On the other hand, our decentering is a kind of curse because it can lead us to abstract ourselves far away from the consequences of our actions. We invent weapons of mass destruction, promote personal wealth and comfort beyond any pragmatic usefulness, divorce the means from the ends in our behavior, and forget that we depend on other people and organisms for our very sustenance on a moment-to-moment basis. In other words, we can epitomize a kind of evil power and imagine that we are wholly exempt from the effects of it. We can abstract ourselves out of the immediate context for both good and ill to ourselves and others.

This uniquely human capacity for abstraction is almost never mentioned in current debates about human meaning. Since the advent of what I call 'the myth of biological salvation' – biological ideology as a means of feeling safe from misery and humiliation – we have tended to reduce human meaning to various 'strategies of adaptation.' These are then compared with the behavior of other animals and/or explained through some imagined calculus of genes and environment. We in the helping professions seem to have chosen this particular historical moment to reduce human meaning to biological ideology. Looked at as a kind of decentering, the contemporary myth of biological salvation is a narrowing of our imagination to portray ourselves as *less* complex than we are, reducing the person to process, organism, interactive systems without intention or desire or imagination.

In psychology and psychiatry especially, this collapse of human meaning into images and descriptions of reactive processes, has set us adrift. Those of us who work therapeutically with individuals, relationships, families, groups and communities to alleviate human suffering, may have forgotten how to reason about human meaning. We may have forgotten how to ask questions about intentions, to examine motivations, to look at personal history in terms of its patterns over a lifetime, and so on. The myth of biological salvation dictates that the human services will pose questions that lead to biological answers, will want to understand clients and patients only in order to give medication or brief manipulative interventions.

With the exception of those individuals with specific training in depth psychology – psychoanalysis or analytical psychology or narrative theory – most contemporary psychotherapists and counselors now feel hopeless and overwhelmed if they cannot 'do something' immediate and material for someone who is suffering. The notion of intentionally entering into the meaning system of a suffering person, in order to understand how and why it is shaped as it is, is ridiculed by those people who espouse the myth of biological salvation. Not only is such therapeutic decentering called 'scientifically ungrounded' (without any understanding of the science that backs it) by the medical and pharmaceutical industry, but it is trivialized and demeaned by popular media and professionals. This is a loss, a forgetting, of knowledge that has clear scientific underpinnings, the kind of knowledge that allows us to remember who we are.

The contemporary mythology of 'genes and environments' is but another human narrative of powers that we do not understand, but hope to control. Its particular strength may be the eventual mapping of certain kinds of life systems and diseases, if the power motives of biologists, and others with a financial stake in the business, can actually be constrained enough to make the field ultimately useful. The Harvard geneticist and zoologist Lewontin (2000) warns that 'A consequence of the intermediate size and internal heterogeneity of living organisms is that they are the nexus of a very large number of weakly determining forces' (92). And 'An organism's life consists of constant mid-course corrections' (93). To be effective as a model of adaptation and change, the myth of biological salvation will have to accept the constraints of biological meaning. Organisms occupy a different niche in physical reality than do simpler physical and chemical processes. Organisms are internally heterogeneous and open systems. Hence, they are not as predictable as simpler processes. *If* the narrative of biological salvation can accurately chart actual living systems, then its strength will be in the mapping of those systems. The greatest weakness of this myth as a world-view is, however, that it offers no personal meaning, no methods for examining the specific questions of a person's life (e.g. Why do I suffer? What's wrong with my relationship? How can I sustain a sense of hope in the face of struggle?).

Different from the other two most recent Western mythologies – humanism and theism – the myth of biological salvation has little to offer in the way of principles, value systems, or guides to moral responsibility. Consequently, people cannot find a compass of personal direction and meaning when they think of themselves as organisms – inheriting depression, being plagued by ADD, suffering from bipolar disorder, or driven to other forms of distraction, such as addictions. It seems to me that pressure is mounting to find a way to help with human suffering that is scientifically defensible as well as spiritually grounded. Such a path would be supported by what we have come to know of a specifically human life, the type of life in which anything is imaginable while many constraints are always present. Such a path would draw on psychology, linguistics, anthropology, economics, and history as the important *human sciences*, although it could also be grounded in the natural sciences, especially biology, without being reductive to those sciences of less complex events and organisms.

Dale Mathers has given us a map for just such a path in *Meaning and Purpose in Analytical Psychology*. With his extraordinary wealth of knowledge, Dale integrates the most important and helpful insights from systems theory, linguistics, semantic theory, constructivism, developmental psychology, psychodynamic psychology, psychotherapy, psychoanalysis, analytical psychology, and medicine. And he does all of this with consistent humor and engagement. Along the way, he even tells us about himself and his work with his patients! In providing such a comprehensive picture of the importance of human meaning in the transformation of human suffering, Dale never loses his way in a maze of contradictory facts. Instead, he functions as a trustworthy guide for the reader who can look back over a line of argument and see its consistency. This is a really important book for those people who are in the business of transforming suffering into meaning and purpose. Who among us is not in that business? Those of us who get paid for it should not miss out on following a groundbreaking new path with the help of Dale Mathers. It is my hope that my brief remarks here have clarified the context, and cultural moment, in which this important book has emerged.

Polly Young-Eisendrath, Ph.D.
Montpelier, Vermont
2001

# References

Byrom (1993). *Dhammapada: The Sayings of the Buddha*. Boston, MA: Shambhala Press.

Lewontin, R. (2000) *The Triple Helix: Gene, Organism, and Environment*. Cambridge, MA: Harvard University Press.

# PREFACE

Sharing in a person's search for meaning brings intimacy, increases mutual respect, and deepens integrity. It may help us recognise and accept the causes of suffering and wish to seek the means of their cessation. Meaning is a central concept in analytical psychology, examined in depth by Jung's close colleague Aniela Jaffe in 1970 who said any search for meaning ultimately leads into an inner realm, and becomes a mystical experience.

In this approach to meaning and purpose a central concept is *between*, my name for the liminal places where meaning condenses, at our thresholds of awareness; doorways into the misty space-time between patient and analyst mirror the space between ego and Self, Self and collective. I will explore how this space is boundaried and what controls the flow of information through it. As children, we understand what a thing is for when we can see what it does, when we can play with it. If playing with meaning is disordered, then our capacity to reality test, to orient in space-time, to form and use symbols, to communicate between ego and Self, Self and other becomes dis-eased. If meaning cannot change easily, meaning-making systems in the psyche tend to premature closure, creating meaning disorders.

Meaning is, by its nature, fluent and ever-changing. Change involves *not knowing*, tolerating uncertainty. Changing a meaning may, coincidentally, relieve 'dis-ease'. However, perhaps some suffering is beyond meaning: we can't make sense of the senseless. However, if facing unendurable suffering, we can stop searching for meaning. It may take years to accept we don't know why *it* happened to us, and nobody can know – indeed, sometimes, *not knowing* is the best answer.

*Not knowing* is a paradox. Meaning has theoretical limits, and, paradoxically, we cannot know what they are, as meaning is an open system. Like a quantum electron – the more we define one of its properties (mass, velocity or position) the less we can define any other. This clinical text re-presents analytical psychology from the vertex of meaning. I hope you will find 'Meaning and purpose' are useful concepts in ordinary down-to-earth therapeutic work, in assessment, and in forming diagnostic and prescriptive tools. I have tried to apply this theoretical re-framing to what goes on in therapeutic interactions, to what is meant by the transference of expectation of relationship from the past into the here and now.

Chambers dictionary says 'To analyse' means 'to discover the general principle underlying an individual phenomenon by resolving it into its component parts', that is, to move from the complex to the simple, to find underlying forms beneath overarching content, finding a repeating, fractal pattern in Chaos. Fractals are 'shape and structure with a special pattern of regularity in their seeming randomness, a self-similarity, in that at whatever magnification these structures are viewed they still look much the same' (Bullock and Trombley 1999: 334). The patterns of a fern's leaves or frost on a windowpane are fractals and so is a coastline. The cover shows a fractal, produced by mapping points generated by the Mandelbrot Set (named after the Polish mathematician Benoit Mandelbrot). A fractal shape, like a coastline, and like meaning, retains self-similarity: no matter under what magnification it's seen. (Gleick 1987: 161–2) Patterns remain the same, though the scale changes. As order emerges from chaos, meaning forms.

Like Yin and Yang, good and evil, day and night, *solis* and *luna*, man and woman, it isn't possible to say where one concept changes into its opposite. We negotiate fractal boundaries for meaning *between* Self and other. We move to and fro across such boundaries during analysis, recognising patterns. Take 'early infant experiences' as being a 'temporal fractal' – for infants, like the systems studied by Mandelbrot (Gleick 1987: 83–118), also show 'exquisite sensitivity to initial conditions'. Very small changes near birth can have momentous lifetime consequences.

The child analyst Donald Winnicott wisely said 'There's no such thing as a baby'; perhaps there's also 'no such thing as a meaning'? Perhaps the purpose of meaning is to permit fluent negotiation between different parts of the psyche and between the individuals and the collective to which we belong. Perhaps the purpose of this study of epistemology (how we know things) is to allow us to discover wisdom – what to do when we do not know – or, as there are no answers, to ask ourselves better questions about meaning and purpose.

# ACKNOWLEDGEMENTS

To my patients who taught me the healing value of meaning, and whose fictionalised accounts appear here with their suggested improvements and consent. Many friends and colleagues helped me develop these ideas, suggested and contributed lines of research, and gave criticism and support. I would like to thank:

Angie Bray, Jane Buckley, Serge Beddington-Behrens, Derek Bolton, Ann Casement, Moira Duckworth, Jolyon Dupuy, Claudia Grimm, David Freeman, Patricia Hughes, Richard Huxley, Will Longden, Tobe MacCallum, Alasdair Mathers, Marilyn Mathew, Will Meredith-Owen, Mel Miller, Kate Newton, Mary Priest-Cobern, Tore Sodermark, Martin Stone, Yvette Weiner, Carl Williams, Ruth Windle and Hindle Zinkin. My friends from Mid Wales (the Rainbow Dragons), and at the Buddhist Society gave me space and time to reflect. Polly Young-Eisendrath gave wise advice, and has kindly written the Foreword to this book. A special thanks to Rosemary Gordon, who taught me to value open meaning systems; to Andrew Samuels, for the initial vision for this book, his editorial skills, patience and friendship; to my children, Joe and Rosie for loving kindness, and most especially to my dear friend Carola, for her strength and support.

Permission to quote from the following works is gratefully acknowledged:

*Cautionary Verses* by Hilaire Belloc, published by Random House UK limited: copyright the estate of Hilaire Belloc, Peters Fraser and Dunlop Group, Limited.

*The Western Lands* by William Burroughs, published by Macmillan.

'i like my body when it is with your' is reprinted from *Complete Poems 1904–1962*, by E. E. Cummings, edited by George J. Firmage, by permission of W. W. Norton & Company. Copyright 1991 by the Trustees for the E. E. Cummings Trust and George James Firmage.

*The Collected Works of C. G. Jung*, USA copyright, Princeton University Press.

C.G. Jung (1936) *Dream symbols of the individuation process*, transcript of the seminar held at Bailey Island, Maine 20–25 September, by kind permission of Ms. Joanna Renouf.

*A Wizard of Earthsea* by Ursula K. Le Guin, published by Puffin Books, by permission of Theo Le Guin, the Le Guin Childrens' Intervivos Trust.

*The Silver Chair*, by C.S. Lewis, published by Puffin Books, by permission of the C.S. Lewis Co. Ltd.

*Karma and individuation: the boy with no face* by Dale Mathers, first published in the *BAP Journal*, London, by permission of the editors.

*Northern Lights* by Philip Pullman, published by Scholastic Books.

*The Adventures of Tom Sawyer and Huckleberry Finn* by Mark Twain, published by Everyman, copyright The Random House Archive and Library.

# 1

# BETWEEN

In between, there are Doors.
(William Blake, *Songs of Innocence and Experience*, 1977)

## Doors

Meaning is hidden in the ajar, in liminal places and people, in errors, margin notes, frayed edges – when we open to each other, where we play, when we play. Meaning is a property of play rather than a property of a thing, a property of a system changing. If a signal is either on or off, its meaning is either zero or one. Unchanging stimuli cease to attract attention. If a note oscillates, as frequency or amplitude modulate, or a screen changes colour, then information is carried.

Open doors invite in, invite others to join us, carry risks of invasion and intrusion. Closed doors give safety, keep out, carry risks of isolation. Is mental dis-ease a door left too wide open, or a door not open enough? Examining how meaning is made can open closed doors, can insert doors where none existed, can give psychological space for new meanings.

Meaning in an open system is a fluent form, it changes, yet keeps *self-similarity*: like a waterfall, a candle, or the leaves on a tree, patterns of meaning remain constant; a tree keeps its 'treeness', a flame its' 'flameness' whilst the particles making them up change constantly. Meaning has a fluent, engaging, negotiable, experience-near quality as it arises between people. It is intersubjective, requiring (at least) twoness: whether the two be ego/Self, me/you, my group/your group, infant/mother, Cowboy/Indian or Freudian/Jungian.

Purpose, by contrast, is a defining characteristic of a closed system. Life is such a system, having direction *between* where we begin as newborn infants and where we end, in death. With a sense of wonder children ask why . . . what does life mean? . . . how does meaning come into being between me and my mother, me and my family, between the archetypal stuff in my genes and me as I am

1

now? What is 'meaning' made of? What tools do I use to make it . . . what can I do with it? What is the purpose of meaning? What is it for?

I remember vividly a snail I met, aged three, peering at me with its eyes on stalks. I recall my awe at being studied so closely by another living being. All beings are systems within ecosystems, opening and closing repeatedly yet 'I have seen many people die because life for them was not worth living. From this I conclude that the question of life's meaning is the most urgent question of all' (Camus 1970). This involves respectful pluralistic dialogue, as between myself and the snail.

Q: 'What do you consider the greatest threat at present to individual freedom and liberty?'

A: 'The rise of fundamentalism of all kinds. Contrary to received wisdom of the moment, I believe we should oppose all forms of moral absolutism. The simplest way to define fundamentalism is as a refusal of dialogue – the assertion that only one way of life is authentic or valid. Dialogue is the very condition of a successful pluralistic order.'

(Giddens 1997)

Or, as Jung said, contrasting theory with dogma:

> For a certain type of intellectual mediocrity characterised by enlightened rationalism, a scientific theory that simplifies matters is a very good means of defence because of the tremendous faith modern man has in anything which bears the label 'scientific'. Such a label sets your mind at rest immediately, almost as well as 'Roma locuta causa finita: Rome has spoken, the matter is settled.' In itself, any scientific theory, no matter how subtle, has, I think, less value from the standpoint of psychological truth than religious dogma, for the simple reason that a theory is necessarily highly abstract and exclusively rational, whereas dogma expresses an irrational whole by means of imagery. This guarantees a far better rendering of an irrational fact like the psyche.
>
> (Jung, *Collected Works* (*CW*) 11: para. 81)

Searching for purpose, asking what is life for, is a common experience. Once upon a time, as children, we all asked such open questions. Unfortunately, as we 'grow up' we seem to forget. In Douglas Adam's Sci-Fi classic *The Hitch Hiker's Guide to the Galaxy* (1979: 125–30, 134–5) the mightiest computer in the universe, Deep Thought, labours for millennia to answer the question, 'What is the meaning of life?' Eventually, it says '42'. No-one can answer questions of ultimate meaning. As Jung's secretary Aniela Jaffe (1970) suggested in an earlier exploration of this field, 'meaning' may itself be a collective myth, intrinsic to language.

Meaning is an *act of communication*, rather than a *communication*. As the sixties pundit Marshal McLuhan said, 'the medium is the message': form is more important than content. Reviewing Jaffe's idea of myth as a field of meaning with 'new technology' may let us learn to deconstruct meaning, our own or another's. The technology I am going to use is semantics, the science of meaning, and systems theory. Using these tools we may learn to take analytic theoretical myths and dogmas apart, maybe learning new ways to validate analysis, or, if not, just learn how to ask better questions.

Analysts are paid for an ability to name percepts. It is an art and a craft, and not a science. And, like artists and craftspeople, we use sciences (like medicine, psychology, anthropology, sociology and semiotics). Agreement on naming percepts defines the form of analysis: in clinical practice, the first step in its' transforming work is naming the problem. Years may be needed to establish the trust necessary for this to happen. As the old joke says,

*Q:*   How many analysts does it take to change a light bulb?
*A:*   Only one, but the light bulb has to want to change.

Change is an inevitable consequence of movement through time. Perhaps, like the archetypal psychologist James Hillman (in Hillman and Ventura 1992) we hope a magic combination of therapy and theory may make the world a more human, better place? A child-like hope? Yes! To explore meaning, we need to play. So, analysis is play? Yes! If therapy is what happens when two people are together in a room and both get help, then a therapeutic purpose of analysis is for both participants to become 'better'. But 'better' at what?

Here's a word-play with 'better'. Everyone gets sad, knows pain and soul-searing distress. Does 'better' mean 'better than I feel when I feel like that?' Well, no. Nothing and no-one could or should stop such feelings, they're human. How about 'better' meaning 'able to change the rate of change of meaning, to speed up or slow down the meaning-making process'? or, 'able to devise new meanings from percepts' or, 'able to share my percepts more openly with others, to reality test, to obtain collective validation . . .' or, simply, 'to feel *more* . . .'. You may or may not agree, but you're playing with an idea. As philosopher Anthony Kenny points out, what 'better' (goodness) means can vary:

> The criteria for the goodness of a thing depends on the nature of the thing in question: an earthworm who does well the things earthworms do is a good earthworm, no matter whether anybody wants an earthworm or not. The criteria for the goodness of a state of affairs depend upon what people want: good weather is not weather which is good of its kind, or which does well the things which weather does, but weather which enables you to do well whatever it is you want to do.
>
> (Kenny 1963: 221)

As we build meaning in sharing this text, we share naming percepts. This allows new meaning and purpose to emerge. When we play with meaning, change occurs in the collective and ourselves. New questions arise: for instance, what is the purpose of meaning?

## Ego, Self and meaning

Exploring meaning in depth psychology is cursed by attributing reality to abstractions, concepts with no existence in space-time. That process, called reification, is a form of premature closure. To talk about the imaginary and symbolic as if they are real gives a comforting, protective illusion that we know what we're talking about. It's like pulling the bedclothes over our heads as children, hoping that the dark, unknown and mysterious will just go away. We can't open our heads and find Self or ego. They don't show up on even the most sophisticated brain scans. They are explaining devices (heuristics), invented to give ways of talking about differing modes of perception. Time-bound perception is called egoic, time-free perception is called Self (Weiner 1996 and see Chapter 7).

If we can't tell Self from other and are in a time-free state of psychic fusion then we can't make our own meaning: 'I' doesn't exist, Self has to open for it to do so. For, if everything means the same, there is zero meaning: if there is zero meaning, we feel like a zero (we're depressed). Then things mean only one thing; for example, 'it's my fault'. We may get explosively angry all the time, or implode into a 'no-meaning' disorder, or, to compensate, become inflated, grandiose, manic – projecting our own meaning everywhere, unable to see anyone else's.

Competing theories (analytical myth-systems) describe such events. But asking 'Is depression caused by maternal deprivation, low serotonin levels in the limbic system or the unfolding of archetypal patterns?', is like asking who makes the music in a rock band – front row (lead guitar and singer) or back line (drum 'n bass)? Each do, both do, all do, some do, and sometimes none do! A rock band, a crowd (even a Chinese Menu) are like Self – holistic units made of different parts with different functions. Ego is like one individual musician, hearing things from their point of view.

Ego and Self form a system. The words describe boundary phenomena, not real things. The boundary is between functions, not between structures. Sometimes boundaries between Self and ego, Self and other are so fragile we fragment, we can't play our own instrument or hear others' music. If we can't tell Self from outside world we may become paranoid: literally 'beside the Self' (Greek: παρα, para. – beside; voιoσ, noios – Self). In a (fictional) two-part system, movement of information from Self to ego does not equal movement from ego to Self. The first movement describes a large a-temporal information system downloading to a smaller one (as from Internet Server to terminal), the second a small temporal system uploading. Imagine the first as 'God calling Moses out of the burning bush', the second as 'prayer' if you relate more easily to religious metaphors than those from information technology.

Boundaries crucial to meaning-making lie between ego and Self, and Self and collective. As mammals, humans mother in a social, tribal, setting. The relationship (mother to collective) is the earliest protection of a newborn Self *and not* 'the mother'. In the story of Jesus, Mary could not have saved Him from the 'Massacre of the Innocents' alone; protection came through a collective response, the compassion of the Wise Men acting as Angels (a Hebrew word meaning messengers) of God, telling her and Joseph to flee to Egypt (Matthew's gospel, Chapter 2).

Individuation (Jung's name for becoming who we truly are) is an act of separation from an individual mother and of opposition to collective norms (the social mother). It challenges individual and collective to adapt to change, to explore new ways of making meaning. Analytical psychology itself is a product of Jung's own individuation, culturally appropriated, now changing and challenging the way societies work.

## Meaning disorder

I'll introduce a new term here, *meaning disorder*. If parts of the perceptual apparatus are missing from birth (in blindness) this is a *congenital* meaning disorder. Sometimes, meaning is trapped in the body in hysteria, hypochondria or psychosomatic illnesses – *body* meaning disorder (Chapter 4). We could think of 'being beside the Self' as a *too much* meaning disorder: as in schizophrenia, or on hallucinogenic drugs when the mind is flooded by incoming information and can't sort signal from noise. Depression is a *too little* meaning disorder. And, like the famous British Rail excuse about trains not running in winter because of 'the wrong kind of snow', we may have the *wrong kind of meaning*, and be subject to stigmatisation because of difference (we're female, or gay, or black, or Jewish . . .). Stigmatisation is a *social* meaning disorder.

Sometimes the psyche has not come together enough to form meaning from percepts, as in Kanners' syndrome (early infantile autism) – a *congenital primary* meaning disorder. Other times it is fixated at an early developmental level due to lack of a supporting early environment (functional autism) as in borderline and narcissistic personality disorders – *acquired* primary meaning disorders. Meaning may be too closed, as in obsessions and anorexia; temporarily overwhelmed in bereavement or following major trauma, torture or brainwashing (post traumatic stress disorder: PTSD) These are *secondary* meaning disorders.

Congenital meaning disorders indicate certain components of the meaning-making process have never worked properly: the hardware is broken or missing (in blindness, for example). In primary meaning disorders, the hardware is fine, but the software is not installed correctly. In secondary meaning disorders, the hardware and software are both fine, have worked, but the software can't handle a sudden dramatic change in the input. In social meaning disorders the hardware and software of the individual are fine, but society treats their signals as noise.

Reframing psychopathology as meaning disorder, will, I hope encourage communication between competing clinical and theoretical models by giving simple words in ordinary language to describe psychic processes. Think of psyche as an information system which opens and closes. Analysis, 'the talking cure', is a descriptive, cathartic, educational and integrative process in which words are crucial. However, to understand what the psyche does, and its semantics, we have to go beyond reified words.

To give meaning in the system (Self-ego) involves mirroring. We learn to give meaning to the system (individual-collective) depending on what we learnt in the system (mother-infant). Approaching meaning from the system (individual-collective) uses archetypal metaphor, myth, and culture to give theoretical explanations: using the system (ego-Self) sees meaning developmentally. Developmental theory, obviously, has future temporal direction, archetypal theory requires past temporal references (memory). Whether we say 'X suffered severe narcissistic injury as a result of failure of early attachment' or 'an archetype could not express itself, could not "unpack", could not "install and run properly" ', we are saying the same thing.

Developmental theory views psychic structures from the point of view of ego, and archetypal theory, from Self. Both are true, each is true separately, neither is true alone. We metaphorise relationships between concepts (ego and Self, Self and collective) when we talk about 'mothers and babies' or 'unfolding archetypes'. To individuate, ego, Self and collective, like analyst, patient and the interactive field between them, need shared language which has to include unknowns and oppositions to produce strong affects (feelings). The theoretical language we use matters less than what we intend for the narrative: what such narratives *signify*, their purpose. Let's take it that meaning forms at the boundaries between time-bound and time-free perceptions. To summarise, timeless Self unfolds through time-bound ego to make meaning. What do I mean? I mean play.

## Play

Play, like analysis, is a *between* experience. The paediatrician and psychoanalyst Donald Winnicott in *Playing and Reality* said:

> Psychotherapy takes place in the overlap of two areas of playing, that of the patient and that of the therapist. Psychotherapy has to do with two people playing together. The corollary of this is that where playing is not possible then the work done by the therapist is directed towards bringing the patient from a state of not being able to play into a state of being able to play . . . I make my idea of play concrete by claiming that playing has a place and a time. It is not inside by any use of the word (and it is unfortunately true that the word inside has very many and various uses in psychoanalytic discussion). Nor is it outside, that is to say, it is not a part of the repudiated world, the not-me, that which the

individual has decided to recognise (with whatever difficulty and even pain) as truly external, which is outside magical control. To control what is outside one has to do things, not simply to think or to wish, and doing things takes time. Playing is doing.

(1971: 44 and 47)

Analysis *is* play. Both activities occur in time and out of it, neither in time, nor out of it. This is a paradox, yet one all children understand. A personal example: at nine, I'm a new kid on the block, my family have just moved to Belfast. It's a scalding June day. I'm out hunting in torn jeans, feathers and war paint. Pat, the first boy I meet, has a Marshall's hat and a six gun. As I snick my arrow, he draws fast and drawls:

' . . . can't shoot 'less youse say "Proddest'nt or Cat' lic" '.
He glares. I hesitate, flicking long white hair out of my eyes.
'Hey, Red Skin! what does your parents b'lieve?'
I look at my bare feet . . . what is he talking about?
'Um . . . in the Great White Spirit?'
Pat, angry, shrugs, says, 'No, fer real . . . ?'
I rub my bare chest . . . bare, like a navvy . . . a worker? . . . Oh, I know!
'Um . . . in the power of the Class Struggle!'
Pat thinks a bit, then, relieved, his freckled face breaks into a big smile.
'Hey, your Da's really a Red . . . ?', says Pat.

Later, skinny-dipping in the River Lagan, floating on our backs, Pat, a red-headed cowboy, tells me he's only felt safe before playing with other Catholic boys. As an ash-blonde Red Indian, I tell him I don't know what Catholics are. He can't believe it. His word 'Catholic' is outside my meaning system, just as 'Red's' (communists, my tribe) are outside his tribe's meaning system. As boys, our system (cowboy/Indian) wins over (Catholic/communist). Naming *our way* gives us a free, safe, closed system to play in. Through play-fights and real fights, Pat and I became firm friends.

As a scruffy, barefoot kid playing 'Cowboys and Indians' I'm both Dale (my parents' son) and an 'Indian'. Meaning here depends on purpose, – whose? Mine, my new friend Pat's (the Belfast Cowboy), or my mum and dad's? If one of our mums shouts 'dinner time', play goes on hold. Making and unmaking meaning, negotiating meaning with others is Self's purpose. The purpose of play (analysis) is to be able to play (to be able to play with concepts, to learn how to symbolise). Purpose, defined by Chambers dictionary, is 'an idea or aim kept in the mind as the goal towards which effort is directed'. 'Directed' is a movement through time, an educative process. (The Latin word *educare* means to draw out.) Play-time is *between* time: both time as series (ego time, mum's time, meal time) and time as parallel (Self time, Cowboy and Indian time).

In depth psychology, the study of knowing (epistemology) and the study of symbol decoding (hermeneutics) help us clarify competing concepts about communication from unconscious to conscious with developmental and archetypal metaphors. The former theories use ego (serial) time, the latter use Self (parallel) time. Caricature them. Say the first is 'Freudian', 'classical', concerned with order and structure – closed systems, 'Cowboy' time (cowboys mend fences): the second is 'Jungian', 'romantic', concerned with chaos – open systems, 'Indian' time (Indians don't fence buffalo, they hunt them). Both are valid modes of signification.

Open signification ('this isn't a finger, it's a gun') is essential to play. Play occurs in simple meaning systems, *whether or not they have any basis in reality*. Play requires we limit our set of logical operators to make a safe, well held, closed myth-system. Preference for one form of myth (Indians, Jungians) over another (Cowboys, Freudians) comes from Self and has genetic components as well as from the environment. Sometimes closed systems work better, sometimes open ones do. I much prefer open systems. It's a question of whether the doors between conscious and unconscious feel safer open or closed.

Security is one purpose of a door, escape is another. Doorsteps, thresholds, *betweens* (*limen* in Latin) . . . liminal space-time is where meaning is negotiated: at the breast, in weaning, on our first day at school, through adolescence and its *rites de passage*, to marriage, child rearing, ageing and funeral rites. Approach meaning supposing we are 'built' as meaning-making, purposive neuropsychological systems. Our systems, like doors, can open (perceive change) and close (digest change). The adaptive value, or wisdom, of either movement depends on reality testing. And, as a 'Red's kid', how could I understand reality except as a political negotiation?

Consider the difference between development and aid. When you're starving, you need food *now* (aid . . .). Then you need political control of the means of production to prevent starvation recurring (development . . .). Aid is a simple, closed system response, with the form: 'problem – solution'. Development is a complex, open system, with the form: 'problem, solution; problem changes, new solution . . .'. Like analysis, development concerns forming positive and negative feedback loops. Analysis is not aid, it is development based on the principle, 'from each according to his abilities, to each according to his needs' (Marx 1875). The social purpose of depth psychology is creation and maintenance of psychic and social systems which can *both* open *and* close to new meanings, or, misquoting *Star Trek*'s famous split infinitive 'to boldly play where no man has played before'.

## The place of meaning in Jung's life

Depth psychology is a collective noun for psychoanalysis and analytical psychology, Freudian and Jungian traditions together. Donald Winnicott described the difference between the two:

> Psychoanalysis had much difficulty in adjusting to the needs of those who see and hear first and think last. Jungians, by contrast, have tended to cater for those who conceptualise without verbal juggling, and some think Jungians are not as good at logic and shared reality.
>
> (1989)

This text is on theory by a clinician, on logic by someone who sees and hears first, on theology by an atheist: a Marxist child and a Buddhist adult. In Zen, meaning is always negotiable. Postmodern? Perhaps. Deconstructionist certainly, as in *If You Meet Buddha on the Road, Kill Him!* – title of the analyst Sheldon Kopp's book on meaning and mental illness (1978). Buddhism has a depth psychology too, which I will refer to from time to time as a contrast, a different, Middle Way.

'The Way' in analysis is through interpretation. Understanding what meaning *means* is interpretation, which can't be value-neutral. The *act* of interpreting means more than the content of the interpretation: the form, a continuing demonstration, session by session over years, that interpretative acts can be made despite the patient's (and the analyst's) best unconscious efforts to smash 'goodness' to bits.

To see depth psychology without Jung isn't possible. To see it with him (not as his) we need to sense who he was and why he (and others) built it. To see the central place meaning has in depth psychology, we need to sense the meaning of meaning for Jung and Post-Jungians. For depth psychology, the search for better meaning is fundamental. This tradition began with Jung, who, quoting his friend and colleague, the American philosopher and psychologist William James, said:

> You must bring out of each word its practical cash value, set it at work within the stream of your experience. It appears less as a solution, then, than a programme for more work, and more particularly as an indication of the ways in which existing realities may be changed. Theories become instruments, not answers to enigmas, in which we can rest. We don't lie back upon them, we move forward, and on occasion, make nature over again by their aid.
>
> (*CW* 4: 86)

I'll argue later that Jung was, philosophically, a transcendental idealist, despite his frequent claims to the contrary; that is, he believed we experience *inside* what we project *outside*. Meaning is internally generated: meaning-filled images themselves arise from the collective unconscious. This view has long been held in the East, in the concept of Maya, the world as illusion. Internally generated meanings require validation by the collective, to avoid solipsism (private language). Jung and James were constructivists. Out-there reality is built: how it's built depends on who builds it, and why.

Constructivists hold we share co-responsibility for the construction of meaning (Hall and Young-Eisendrath 1991). There are 'out-there worlds' of course, but we perceive them *our* way – my way may share your way, becoming a 'Middle Way'. And, as a Buddhist I'd agree that 'in Buddhism, there is a strong understanding that everything (from money to shit) is transcendent, and that we must engage in our experience with a kind of democracy of appreciation' (Young-Eisendrath 1997a).

The way that can be named is not the way, it's Tao (McNaughton 1971). Tao, a constructivist perspective like Buddhism and depth psychology, says the structure of psyche itself gives us our only access to the phenomenal world and the collective – an idea Jung found in Kant and Schopenhauer (strongly influenced by Buddhist thinking) (see Khong and Thompson 1997). Meaning exists with its history. However, as Hegel said, 'What experience and history teach is this – that people and governments never have learned anything from history, or acted on the principles deduced from it' (1807a).

There isn't one background to analytical psychology. We come to its history with our stories, constructing different meanings to suit our needs: 'is this his-story, her-story or our-story? Which version of Jung is he giving us? What has this to do with meaning and purpose?'

To answer, try this mental exercise:

> Imagine a corridor through time. It begins at birth and ends at death, with doors. Imagine your life, you own personal history. As you do, ask yourself what it means . . . what your best friend and worst enemy are going to say in their accounts of your life . . . when you die, what are you going to say?

History is a set of doors from a time corridor. It appears there's an external world to which we relate, in which we exist and an internal world from which the narrative comes. But this is an illusion. As Herman Hesse put it, 'Nothing is outside, nothing is inside; for that which is outside is inside.' (1974: 258–70) We exist in a *between*, as a fleeting movement in a time corridor. Ghosts. Jung, like any other dead person, exists this way. My construction of him is not empirical. I never met him. I know a woman who did: Marianne Jacoby, a brave communist Jewish refugee who fled Berlin in the late 'thirties. She analysed with Wilhelm Reich, Toni Wolff and Michael Fordham, and helped found the analytic school where I trained, the British Association of Psychotherapists. She said:

*M:* . . . you just make sure you tell them he was big.
*D:* You mean . . . ?
*M:* Huge . . . over six and a half feet tall. Built like a mountain, with a big loud voice and a big loud laugh.
*D:* What impressed you most about him, then?
*M:* Oh, that's easy. His laugh.

Jung exists now as a memory to those who knew him, and in his *Collected Works*: unfortunately, a collection, a lumber room rather than a library, an unpacking of his creative mind. He exists in historical perspective: in Henri Ellenberger's essay on Jung in *The Discovery of the Unconscious* (1970: 657–748); in sanitised versions, like *Jung and the Story of our Time*, by Laurens Van Der Post (1976); in hagiography, *Jung*, by Barbara Hannah (1991); in apocryphal 'autobiography', *Memories, Dreams, Reflections* written mostly by his secretary Aniela Jaffe (1970), heavily edited to hide the importance of Toni Wolff. He exists in apologetics, (Smith 1996), in pictures (Wehr

1989), in post-structuralist texts (Gallant 1996) . . . and, last but not least, in Richard Noll's unauthorised versions – *The Jung Cult* (1996), and the blockbuster sequel, *The Aryan Christ* (1997). Both of these, though marred by poor scholarship (Shamdasani 1998), by showing a human, fallible Jung enhance his legend (Groocock 1998).

Pluralists may like to continue with the postmodern Jung of *The Plural Psyche* (Samuels 1989a). All deserve reading, all have different meanings and purposes, all are constructions, rather than 'objective truth'. All agree it's important that Carl Jung was the son of a clergyman who had doubts about his faith, and that, as a child, Carl puzzled about 'meaning'. In *Memories, Dreams, Reflections* he describes being a small boy sitting on his own special stone, wondering if it was the stone or he which was thinking, which was alive, like the famous Taoist story of Chuang Tzu and the butterfly: 'Chuang Tzu dreamed he was a butterfly. When he woke, he didn't know if it was Chuang Tzu who had dreamed he was a butterfly, or if he was a butterfly now dreaming he was Chuang Tzu' (Jung 1989: 35; Suzuki 1997: 251).

Less well known is his mother's depression and admission to a sanatorium when Carl was three and a half; her two personalities: daytime, Earth Mother; night time, Witch Mother (Smith 1996: 16). I'll not analyse Jung or reconstrue his work in terms of his neuroses and psychoses. It isn't necessary. Any kid can imagine what it's like when mother is *not there*, she's off her head and in the lunatic asylum. Worse, as you grow up, the other village kids know it too – what shame!

This experience makes you sit on stones when you're three and a half and wonder which is alive, you or the stone? Which version of his story will we choose? I prefer a version which remembers Carl Jung had a splinter of the Devil's mirror in his heart, like Kai, the boy in *The Snow Queen* found by his faithful friend Gerda sitting on the floor of the Snow Queen's Palace staring at broken ice letters on the floor, which, if put together, spelt 'Eternity' – as long as an hour when you're three and a half and your mother has gone (Andersen 1986: 174–93). Where's the meaning in that? There isn't any.

An eloquent Jungian theoretician, Beverley Zabriskie, describes such experiences in her paper 'Thawing the frozen accidents' (1997). She names them *frozen moments* or *moments-that-are-complexes*. Meaning comes out only one way. It's a closed system. No matter how often we replay such moments, they mean the same – abandonment, abuse, loss, defeat. Jung had a closed door somewhere in his own time corridor, was always on that stone, wondering who was alive. Some of him stayed fey, dreamy, 'with the Spirits' – what we Scots call 'away with the fairies'.

His family presented meaning to him in terms of spirit, either the Holy Spirit or 'Spirits'. Father was a Swiss Reform pastor (a particularly closed, fundamentalist myth-system) and mother a spiritualist (Smith 1996:14). Carl saw paranormal events: a bread knife mysteriously split in a closed drawer, a grandfather kept a chair in his study for his dead wife, mother held seances. He wrote his doctoral thesis about his cousin Helen Preiswerk: a medium, an hysteric or madly in love with her older cousin (or all three?) (*CW* 1: paras 1–150) He spoke vigorously in debates in the Zofingia Club (a student society) on psychic research, philosophy and religion. His life work could be read as an attempt to come up with different, perhaps better, meanings than father's failed faith or mother's metaphysical melancholia.

This spiritual preoccupation could support Noll's shrill assertions about Jung 'founding a religious cult', and his reconstruing depth psychology as one of the most successful pyramid sales devices in history. However, neither Jung or Post-Jungians are interested in doling out religious meanings (far less purposes) off the peg. We are interested in finding out how meaning may be made, if it be made well or badly; in the aesthetics of meaning; in semiotics, the science of meaning – the 'depth' of depth psychology.

And the psychology? Translating from Greek, it means 'soul, spirit, mind, butterfly'. In the Greek myth, Psyche, beloved of Eros, suffered the envy of Aphrodite (his mother). Psyche is an old-fashioned word for a looking glass on a stand, suggesting both *Alice Through the Looking Glass* and mirroring – especially of the face (persona). These associations lap round the study of the knowledge (λογοσ) of mind (πσψχηε), which in its most dramatic form is called parapsychology – 'science in Wonderland'.

Jung's interest in parapsychology and his views about 'inner and outer reality' locate him firmly within the nineteenth-century Anglo-American psychological tradition, with William James (who invited him to Yale for the Clark Lectures; with whom he stayed and corresponded (Shamdasani 1990 and 1995; Taylor 1996). Both were interested in psychic research, seeing religion and spirit as proper objects for psychological investigation, as did the group around the English psychologist F. W. H. Myers which formed the Society for Psychical Research to explore *sub-liminal* consciousness.

I italicise sub-liminal (beneath the threshold), as that group first theorised meaning as arising from the sub-liminal, between conscious and unconscious, primary and secondary process thinking.

Jung's search for meaning continued during his career at the Burgholzli Clinic. Treating severely psychotic people, he researched differences between the major functional psychoses, schizophrenia and bipolar affective disorder (*CW* 1: paras 187–225). In these psychotic states, attempts to make sense of the senseless are called 'effort after meaning' (Jaspers 1959).

For example, I once met a man

when I was a young psychiatrist. He peered into the ashtray in my room, found three cigarette butts then looked round carefully . . . down at himself, over at me, across to his social worker. Slowly , he smiled, then said,
' . . . Aha!'
In that moment, 'he knew' . . . meaning dawned. 'Them butts'. He gave me a conspiratorial look. 'You an' me, innit doctor?' Carefully, he touched each in turn. One had lipstick on it. A confirmation. 'You an' me an' . . . 'er. 'Ere in this f***ing room.' He touched the ashtray . 'You two is goin' to do me up like a kipper.'

We did. We admitted him to hospital just as his 'voices' had promised. This man was thinking magically, in that counterpoint reality which Freud named primary process thinking. It privileges inner experience, and is a shared object of study for parapsychology and depth psychology. Analysis looks at movements between primary and secondary process (every-day) thinking. Reality testing requires movement between them, between unconscious and conscious. Meaning comes from the no-man's land of dreams and synchronicities, which validate our experience to help us adapt to environmental change. This adaptive function is, I believe, a primary purpose of meaning: it confers developmental, evolutionary advantages. Open, fluent meaning systems are better able to adapt to environmental change than closed ones.

The result of analysis is not, as sometimes imagined, development of psychic ability; analysts don't mind-read or have magic powers. However, there are different awarenesses after analysis, increased ability to tolerate uncertainty, to avoid premature closure and sustain ambivalence (pluralism). We can stay longer in transitional space (Winnicott), the 'third area' (Schwartz-Salant 1989), the 'intersubjective field' (Atwood 1994) – in *between.*

## Time distortion and the word association experiments

Ghosts, spirits and mediumistic activity are liminal, like analysis and play (recall, the Latin word *limen* means threshold, doorway or boundary marker). Hermes, (Mercury) Greek god of Shepherds and Magi, symbolised boundaries; edges of farmland were marked by a (phallic) stone, called a herm (Kerenyi 1951). Hermes conducted souls in the underworld, a ghost's taxi-driver. Meaning is haunting, it comes from the 'Ghosts and Empties' in our lives (Charlton 1997). Psychic research theorises ghosts as 'frozen moments' in time's doorways (Gregory and Kohsen 1954; Tyrrell 1943). Like ghosts, meanings are situational constructions. Their existence depends on who is looking, through which door from the time corridor.

Time distortions characterise psi (psychic) phenomena. Psi processes don't seem governed by space-time constraints. They happen with an immediacy which suggests a purpose-led (teleological) cause. Psychological complexes have a similar immediacy and create similar distortions: for instance, time loops or stands still in repetition compulsions. Psi events mark deep, unconscious changes: like poltergeists in adolescence, or seeing a ghost after bereavement.

In the Clark Lectures (*CW* 2: paras 939–1014; *CW* 17: paras: 1–79) Jung described the word association test, which temporarily captures the unconscious overwhelming conscious – a prelude to psi experience. In the test, a list of words is given, and the subject responds by saying the first word which comes into their head. Both content (words) and form (time delay between stimulus and response) give information. Time delays result from sub-liminal perception of associated painful feelings. Words are made to lose meaning. This is a (transient, acute, rapidly remitting) primary meaning disorder.

Jung suggested long delays showed the existence of unconscious complexes. (More advanced technology, but similar techniques, are used in modern lie detectors.) Freud's enthusiasm for Jung came from the latter's world-wide reputation as an experimental psychologist, whose work provided hard evidence for the existence of the unconscious, and, therefore, validated Freud's theories. And Jung needed Freud's theorising to make sense of his results:

> This concept he called repression: the mechanism by which a conscious content is displaced into the unconscious, defined as the psychic element of which we are not and can never be conscious. The concept of repression is based on

repeated observations that neurotics forget significant experiences or thoughts so thoroughly one might easily believe they had never existed ... it is possible to demonstrate this phenomenon experimentally, by the association test.

(*CW*. 4: para. 210)

This, Jung's major scientific contribution, is central to understanding concepts of meaning in depth psychology. Repression is a fragmenting of painful perceptions so thoroughly they can't be put back together. The record is erased, then the record of the record ...

## Memory and reconstructive imagination

To develop the argument: the Royal College of Psychiatrists recently published a controversial report into False Memory Syndrome. Brandon *et al.* (1998) argue memories of abuse 'recovered' during hypnotic regression, therapy or analysis are not necessarily memories of real historical events occurring as described which could have been independently witnessed, could stand forensic investigation or form a basis for legal action. They do not question the grim reality of childhood sexual abuse, or that such trauma can be repressed. It's undeniable, it predisposes to adult depression; abused kids may go on to abuse, or, at worst, become serial killers (Turco 1997).

The authors point to profound differences between 'out-there' and 'in-here' experience: reality in a collective setting versus reality as felt. The idea of children having sexuality (and being sexually exploited) was anathema to polite Viennese society. It shows Freud's great personal courage that he persisted with his theory of infantile sexuality in the face of passionate, intemperate and anti-semitic abuse. Jung's clinical work (and personal experience of child abuse – Kutek 2000) made him support Freud, but he didn't agree sexuality explained 'everything'. Instead, he felt infantile sexual *fantasies* – incest fantasies in particular – are vital to installing adult sexual functions.

Repression and child sexual abuse are not related causally. Infants have sexuality. Painful memories are repressed. Infantile sexuality does not cause repression, repression does not always result from infantile sexuality. The word association experiments show that, due to repression, painful experiences are rarely recalled correctly, nor are they always caused by repressed infantile trauma. Freud explained repetition compulsion as an attempt to return to the scene of the crime – relive the trauma, but this time have a different result. Freud suggested when trauma can't be worked through, when it is repressed, then resentment from the past is carried forward (Freud 1898): the German word for this is *Nachtraglichkeit*.

This key concept resurfaced in a development in depth psychology made by the Harvard psychoanalyst Arnold Modell (1990: 60–74), based on the pioneering neurobiological work of fellow Harvard neurobiologist Gerald Edelman (1987) who proposes: 'memory does not consist of a permanent record in the brain that is isomorphic (same shape) with past experience, but rather, that memory is a dynamic reconstruction that is context bound and established by means of categories.' Considerable evidence supports this neuro-biological basis to the constructivist argument about meaning, validating psychoanalyst Charles Rycroft's view that 'memory is reconstructive imagination' (1981).

Memory isn't at all like a book, photograph, or block of data on a computer disc. There is no 'hard copy'. Memories are put together anew each time from information stored throughout the whole brain. The process is holographic (Zinkin 1987): a colour here, smell there, sound in another place. Reconstruction (an act of giving meaning) is organised by what we felt at the time of the original percept and what we feel now becoming synchronous. This is a bridge between dynamic and organic psychiatry, analysis and biology. We can explain meaning in terms of social setting as well as events in our brain cells: the linking concept is feeling, the events having *self-similarity*.

Feeling, a technical term in analytical psychology, is not the opposite of thinking, nor is it 'to express emotion'. It means *to attach value to percepts*. Similar percepts produce similar feelings and lead to similar re-imaginings. Memory is driven 'top down' (from cortex to thalamus) not 'bottom up' (from thalamus to cortex). What we see and hear 'out there' is determined by what we expect to see and hear, rather than what is objectively there. As Kant said, 'percepts without concepts are blind'. This is why internal reality is nearly always believed over external reality (why Pat initially assumed I, an unknown 'Red Indian' boy, was a threat). The unknown challenges meaning systems, requests them to open.

## Semiotics, cybernetics and ecology

Semiotics is the science of meaning. It studies meaning-making in individual and social systems. Systems theory provided the idea of 'opening and closing systems' (Bertalnaffy, 1968). I'll play cybernetics and ecology, derivatives of systems theory against depth psychology throughout this text to approach meaning 'independent of semantic differentials resulting from power gradients' – a technical way of saying 'those who get to give words meaning are those in power': 'It's bedtime, Chief,' said my mother. 'Why?' I argued, wondering whether I could scalp her. 'Because I say so!'

A Marxist might claim: 'Capitalists have power, they expropriate the labour of the workers'; a capitalist may say 'Greed is good: it brings profit'; a Christian might say 'Jesus saves'. It's hard to escape beliefs, 'theories of everything', but, as the American journalist H. L. Mencken said, 'for every difficult and complex problem, there is a solution which is simple, uncomplicated, and wrong!' Meaning is a system, not a belief, and has to be studied as a system.

Cybernetics (Greek: κιβερνετος – helmsman, navigator) is 'the comparative study of communication processes and automatic control systems'. Norbert Weiner (1948) described how parts of systems interact through feedback loops: whether it is water flowing from a sink turning off a tap (negative feedback) or incoming signals from a rock guitar hitting outgoing signals from the amp, making 'white noise' (positive feedback) – or output from a dysfunctional parental couple provoking a child to autistic withdrawal (Axline 1969), suicide, or the chronic suicide of addiction.

Perception and memory are multiple feedback systems, tending to close around self-similar feelings. Our brain's most essential task is not reconstructive imagination, but the 'choice' *not* to – not to use negative feedback to damp incoming signals so that (except in psychosis) we don't get information overload.

Self steers, like a Polynesian mariner guided by sub-liminally perceived currents, stars and the smell of the land. Polynesians also invented surfing: its lesson is everyone falls off their board sooner or later. 'I' (which is all 'ego' means) continually falls off the time-wave of Self. Self is a dynamic open system like ocean, wave and surfer. Working out which logical operators work in a meaning system is surfing with semantics. Logical operators are statements which get a system to do something. They can be simple: {if/then}; {and/or}; {both/and}; {either /or}; {when/if} – or complex: – {both/and/ neither/nor}; or {if/and/then/then}.

Psychological 'complexes' (closed feedback loops) usually use simple logical operators. The anthropologist Gregory Bateson (1973) described one in his classic 'double bind': a 'damned if you do and damned if you don't' logic, characteristic of sado-masochism: 'Whip me, whip me,' begs the masochist, 'No,' jeers the sadist. Resolving complexes usually means changing simple logical operators to complex ones, creating new meaning possibilities, like this: in phobia: *If* I see a spider *then* I am afraid – becomes – *if* I see a spider *then* I am afraid *then* I use my memory *then* I remember I was afraid of my mother, *then* I realise that my mother is not the spider, i.e., {if/then} becomes {if /then/then/then . . . }. In depression: *If* I feel bad *then* it's because I am bad – becomes – *if* I am feeling bad *and* I believe its my fault *then* that's an omnipotent fantasy *and* it's not my fault *and* I don't have to feel bad, i.e., {if/then } becomes {If/and/then/and/and}. In paranoia: *If* I do X, then they'll kill me . . .

Analysis works out which logical operators are used, through the transference and counter-transference, discovering who is being and feeling what for whom. When complex logical operators replace simple ones it is easier to tolerate an open system, easier to play. As we learn to handle more complex logical operators we increase creativity, gain a sense of humour, integrate with our social matrix, tolerate difference, learn to live with uncertainty – we individuate (Read 1974: 241–3), being both more ourselves and more linked with the collective, our eco-system.

Ecology studies man in his environment (Greek: οικος – house, λογοσ – knowledge). Freud's stated aims for analysis were 'to love and to work, to replace hysterical misery with common unhappiness'. In ecology, 'better' (goodness) means sustainable environmental adaptation. Marx's famous distinction between architects and builders 'An architect has a concept . . . a builder merely builds', is helpful here (1961a). Political issues are about money and power, supply and demand – social ecology. Analysis only exists in a social context, and must accept the reality of its social frame to approach meaning (Samuels 1995).

Analysts' interpretations are intersubjective, therefore subjective and prejudiced. My prejudice is towards open meaning systems, as they have a greater adaptive potential. We're all capable, somewhere, of being fundamentalists: yearning for safe closed systems, bounded by our fears and primitive infant-like terrors. Interpretative acts challenge closed, over-determined systems; which, by constant repetition, become mistaken for percepts. As Louis Zinkin, my late supervisor, told me, 'There are strange effects at boundaries.' The next chapter looks at the strangest effect of all – individuation.

# 2

# INDIVIDUATION

Full fathom five thy father lies;
Of his bones are coral made
Those are pearls that were his eyes
Nothing of him that doth fade,
But doth suffer a sea change
Into something rich and strange.
(William Shakespeare, *The Tempest*, Act 1. ii)

## The transcendent function

*The Tempest* opens with a 'Night Sea Journey': a handsome lad shipwrecks on a desert island, starting his hero-quest. As the T-Shirt says, 'Life's a beach': for Ferdinand, shipwrecked hero, literally true. Beaches, where the sea of unconscious meets islands of ego, are liminal places where we play: innocent child, sultry young surfer, relaxing parent, dozing grandparent. Play is free movement between ego and Self, Self and collective, between time-free and time-bound percepts, enacting our creative, transcendent function. In *The Tempest*, Shakespeare played out an internal drama, projecting what psychoanalyst Heinz Kohut (1971) calls 'self-objects' (symbolic self-representations) on to current events. The characters resemble Shakespeare's 'sub-personalities' (Assagioli 1973: 74–7, Redfearn 1985: 88–100); aspects of his Self, reworkings of his developmental history *and* projections of archetypal, collective images.

A hurricane shipwrecked the incoming Governor of the Virginia Company on Bermuda in 1609, which was 'dear' to Shakespeare, with a fortune invested in the Company. He worked through his ill-fortune and loss of value in Ferdinand puer, eternal youth and Prospero senex, wise old man. Characters are archetypal images: Miranda, anima; Antonio, evil shadow; Caliban, ugly trickster; Ariel, nature spirit – puer/trickster, Hermes. There is even a terrible witch mother, Sycorax. Prospero is Shakespeare, perhaps fore-knowing, when he breaks his magic wand (Act V. i, 50–6) he'll say farewell to his books: this was his last play.

Hermann Hesse used theatre as a metaphor for individuation. In *Steppenwolf* (1951), his semi-autobiographical shadow, the archetypal anti-hero, HH, learns wisdom in the Magic Theatre, with its daunting sign, 'For Madmen Only'. It feels like madness to ego to relinquish omnipotent control. During individuation, a Night Sea Journey to a far distant shore (*CW* 5: paras 349–61), ego may feel like Osiris, the Egyptian Lord of Death and Rebirth, set adrift on the Sea in his coffin by Set, his evil shadow-brother. After a heroic quest, Isis, his loyal wife and sister, frees Osiris from a tamarisk tree. She also has to 're-member' him, as his phallus got lost in the process (Wallis Budge 1967: xlviii–liv). Individuation works against castration anxiety, against impotence and for creativity (Neumann 1989: 220–56.)

> Individuation is a process, not a state. It is a continuing process that involves the search not for perfection, but for as much wholeness as possible. In other words there are no 'individuated' persons only individuating persons. Individuation involves the development of ever-growing awareness of one's personal identity, with both its 'good' and desirable quantities and ego ideals as well as its bad, reprehensible and 'shadow' qualities. It encompasses an ever-growing consciousness of one's separateness, the development of oneself as a whole and unique person, relatively detached from personal and social origins and concerned to discover personal values. One becomes conscious of existence as an organic unit, separate from the collective, separate but not detached and impervious to the community's needs.
>
> (Gordon 1998: 267)

Individuation involves separation, loss and facing the reality of death: Ferdinand mourns the loss of his father. Through the tasks of adolescence (work, sexual relating, leaving home) given him by Prospero, he matures. His 'change into something rich and strange', results from contact with Self along the 'ego-Self axis' (Edinger 1962); represented by Ariel, connecting Ferdinand to Prospero (like Hermes/Mercurius, who guides souls to his Uncle, Hades, Lord of the Dead. His Roman name is Pluto: ninth planet, astrological ruler of gangsters, revolutionaries and the plutonium plutocrats of the global military-industrial complex).

Individuation concerns answering questions Hades (Osiris) might ask us when our soul is weighed before him. If 'ego-Self' links are secure, ego no longer has to rule the psyche like a Hitler – it can play: a youth in winged sandals, neither trapped in the Humpty Dumpty eggshell fragility of severe narcissistic wounding or lost in the All-the-Kings-Men raging, invasive hostility of boundariless 'borderline' defences. These are primary meaning disorders where ego continually falls (and feels) 'off the wall', and Self shipwrecks into purposelessness.

Normally, meaning and purpose develop *between* person-ego and system-ego as we grow from egocentrism to ego-adaptation (Guntrip 1971: 103–41). As the analytical psychologist Edward Whitmont said: 'individuation means not only a conscious relationship to interpersonal reality and social collectivity. It includes developing the ability for introspection no less than for experiencing, playing with, feeling for, and fulfilling one's calling in outer reality' (1982: 340). It is 'the development of a psychological individual as a being distinct from the collective, a differentiation which is a natural necessity allowing the better survival of a social group as its members are more able to adapt to change' (*CW* 6: paras 757–62).

Jung's definition includes collective relationships, yet opposition to social norms is inevitable when we negotiate between individual and collective (*CW* 6: paras 757–62). If meaning is not free choice, purpose can't be: when we face meaning-in-a-complex, or a *frozen moment*, we feel pointless, as well as meaningless. My patient Dekk had such a moment during a row with his wife. The frightened look in his son's face immediately took Dekk back to childhood, seeing rows between his parents. This made the present-day argument suddenly become pointless and meaningless: re-membering, re-learning to make meaning, is a precursor of individuation. This takes place in the transference–counter-transference dynamic. As Melanie Klein said:

> when pre-verbal fantasies and emotions are revived in the transference situations they appear as 'memories in feelings' as I would call them, and are reconstructed and put into words by the analyst. In the same way, words have to be used, when we are reconstructing and describing other phenomena belonging to the early stages of development. In fact we cannot translate the language of the unconscious into consciousness without lending it words from our conscious realm.

> (1987: 5)

In transference, discrete acts of meaning-making are examples of the transcendent function:

> there is nothing mysterious or metaphysical about the term transcendent function. It means a psychological function comparable in its way to a mathematical function of the same name, which is a function of real and imaginary numbers. The psychological 'transcendent function' arises from the union of unconscious and conscious contents.
>
> (*CW* 8: para. 131)

Jung emphasised the role of archetypes and the collective unconscious. He felt forming a stable identity and persona by differentiation from the archetypes was a prerequisite for individuation. Sexuality, incest and primal scene fantasies are archetypal patterns (*CW* 16: 353–61) which transform internal objects, archetypal images and symbols. His view contrasts with insights by London analyst Michael Fordham and the developmental school whose theoretical myths are, surprisingly, closer to Eastern ideas than those of the classical school.

Both developmental and Buddhist perspectives understand Self gradually unfolds from potential to actual. This begins before conception and continues after death. Not that developmental Jungians necessarily believe in reincarnation or karma; they recognise the social, historical context of an individual extends before and after a lifespan. Both consider pathologies of individuation produce autism, inflation, depression and psychotic illnesses (*CW* 9i: para. 495) – primary meaning disorders. And both treat the outer world *as if* – that is, as if *constructed*. I'll look at how constructive processes develop from infancy to adulthood in the next chapter. First, I'll illustrate how the concepts ego, Self and shadow interact in naming objects, in the metaphor of the Night Sea Journey.

## The Night Sea Journey

Jung used this phrase to name development of the transcendent function in adulthood. He felt 'for a young person it is almost a sin, or at least a danger, to be too preoccupied with himself; but for the ageing person it is a duty and a necessity to devote serious attention to himself' (*CW* 8: para. 785). Classical Jungians see individuation as a lifelong, Self-guided movement. Its time-envelope opens maybe in parental courtship, and is embodied in the Primal Scene as sperm meets egg and unfoldment of genetic material begins (Samuels 1985b: 111–34). At death, the personal envelope closes, but the social envelope remains open. For individuals, death carries a fear of not-being: existential despair. However, though death is unknown, it does not follow that the unknown is death. The teleological point of view of analytical psychology holds life and death – *both* have purpose. Teleology (Greek: τελεοσ, teleos, ending) interprets life-events by purpose (what they let happen) rather than causalistically (what happened *then* to make this happen *now*?) Analysis challenges habitual logical operators, and prevents time becoming a closed loop.

Meaning is opened by metaphor, by the transcendent function, through enactment and symbol formation. Meaning may close in life's shipwrecks but can be reopened in transference and counter-transference, as traumatic moments rework. This needs the support of culture, tribe and family, where social and religious rituals mark *rites de passage*. Culture humanises archetypes through art: artist, author and actor validate enactments and provide symbols; as true of the Ancient Greek healing plays at Epidaurus as it is for the TV soap-operas contemporary adolescents devour. Rather than seeing teen angst as resulting from psychic storms (ours or our parents'), suppose it is intrinsically part of human evolution, part of a hero-quest?

Individuation, like initiation, hurts. Feelings change as we humanise archetypes and rearrange internal objects. This is *meaning-making* (speaking 'Jungian') or, *Self-cathexis on to self-objects* (speaking 'object relations'). Cathexis (Greek: Χατηεξις, holding) is psychoanalytic-speech for charges of emotional energy attached to ideas or objects. (For example, as a vegetarian, steak has, for me, a negative cathexis.)

Analysts look on cathexis as purposive; containing forward temporal perspective (hope). Purpose, and hope, are a Self's navigation aids. Self uses ego to detect emotional energies using meaning-maps and feeling tone. As they emerge in body-language (gestural praxis), we track *form* rather than *content*. We unconsciously communicate value patterns in sub-liminal perceptions. If you blush when I refuse steak, I sub-liminally guess you're embarrassed or annoyed and may start apologising or explaining. I don't think this out, or consciously attend to your gestural praxis – unless I'm in a different culture.

Stultified behaviours show how much cognitive activity a person is giving to a social task: if excessive (as in stammering), it's as painful as watching a child with Asperger's syndrome trying to make meaning with shoelaces. Night Sea Journeys increases awareness. As in learning meditation, at first 'be aware of your breathing' changes breathing, later, we simply are aware. This is like learning to ride a motorbike or play an instrument – practice (repetition) links time-bound bodily action and time-free intention. Problems with linking show up as speech delays in the word association test. We can study these problems using the science of meaning.

## Semiotics

Swiss linguist Ferdinand de Saussure's innovation in semiotics (Greek: σεμειον, semeion, sign) was to introduce two terms: 'synchronic' – meaning as a whole at a given, timeless moment – and 'diachronic' – meaning developing over time (Ullman 1962: 7). He describes a pluralistic concept of meaning (Cobley and Jansz 1997: 8–17). Till then, semioticians divided into two camps: one, with German philosopher Gottlob Frege, treated meaning as an eternal, timeless property of a sign, the other, with Frederick Engels (Marx's collaborator) treated meaning as time-bound, therefore always negotiable (Cohen 1962: 22–3).

Transcendent experience is both time-free (synchronic, of Self) and time-bound (diachronic, of ego). A synchronic narrative is all the scenes of a movie, all the actions in a life, at once: a diachronic narrative is a film, life, in its usual, sequential way. New York analytical psychologist Ann Ulanov reminds us ego and Self are metaphysical concepts which 'conceptualise the human tendency to personalise any relationship, even one to transpersonal realities such as God, society, or the values and truths held to be of supreme worth by individuals and groups' (1982: 68–85). Meaning forms in an intersubjective space, neither you nor I, ego or Self, time-bound or time-free, yet, mysteriously, all (*CW* 8: paras 145–8).

Jung observed intersubjectivity through transference and counter-transference (*CW* 16: paras 283–4, 422 ff.) which psychoanalyst Wilfred Bion described as made of atoms of meaning. Pre-sense experience (beta elements) are transformed by mother's reverie into alpha elements, nameable experiences: 'alpha function whether in sleeping or waking transforms the sense impressions related to an emotional experience, into alpha elements, which cohere as they proliferate to form the contact barrier' (1962: 6–7). 'Alpha function' is Bion's shorthand for how meaning-values grow as sub-liminal percepts become nameable feelings; 'contact barrier' is the liminal zone, *between*, called the autistic barrier by child analysts Frances Tustin (1981: 143–4) and Michael Fordham, who described autism as 'a disordered state of integration, owing its persistence to failure of the self to deintegrate' (1976: 88).

Now, individuation, could be a 'man's heroic quest' (Bly 1990) or a 'woman's healing journey' (Estes 1996), but, by emphasising individuation as an 'effort', like the Calvinist notion of 'justification by works' it becomes another task for ego to perform. However, in *Aion* Jung said wholeness arises from the playful, timeless qualities of Self – not by 'effort' (*CW* 9ii: paras 43–67). Ego is a time-bound area within Self. Individuation, more than awareness of uniqueness, is awareness of temporal limits to meaning; ultimately, personal meaning survives as a creative heritage – children, work, art. This, in turn, brings a humbling realisation: *my meaning and purpose are no-one else's*. Yet, the more we're touched by Self, the more we join the collective and the more our units of meaning can change. We move from dependency, to interdependence – not independence (an egoic fantasy).

## Dependency

In *The Tempest*, young Ferdinand is sacrificed (shipwrecked) to win the princess, Miranda. The young men I'll describe here played sacrificial roles in their families. Like candidates in a Dionysian initiatory mystery, heroic sacrifice establishes potency, which, like heroin, is highly addictive. Individuation means negotiating twoness: between {ego and Self}; {infant and mother}; {individual and collective}; allowing 'both/and' experiences, rather than co-dependence, when one exists only to meet the need of another, or the either/or of 'heroic' independence, with its clear moral distinctions between right and wrong.

In dependency, little moral distinction between right and wrong is possible due to a failure of purpose. The main logical operator is 'neither/nor': dependents can neither flip nor fly, fight or flee. A child-like frozen persona oscillates between terrifying fragmentation in borderline defences or the suicidal existential despair of narcissism. A death wish becomes a 'strange attractor' in the psyche, thoughts orbit it but never escape. It is as if the no-man's-land between ego and Self is a 'mine-field': in narcissism, everything is *mine, mine, mine*. Ego has fragmented into the potential space between it and the Self. The pain intrinsic to negotiating this 'contact barrier' (mirrored in the barrier between ego and outside world) is suspended by repetition compulsions.

Rituals, religious or obsessional, sexual or drug related, are comforting. The price is remaining *between*: in a 'mine field', a closed egocentric system, with a shadow life where power has replaced love. Persons or things on which one depends have non-negotiable loci of control. Relationships to Self and others are sado-masochistic: rubber and leather may physically enact a 'contact barrier', pushing your money (value) through a needle in your arm is a masochistic Self-attack (Cowan 1982: 95–114). Rosemary Gordon (1993: 274–89) suggests masochism is shadow of the archetype of sacrifice and mirrors the archetype hero/heroine. The hero's battle for deliverance from the mother (*CW* 5: 419–63) with its peril, sacrifice and reward mark it as an initiatory quest. Drug use is an *as-if* initiation (Zoja 1989). Now, individuation involves initiation; whether phallic, masculine, yang, 'hero's quest', or uterine, vaginal, feminine, yin, 'healing journey' – the adolescents described here were unable to make a hero's journey and reach initiated, potent, purposeful manhood.

### Clinical examples

Dekk is a successful young TV actor. He calls himself 'son of Holloway Woman' (a women's prison in North London). He was born there to his unmarried teenage immigrant Irish mother. Family myths include 'grandad ran guns for the IRA' – a 'terrorist bastard' or 'hero of liberation', depending whether you wear Orange or Green. Dekk's family were dirt poor; crime (envious attack) was an aspiration, father was an alcoholic young burglar. Dekk grew up living on his wits, was a rent boy at fifteen, taking 'dope and downers', until he found heroin (like Jim Carroll, author and hero of *The Basketball Diaries*, 1997)

Success in a straight's world breaks his myth. He's the family shadow, 'rich, bourgeois and English', with a delusional belief he's a murderer. He explains murder tops the crime hierarchy, as ultimate crime. A serious suicide attempt at seventeen led him to a therapeutic community, then into Narcotics Anonymous. Success betrayed the street kid he'd been, directed inwards his sense of betraying, and being betrayed by, his family. A session might have been like this:

> 'Kids from families like mine ain't supposed t' make it,' he says . . .
> Turning from me or anything I say. Been here before . . .
> '. . . your kind don't know fucking shit about what I've suffered, what I'm going through now . . . you don't care, you can't care. Nobody did, nobody does, and nobody's going to . . .'

His face, an empty mask. Now, why . . . where's the feeling gone . . . shit, my guts hurt! Thinking's stopped too. So, why? What's he up to? I'm angry, what does he know about me? . . . hey! I'm so full of my own stuff I've killed Dekk off. Right now! I'm not thinking about him . . . I feel murderous. Bastard! He's done it again! Just when we're getting somewhere . . . what was it Bion said . . . 'alpha elements cohere as they proliferate to form a contact barrier?' Oh. So Dekk's body says ' . . . don't touch me' But the eyes? A small unwanted kid, too scared to cry. From somewhere I hear my voice . . .
'Mmm. Like River Phoenix . . .?'

Gently, I named another young film actor, Dekk's hero, who also confused hero with heroin, and shipwrecked on the pavement outside an LA nightclub one Halloween, dying of a massive overdose. Dekk's tears fell as his eyes met mine.

A private, closing meaning-system was re-entered using a 'culture carrier' (River Phoenix) with whom he could identify, giving his Self collective support. No longer isolated, openly sharing feeling, *memory in feeling* became *memory as feeling*.

Dekk told me of his wish to murder me. He'd seen my worn black leather bike jacket in my hall, started talking about bikers, imagining I'm from a shadow family, but somehow 'made it'. He envies me. I said imagining me as 'a Hell's Angel' means he knows I'll survive his envious attacks (unlike his father, who left when he was ten). I admit I envy him his fame, but not what it has cost. He laughs, we share twoness, joke about parallels between theatre and analysis (he tells me about Ferdinand in *The Tempest*).

Later, Dekk had a 'drama', a blazing row with his wife. Till now he'd felt afraid to, in case he'd kill her. He went to hit her, but his son gave him a dirty look. Retelling this, Dekk froze, suddenly back in mother's kitchen, a skinny kid watching father belt his mother, and knowing he'd be thrashed next. My throat went dry, I felt sick.

It goes around, rage. From father to me (for pointing it out), to Dekk's son for getting through to him in a way he couldn't with his father. In the session feeling is recognised: not acted on, named. Sensation connects to feeling, tears . . . of rage and relief. Dekk left after five years of once and twice a week therapy, no longer afraid of success.

Then – Ben. One hot summer day a barefooted boy in a torn vest and dirty jeans knocked on my door, tan face hidden by long dark curls. He held a battered guitar like a teddy bear and had white scars on his brown arms, made at sixteen, when he was expelled from school. He said, 'Pain's better than feeling nothing.' Outside his mother waited in a limousine. She'd brought him straight from the Los Angeles 'plane; he'd been a surf-bum, taking crack daily. A serious suicide attempt (not his first) made his beach buddies ship him home. He said, 'I don't have no home,' – he'd live on the street rather than with his family.

Ben's millionaire father had many houses and mistresses. Mother had many houses and boyfriends. As third, much the youngest child, Ben's myth was 'baby save our marriage'. But, nannied on day one, mother's pet was ignored by father, elder brother and sister. In boarding school at four, then at an exclusive public school, he was cruelly bullied and often ran away. Life became long-haul flights between warring parents.

He first got drunk at eleven, stoned at twelve (he smoked reefers daily), started cocaine at sixteen. He tried heroin but didn't like it, it made time *freeze*. He said drugs replaced love, 'a smoke mother is always there'. We explored his deliberate self-harm as shadow, revenge for being unvalued. The story of Abraham and Isaac reconnected him to his Jewish roots, renamed 'addiction' as self-sacrifice, atonement, initiation, and a scapegoat – 'who habitually caught the bad conscience, perceived the denied shadow and felt responsible for it' (Pereira 1986: 33).

Ben cried hard, tears soaked his vest. Deeply shamed, he shouted 'mummy's baby'; a taunt thrown, now turned back. I felt his shame, empathised with his wish to fight helplessness by 'being a street tough', and linked this to masochism. He wrote a song about it for me, which moved me to tears. Ben saw me cry and realised what he brought, including his tears, was valued. Trust deepened. By winter, he'd found a scruffy denim jacket and sneakers, shaved his head, moved from the street to a squat, got work as a labourer and joined a punk-rock band. Over two years, he came to accept that his friends and I valued him. He left for a year, then his mother died tragically. He came back rather than use hard drugs, had an atonement with his father; but wouldn't take his money, except for part of my fee. He busked in the subway for his share, bringing me a hatful of loose change. He dreamed:

> I'm on top floor of a ten-storey apartment block. An identical block is ten feet away. A boy on the windowsill opposite

talks to his unseen mother. He's trying to get across to me. He jumps, but I can't hold him. He falls to his death in the street below.

Ben associated: 'I'm a Gemini', meaning, for him, searching for but never finding his 'mirroring twin'. The Self–chosen 'fall' from rich kid to street kid was an attempted Night Sea Journey from a 'terrible witch mother', like Dekk's rise to fame. Both enacted the family shadow, two shadow children living on frozen tears.

Drugs, as suicide analogue, as a death-wish which holds the psyche together let ego remain 'person-ego', internally driven, closing tighter and tighter, cutting off from Self and society. The issue was whether these youths were 'mummy's boy' or 'father's son'. Their deep shame as objects created for mother's pleasure which failed meant their creative gifts (acting and music) had no value. The solution: flight to the inner world and self-punishment to say 'Look what you made me do.'

Masochistic strivings threaten to destroy Self, which is felt as a threat: to be offered good things if you have no sense of inner goodness is like an envious and sadistic attack (Money-Kyrle 1971). To be made aware of the possibility of meaning when deprived of the capacity to make it is torture. 'The masochistic phenomena which we find in neuroses represent a pathological modification of the Dionysian tendencies which seem to spread through the world' (Horney 1946: 248). Dionysus, god of intoxication, is an ecstatic masochist (Cowan 1982: 95–114). Masochism is a closed system in which to lose is to win, 'the bottom is always on top'. Victims create guilt in persecutors, damned if they hit and damned if they don't. Jung describes the underlying object relations of this twisted path to individuation in *Symbols of Transformation* (*CW* 5):

> It is as if the libido had suddenly discovered, in the depths of the unconscious, an object which exercises a powerful attraction . . . we have to suppose a rather exceptional condition, for instance a lack of external objects, which forces the individual to seek a substitute in his own psyche. It is hard to believe this teeming world is too poor to provide an object for human love – it is rather the inability to love which robs a person of these opportunities. The world is empty only to him who does not know how to direct his libido towards things and people, and to render them alive and beautiful. What compels us to create a substitute from

within ourselves is not an external lack, but our own inability to include anything outside ourselves in our love. Resistance to loving produces the inability to love, or else that inability acts as a resistance. Part of the psyche really wants the external object, but another part of it strives back to the subjective world, where the airy and lightly built palaces of fantasy beckon.

(*CW* 5: para. 253)

A dependent ego-complex, unsure of its omnipotence, attempts to replace Self. This is dependency, individuation's shadow. If a child is 'mommy's little angel' (like Ben), then shadow is the Hell's Angel he wishes to be (and for Dekk, vice versa).

## Meaning: an adaptive psychological structure

I work with many artistic people who wrestle with dependency. It seriously impacts on their creative ability. Jung mostly worked with highly motivated, wealthy *haut bourgeois*. Having everything material life could offer, they too experienced crises of meaning, due to losing attachment to the Spiritual (transcendent). Jung addressed this emptiness, letting people re-experience a numinous (awe-filled) relationship in the here and now: in their transference to him as the 'wise old man'. Like all analysts, he carried a projection made by ego of timeless Self.

He knew the value of decoding psychic projection by reference to the natural world from his medical studies and in his studies of Paracelsus, the great fifteenth-century alchemist-physician. 'The light of nature is an intuitive apprehension of the facts, a kind of illumination. It has two sources, a mortal and an immortal, which Paracelsus calls "angels"' (*CW* 13: para. 14). An angel is a messenger from God, from the Self. See them as metaphoric, rather than literal (with wings and haloes) and imagine them as very small, existing at neural synapses. Jung's biological perspective on meaning used ideas from ecology and analysis, asking, as a biologist may of a living structure, 'What's this *for*?'

American psychoanalysts Malcolm Slavin and Daniel Kriegman in *The Adaptive Design of the Human Psyche* (1992: 55–80) synthesise ideas from structuralism, Chomsky's linguistics, developmental psychologist Daniel Stern, and neurobiologist Gerald Edelman to produce an answer. They show meaning evolves from *deep structures* in the psyche: we call these archetypes. The Darwinian idea of adaptation overcomes philosophical problems created by reductive explanations which bedevil science in general and psychoanalysis in particular. It argues that we are pre-programmed to make meaning and use language, adaptive psychological structures resulting from genetic experiments which gave evolutionary advantage.

Meaning-making structures operate in a relational environment, shaped by family and culture (see Jacques in Chapter 8). There is no biological need to see meaning as defence against psychic pain, or 'drive reduction', as suggested in Freud's early model of mind. Analytic constructs do not need to derive from nineteenth-century hydraulics, for we can observe these structures in their long process of evolution.

Anthropologist Gregory Bateson (1973: 375–86) gave meaning a cybernetic explanation: not by deriving cause from effect, asking rather, given the restraints on any living system, why does an event *not* occur – in this case, meaning? Cybernetic maps of systems look for transformations which move information, allowing that 'a map is not the territory'. The bio-system might be our neural synapses or society, for in human behavioural systems, especially religion, ritual and whenever primary process dominates, the name often is the thing named. Bread, in the Mass, is the Body of Christ, the wine is the Blood.

There are differences between the context in which a name is given and the name itself. For instance, taking the word 'mother' – *my real mother out there*, or *my internal image of mother* – both are valid uses, but different in context. Distinctions between inner and outer worlds are a useful heuristic (explaining) device, I'll discard them later, as, from a constructivist perspective, the distinction is artificial; after all, there's only one world, no matter how described. If individuation is a normal biological process, then asking, 'Why is it not occurring in this person?', frames psychopathology as *meaning disorder*, a metaphor for difficulties in the ego-self relationship.

## Consciousness

Meaning-making requires functioning neuroanatomical structures and cognitive processes. Medieval anatomists believed the pineal gland was the third eye, seat of the soul, home of the self, creator of meaning. Brain research finds self as cybernetic nets, interconnected brain areas, where neurones enmesh like the branches of trees in a forest. Billions of interconnections create tendencies to pattern the outer world in particular self-similar ways, that is, to make gestalts –

to look for closure (Davison and Neale 1978: 483–9; Walsh 1978: 18–26).

Over-determined self-similar patterns are called complexes, areas of diminished reality testing. For example, if typing, or playing the piano, we might hit the wrong key, go to correct the error, but hit the wrong key again! We take in the error, but not the cause: tiredness, boredom, frustration, ignorance or lack of practice. This happens in depressive and obsessive ruminations, painful incidents replay endlessly, as if this could magically change what's already happened.

Analytical psychologist Anthony Stevens (1982: 247–75), summarised evidence about hemispheric functioning: suggesting our left brain performs tasks needing concentration, attention and language and distinguishes parts from wholes (it deconstructs – closes). Our right brain deals with phantasy, spatial awareness and 'gestalt formation' (it constructs – opens) (see Blakeslee 1980). The corpus callosum bridges the hemispheres. Its functions don't correspond to ego, or Self: thinking they do confuses neuronal message with neural medium. Consciousness depends on arousal. Cognitive psychologists suggest:

> Consciousness is a process in which information about multiple individual modalities of sensation and perception are combined into a unified multi–dimensional representation of the state of the system and its environment, and integrated with information about memories and the needs of the organism, generating emotional reactions and programmes of behaviour to adjust the organism to its environment.
>
> (Thatcher and John 1977: 162)

Jung said:

> the relation of psychic contents to the ego, insofar as this relation is perceived by the ego. Relations to the ego that are not perceived as such are unconscious. Consciousness is the function of the activity which maintains the relation of psychic contents to the ego.
>
> (CW 6: para. 700)

This is awareness (apperception). Cybernetic (system based) and ecological (environmental-adaptive) models metaphorise consciousness as 'Internet': accurate, as it depends on a nerve net, the Reticular

Activating System – RAS (reticulum is Latin for a string bag, or net). Located in the pons (the bridge between spinal cord and brain), continuous with the medulla below and midbrain above, the RAS determines arousal, mediates pain, maintains respiration and heart beat. It's almost entirely beyond conscious control, except in a few yogin, who can reduce arousal at will.

We're born able to be aroused, to gaze, suckle, open and close to stimuli. Arousal is triggered by innate releasing mechanisms: genetic, inborn, typically mammalian, dependent on mother's and baby's cognitive and neuropsychological software and hardware playing together. Millions of information processing tasks driven by pre-programmed motor systems unfold when an infant studies a face, feeds, and digests both food and experience. Object relations theory asks of this experience questions like 'Is the play between nipple and mouth a power struggle or mutual love? . . . how is that reflected in a person's present relationships? Can they open and close to objects? Can they play?' These theorists see the analytic task as allowing free play, free movement of objects: individual freedom. Developmental metaphors concentrate on power struggles between nipple and mouth as archetypes for 'the Hero's battle for deliverance from the mother'. As Nobel Prize winning Italian author Elias Canetti put it:

> The concept which I have put forward of digestion as a central process of power holds for the mother too, but in her case the process is distributed between two bodies and is made clearer and more conscious by the fact that the new body, for whose nourishment she provides, is separated from her own. The mother's power over a young child is absolute, not only because its life depends on her, but also because she herself feels a very strong urge to exercise this power all the time. The concentration of the appetite for domination on such a small organism gives rise to a feeling of superiority greater than that obtaining in any other habitual relationship between human beings.
>
> (1984: 221)

He is describing a power gradient which determines locus of control. Fordham suggested envy-as-twoness emerges in the systems {Self/emerging ego} and {ego/all-containing Self}. Events in the system {infant/mother} parallel those in the systems {Self/ego} and {Self/other}. Notice, as Canetti said, power gradients differ: the players are not reversible. Self is always bigger than ego, always has power.

## Autism and semantic deficit disorders

If no eyes, no gaze. Blindness is a congenital meaning disorder of visual perception. If our parietal lobes don't function, then, though we gaze, we have a learning difficulty in locating objects in space-time (either internal or external). 'I'm clumsy. I crowd you when we meet. I've no sense of boundary. You find me intrusive, I find you unlocatable ... I can't find you.' This is Asperger's syndrome: a congenital meaning disorder (Attwood 1998), others include deafness, semantic deficit disorders (including the dyslexias) and early infantile autism (Kanner's syndrome).

'Autistic', to psychiatrists of learning disability is a congenital, severe failure of information processing. It is movingly described by the child analyst Virginia Axline in her classic work *Dibs: in Search of Self* (1969) and defined as:

> A syndrome present from birth at or beginning almost inevitably in the first thirty months. Responses to auditory and sometimes to visual stimuli are abnormal and there are usually severe problems in the understanding of spoken language. Speech is delayed, and if it develops is characterised by echolalia, the reversal of pronouns, immature grammatical structure and the inability to use abstract terms. There is generally an impairment in the social use of both verbal and gestural language. Problems in social relationships are most severe before the age of five years and include an impairment in the development of eye-to-eye gaze, social attachment and cooperative play. Ritualistic behaviour is usual and may include abnormal routines, resistance to change, attachments to odd objects and stereotyped patterns of play. The capacity for abstract and symbolic thought and for imaginative play is diminished. Intelligence ranges from severely subnormal to normal or above. Performance is usually better on tasks involving rote memory or visuospatial skills than on those requiring symbolic or linguistic skills.
>
> (World Health Organisation, Glossary to ICD 9, 299.0. 1978)

In this congenital meaning disorder feeling can't reliably link to sensation, (in Bion's language, beta elements can't coalesce to form alpha elements). Failure to attach value to percepts creates severe social isolation. In Chapter 1 I discussed how Jung's association experiments showed areas of mind can become inaccessible to consciousness: complexes are like 'autistic moments'. Both Freud and Jung knew multiple consciousnesses can coexist in one person, unaware of each other, classically described by Morton Prince (1900), as 'autonomous subpersonalities'. Psychoanalyst Harry Guntrip called this splitting and the severe social isolation it creates 'the schizoid compromise' (Guntrip 1971: 148). Winnicott (1971), his analyst, suggested this term differentiated neuroses from psychoses:

> Those who have had good enough mothering struggle with the ordinary difficulties in human relationships . . . those who have not, have deep seated doubts about the reality and viability of their very self . . . suffering from varying degrees of depersonalisation, unreality, the dread feeling of not belonging, of being fundamentally isolated and out of touch with the world. This is broadly, the schizoid problem, the problem of those who feel cut off, apart, different, unable to become involved in any real relationships.
>
> (1971: 77–8)

Analytically, 'autism' means withdrawal to 'auto-sensuousness'. Self, without ego's navigational aid, is beached, washed up, unable to go ashore or back to sea. Language becomes private. 'Autism' in the analytic sense is a *primary meaning disorder*; that is, the biological hardware could work but has been mis-programmed. I suggest using this term avoids confusion with a rare congenital meaning disorder.

Meaning disorders can begin as disorders of perceptions, which depend on search patterns, or concepts. As Kant said, 'percepts without concepts are blind'. Primary meaning disorder means a failure of *self-similar* patterning, or, taking a term from semantics, sticking to primacy of concept (repetition compulsion). An historical example of primacy of concept occurs in *The Voyage of the Beagle* (1998). Naturalist Charles Darwin noted native people in Tierra del Fuego couldn't 'see' HMS Beagle. To them, 'ship' meant 'canoe-sized boat'. The Beagle was too big to be a ship. It might be a cloud.

This is 'primacy of concept' – conceptual closure. At the other end of the world, the Inuit have over thirty words for snow – conceptual opening. Peter Hoeg in *Miss Smilla's Feeling for Snow* (1996) describes how an Inuit woman, dealing with the unexplained death of a small boy, has an urge to find 'whodunnit'. Her feeling for snow reveals clues ordinary Danes could not see. Detective fiction humanises bottled-up ('autistic', meaning disordered) murderous impulses, as does analysis.

Jung illustrated this using a myth, 'The Spirit Mercurius'. Trapped in a bottle, the spirit is enraged. When freed, and tricked, it's willing to grant wishes (*CW* 13: paras 239–46). Mercurius, like Ariel in his tree, is trapped. Meaning-making is hard when we're trapped by others' constructs, or when consciousness is clouded, if we're 'on the bottle' or have 'lost our bottle'. Maybe we're adrift in a strange country (like Ferdinand), or ill, exhausted or psychotic. In strange situations ego has to reality test continually. This requires a high level of vigilance, which often fails, creating a *secondary meaning disorder*. That is, the hardware works, the software has given way under stress. In order to make clearer the difference between primary and secondary meaning disorder I need to amplify the definitions of ego and Self used in the last chapter.

## Ego

Jung said ego is a complex, whose function is to reality test, maintain identity, personality and temporal continuity (*CW* 6: para. 706). It derives from Self and is defended by both Persona and Shadow. Persona is the mask we present to the world. The term comes from the Greek, the masks worn by actors, as still used in Japanese Noh theatre. Ego is essential for individuation (Fordham 1985: 34–9; Hall and Young-Eisendrath, 1991: 6–7). Consciousness is not a synonym for ego. Jung pictures ego as accessing memory, providing subjective components of conscious functions (first impressions), modulating affect and preventing invasion by the unconscious (Tavistock Lectures, *CW* 18: paras 36–8). Ego is intersubjective, closes and opens (Atwood 1994). Its reality testing gives sensory continuity, secures identities (sub-personalities) which mediate between conscious and unconscious. It's the director of Hesse's Magic Theatre, and presents in dreams as 'dream-ego', the viewpoint with which the dreamer identifies.

Ego gives awareness of the inner world, body, breath, 'me as me' (closing); and, externally, awareness of objects (opening). The first could be called 'person-ego', the second, 'system-ego'. Guntrip (1971: 106) uses Latin terms: 'autoplastic' ego adjusts us to our environment (opens), and 'alloplastic' ego attempts to alter the environment to fit us (closes). I'll use English terms. Now, we can project (creatively imagine) mental processes in any other, or any thing; think of the four year old Jung and his stone (Chapter 1). In children, this is called play; in adults, magical or primary process thinking. We never know if what I call 'red', you call 'red', if what I call 'aggression' you'll call 'assault'. Naming depends on semantic differential (locus of control), so, what gives the names?

## Self

Self is neither conscious nor unconscious, yet both conscious and unconscious. This is a paradox. Jung (*CW* 6: paras 789–91) defined Self as potential, . . . *the whole range of psychic phenomena in man*. Like friendship, it manifests in time, a bit at a time. It's transcendent, beyond understanding . . . like sand on a beach, finite yet uncountable. Self is the infinite potential in our genes, with infinite exits from our life's time-corridor into moments. In object relations theory, ego is primary:

> ego, according to Freud, is the organised part of the self, constantly influenced by instinctual impulses but keeping them under control by repression; furthermore it directs all activities and establishes and maintains the relation to the external world. The self is used to cover the whole of the personality, which includes not only the personality, but also the instinctual life which Freud called the id.
>
> (Klein 1975: 249)

For analytical psychology, Self is primary. It isn't actor, director, or producer. It's the whole show, plus audience, critics, cultural tradition and relationship to the collective. As Jung says:

> The term 'Self' seemed to me a suitable one for this unconscious substrate, whose actual exponent in consciousness is the ego. The ego stands to the Self as the moved to the mover, as object to subject, because the determining factors which radiate out from the Self surround the ego on all sides and are therefore supra-ordinate to it. The Self, like the unconscious, is an *a priori* existent out of which the ego evolves. It is, so to speak, the unconscious prefiguration of the ego. It is not I who create myself, rather, I happen to myself.
>
> (*CW* 11: para. 391)

The child analyst Mara Sidoli (in Sidoli and Davies 1988: 55–61) lists three concepts essential for meaning-making: ego, Self and the archetypes (patterns which function as inborn organisers of experience). By ego she means the social constructs of an individual (self from 'outside', time bound, 'me, now'). Self signifies the psychic totality of an individual, from 'inside', everyone we are or could be. It is time-free, 'all of me, my whole existence' – and a spiritual dimension.

An archetype is an unconscious entity having two poles. One is the body, physical and neuropsychological, complex adaptive behaviours unfolding at developmentally appropriate stages (such as sucking in infancy, or masturbation in adolescence). The other pole is fantasy, internal images from cultural myth-systems which release meaning, installing archetypal patterns (*CW* 8: paras 219–20). Archetypes occur in all people, in any culture, at any part of space/ time. They're verbs, *doing* words – fathering, mothering, courting, mating – not nouns. Individuation is archetypal, and also inevitable, it's the adaptive design of the human psyche. Like change, it happens if we have enough cultural freedom to allow the archetypes to unpack.

Anthony Stevens (1982: 220) says archetypes are 'open-ended systems, like Chomsky's language acquisition device, neurophysiologically based complexes primed to be programmed with the religious/ mythological/moral/"vocabulary" of the culture'. Self, an archetype, may appear in dreams as a ruler or wise being, a mandala figure, or, commonly, as a crowd. Self is a collective noun: sub-personalities, archetypal images, internal objects and self-objects: to *all of which* the Shadow is the opposite, *The thing a person has no wish to be* . . . (*CW* 16: para. 470). Contemporary Jungians at times simplify this to the *opposite of the lived persona* . . . side-stepping a vital moral problem. Shadow is more than the unlived good in an evil person, and the unlived evil in a good one.

In one of my dreams (memories), shadow was a huge traffic cop, standing beside me, a young Hell's Angel, stopped for speeding, calming me down simply by *being there*. Shadow *is* arresting. It looms, we stop. This is not always bad, being stopped was better than having a crash due to reckless driving! As Freud said in *Mourning and Melancholia* (1917) 'the shadow of the parents falls on the object'. Here, collective shadow images (cop and biker) show an internal dilemma . . . do I 'go faster', do I 'slow down and consider others?' The dream reminded me of 'knowledge of twoness', the sense of Other as separate from Self. Fast bikes, a popular image of freedom, produce envy: 'I want what you have, and I'll spoil it if I don't get it.' (In reality, the cop had asked me about my old British bike as well as telling me off.) And, in benign form, twoness is 'gratitude', *I want to share what I have, to thank you for what you have given me*: the cop enjoyed racing me, I felt grateful for his sense of humour. Envy, as twoness, has two forms then, 'envy' and 'gratitude' – one closes, the other opens.

Self uses both envy's positive and negative sides, as explored by Jung in *Answer to Job* (*CW* 11: paras 560–758). In his analysis of the myth of Job, Jung took the dialogue between God and the Devil over Job's fate as metaphor to the dialogue inside Self over the fate of whichever aspect of ego is currently uppermost. Self, to the over-comfortable *embourgeoised* ego can appear demonic, threatening to destroy everything stable. In analysis, this experience is the *nigredo*, the blackening of the alchemical work, or (if you prefer) attaining the depressive position, realising wished-for omnipotence cannot ever be attained.

Jung supposes Self is a given, present from conception or before: Self is fullness emptying into ego. But is the cup half-full, emptying; or half-empty, filling? – a Zen question. Is the fish swimming with or against the stream, deintegrating or integrating? Fordham suggests deintegration is opening of Self to percepts, reintegration is closure of ego to a particular percept and its subsequent incorporation into Self (where it can form a stable internal object) a psychological reference point, a 'golden mean'.

## The ego–Self axis

In making meaning, ego is a primary object for Self. Self and the archetypes are primary objects for the ego. Purpose derives from their connection. Edward Edinger (1962), named this the 'ego–Self axis'. Edward Whitmont (1969: 250–64) believed estrangement of Self and ego link to Fordham's concepts, deintegration and integration.

In deintegration, part of Self 'divides' to act within consciousness, on the ego. As defined by the Scottish object relations theorist, Ronald Fairbairn (1952: 9), ego has adaptive, discriminatory and integrative functions, bridging 'inner and outer', testing reality. It represses disturbing feelings, often by dividing. As a result, it scatters, forming islands of consciousness in the ocean of unconscious rather than being an organising centre, or a 'higher Self'.

Meaning-making requires consciousness and ego. It relies on

unconscious mechanisms to separate ego out from fusion (confusion) with mother. Like analyst Erich Neumann (1989: 268), I am assuming that fusion is a primary state, whereas Fordham assumes the existence of a primary Self. The mechanisms are: (1) denial, a capacity to 'autistically encapsulate' in order to isolate and digest experience; (2) envious splitting, within the ego, of ego from Self, of Self from other; and (3) projective identification, interpreting others' behaviour as caused by our internal needs, as we do as children. I suggest these depend on Self using 'primacy of concept', its own concept of itself and its object relations.

Ronald Fairbairn (1952: 28–58, 82) suggested unfoldment of ego doesn't arise from 'libidinal push'. Reformulating Freud, he suggests our primary need is for others (objects) to relate to. Meaning comes through object seeking, the unfoldment of archetypal patterns in defence of Self (Kalsched 1998: 83–102). (Note that in object relations theory the word 'object ' is grammatical: 'I' equals subject, nominative case: 'he, she, it,' equals object, accusative case. The theory does not say people are *things*, a common and unfortunate misconception.)

For Fairbairn, meaning arises in exchanges between foci of ego consciousness (or sub-personalities). He framed the analytic task as turning closed into open systems. For example, he described depression as warding off feelings of helplessness in the face of premature closure (loss and other exit life events) with illusions of responsibility. Believing we caused failures in our early environment (omnipotent guilt) costs us self-esteem, autonomy and creativity. The myth 'whatever it means, it's my fault' does bring an illusory independence in its corollary, 'If it's my fault, then I can make it better' omnipotent control. Blanket guilt also allows avoidance of looking into what one is really feeling guilty about.

Infantile rage at mother for consistently failing to recognise needs can lead to crippling of the ego. Two sets of internal figures arise: one hidden, highly sexualised and seductive; the other, strongly dominating but sexually rejecting. One taunts and teases, the other bullies and punishes (like Ariel and Caliban). This idea is central to psychoanalyst Mervyn Glasser's (1986) 'core complex'. Glasser defines envious splitting as 'the activity by which the ego discerns differences within the self and its object, or between the self and its objects'. He suggests a sado-masochistic image of mother and infant as a couple can form at the centre of the psyche translating meaning-making into power dynamics, an argument about locus of control.

In cognitive psychology, splitting is necessary to detect boundaries, to tell figure from ground, like the optical illusion which is first two faces, then a chalice . . . back and forth. Ego is primarily a boundary detector, finding meaning as a 'strange effect' at a boundary. As Self exists outside time, and ego in time, time perception must be an ego function (Chapter 7). This is basic to Jung's association experiments, measuring time delays between stimulus and response caused by unconscious complexes 'a recollection, composed of a large number of component ideas . . . the cement that holds the complex together is the feeling tone common to all the individual ideas' (*CW* 2: para. 733).

I'm viewing individuation as an heroic, sacrificial journey, as did the two patients I discussed earlier. Their myths are easy to relate to: most of us try being heroes. We succeed, fail, or die in the attempt. Heroism is an act in opposition to cultural norms, a path to individuation (not the only one). As cultures set boundaries using taboo this creates a paradoxical challenge to human adaptation: how do we construct an ego from Self in a biased, deceptive, relational world (Slavin and Kriegman 1992), which character do we play from all our potential characters? If the ego-Self axis only operates as a core complex, this adaptive potential is severely limited. Dekk showed what this looked like with his obsessive murderous ruminations, and Ben with deliberate acts of self harm.

## Self and collective

Night Sea Journey is a term for making meaning, and a metaphor for sexual intercourse (a boy's 'night sea journeys' often begin in his wet dreams). It is also a metaphor for primal scene fantasies, internal images of what happened during the parental intercourse when our spirit became matter. Jung joked, 'the penis is a phallic symbol' (*CW* 18: 572) – like Prospero's magic wand, or an addict's needle. We could say 'Prospero projected his phallus into the storm', or 'acted out the terrible witch father'.

For Edinger, Whitmont and classical Jungians, and object relations theorists like Roger Money-Kyrle (1971), attention from Self to ego often feels envious, spoiling, inflated, phallic, intrusive, blowing us off course, wrecking lives, casting us ashore on desert islands. Ego then enviously attacks Self . . . saying, 'Self has everything, "I" have nothing.' Self becomes a menacing crowd, attacking closed off parts of the psyche.

London analyst, James Astor (1998: 1–4, 24–31), suggested Jung's psychiatric background led him to create a more open model than

Freud, the gifted neurologist, and that the conceptual openness of Jung's model arises from his appreciation of the collective unconscious, which (as in the clinical examples) provides collective parenting. That is, unconscious projection has value in linking us to the culture, holding and containing both the positive and negative aspects of our psyche. For instance, it could be Jung was himself in an *enantiodromia*, treating the psychotic part of himself by unconsciously projecting it into his patients in the asylum.

In *Symbols of Transformation*, written after breaking with Freud (in 1913), a most disturbed time of his life, Jung described the Night Sea Journey of Hiawatha. I think he identified with this native American culture-hero, and used 'effort after meaning' to contain his disturbance. This is why his text is so disjointed, so full of free associations. Its also an example of Jung using culture to re-parent himself, and find new purpose.

In the myth, whilst crossing the Big Lake, Hiawatha is swallowed by Mishe-Nama, the monster from the depths (the Water Dragon):

> this is the almost world wide myth of the typical deed of the hero. He journeys by ship, fights a sea monster, is swallowed, struggles against being bitten and crushed to death, and having arrived inside the whale-dragon, seeks the vital organ, which he proceeds to cut off or otherwise destroy . . . It is easy to see what the battle with the sea monster means: it is the attempt to free the ego consciousness from the deadly grip of the unconscious.
>
> (*CW* 5: paras 538–9)

Differences between developmental and archetypal perspectives depend on where we place locus of control and temporal focus in the analysing system (a 'mini-collective'). Developmental/sequential time perspectives concern *process*, (what happens here mirrors what happened before with your mother): archetypal/parallel time concerns unfolding of *pattern* (what happens here mirrors what happens everywhere in the collective). Michael Fordham argues 'the hero's battle for deliverance from the mother' recapitulates early struggles at the breast (1995: 150–72), justifying his belief by appeals to infant observation and dismissing Erich Neumann's argument that 'the myth, being a projection of the transpersonal collective unconscious depicts transpersonal events, and, whether interpreted objectively or subjectively, in no case is a personalistic interpretation adequate' (1989: 197).

It's arguable whether Fordham's polemic was motivated by envy: 'Jung's mantle' fell to Neumann, not him. Indeed, Jung remained dubious about Fordham and his developmental project till the end of his life, perhaps because Fordham (as a gifted analyst of children) bluntly diagnosed Jung as a 'childhood schizophrenic' to his face (Smith 1996: 22). Andrew Samuels felt these rivalrous myths in analytical psychology led to 'a third system' (classical) which acts as a bridge (1985a: 11–22). I think he obscures the value of healthy opposition between two continuously useful and *different* meaning systems, which (as for Fordham and Neumann) appeal to different temperaments.

These oppositions exist in other human culture systems. Zen Buddhism has a developmental approach – 'being in the moment', breaking down our ego identification. The Tibetan Buddhist tradition uses an archetypal approach based on active imagination, studying collective patterns, in mandalas, mudras and ritual. Two ways, one enlightenment. Joseph Henderson (1984: 83), describes Self as a container of duality, 'evolutionary and creative, alive in a perpetual becoming, self-contained in a permanent state of being'.

Ego is very small, Self is very big. The notion that ego needs *more consciousness*, that ego could then function in a 'royal' manner towards Self is hubristic nonsense: as in phrases like 'I've been doing a lot of work on my Self' – imagine a drop of water saying 'I've been doing a lot of work on the ocean'. Hubris is psychic inflation, spiritual pride and closure against others who have not 'done a lot of work on their Selves'. London analyst Kenneth Lambert (1981: 141–3) describes Jung's understanding that transference dynamics always operate, projection always occurs, and that they contain infantile, sexual and incestual fantasies. Whilst commenting that Jung did not especially make meaning from infantile transferences, Lambert points out how much he did make meaning from archetypal transference – archetypal images being projected on to the analyst, who assumes a projection of the patient's Self. It is neither analyst nor patient who 'do work on the Self' – it is two Selves, inter-subjectively and (largely unconsciously) sharing meaning.

Preoccupation with the ordinary ebb and flow between ego and Self is symptomatic of any psychopathology. In borderline, paranoid states we imagine 'they' are after us. Narcissistically injured sub-personalities stay preoccupied with how they appear to others, rather than how ego and Self appear to each other. In neither state is there much sense how our combined ego/Self relates to the collective. Without the meaning-stabilising work of individuation, change goes on being experienced *as if* it was opposition rather than difference: 'The only person who knows how to separate himself from the grim law of enantiodromia is the man who knows how to separate himself from the Unconscious' (*CW* 7: para. 112).

This view is supported by the liberating value of well-timed failures of infant, childhood and adolescent environments in natural, adaptive ways. Indeed, I'd say (as a parent), my task is to fail my children gradually and progressively, to be a 'good-enough failure' rather than a 'good-enough father'. A problem for Western cultures so tuned to see things only in terms of success and failure (the first always good and the second always bad) is that it is difficult to accept as natural the flow of events during a life as a series of steps: forward and back, doing and undoing, learning and unlearning. The next chapter examines this in more detail, looking at how children develop their temporal navigation skills.

# 3

# THE CHILD'S DEVELOPMENT
# OF MEANING

Tom's mind was made up now. He was gloomy and desperate. He was a forsaken, friendless boy, he said; nobody loved
him: when they found out what they had driven him to,
perhaps they would be sorry; he had tried to do right and get
along, but they would not let him; since nothing would do
them but to be rid of him, let it be so; and let them blame
him for the consequences – why shouldn't they? what right
had the friendless to complain?'

(Mark Twain, *The Adventures of Tom Sawyer*, 1991: 70)

## A child's theory of mind

In Mark Twain's version of the Night Sea Journey, the Mississippi
River is the collective unconscious and the heroic quest is the boy's
adventuring. Tom Sawyer, an orphan, is escaping his nagging aged
aunt: his friend, Huck Finn, a street kid, is escaping his down-and-
out, violent, alcoholic father. Here, Tom is playing with the idea of
suicide. We think like this when life suddenly loses meaning, when
the universe no longer supports us, when our meaning structures are
destroyed and there's a threat to our very Self (Orbach, 1988: 91–4,
204): through illness (Mary, Chapter 4), parental abuse and neglect
(Mike, this chapter) or (as for my friend, Aman) by collective
betrayal. Aged nine, Chinese troops 'liberated' Tibet and, billeted in
his home in Lhasa, ate his favourite dog before his eyes: a truly
frozen moment.

If our meaning structures are inadequate or overwhelmed; if we
do not have internal 'good-enough' parents (secure internal objects)
then humanisation of archetypal patterns is unresolved, leaving us
with dependency issues (Dekk and Ben, Chapter 2). We make premature use of the collective and its cultural myths for support, meaning structures have to grow with the collective as parent. If we're
defined by others as delinquent, criminal, addict or madman, then

we're marginalised, liminal. If we live childhood for someone else, struggling but always failing to be how we imagine someone else needs us to be, then our childhood is stolen. We become self-marginalising, blaming ourselves for the shortcomings of our parents, family, friends and society.

I emphasise *if . . . then* as it is a child's logical operator. Child-thinking is concrete, slow – child-feeling is quick. It is deep magic, the interplay between two modes of time perception, time-free Self and time-bound ego. Twain eloquently used this interplay in his creative process as, with flow and intensity, he weaves his own childhood into his stories. A kid himself on the Mississippi in the early nineteenth century, Tom Sawyer and Huck Finn are young, wild Sam Clemens, re-told as Hero. Renaming himself Mark Twain, Sam did as we all do, mythologising painful childhood events to give them and himself new meaning.

Developing meaning in childhood requires playing with identity and alterity (otherness), evolving a 'theory of mind' in the process. We do this by observing infants and other kids. We hear their stories, tell stories about ourselves, learn from movies and soap operas and TV game shows and parents. We watch everything they do and take it in. If mum and dad love, we learn to love – if they fight, we learn to mistrust. As Jung said:

> the marked predominance of mythological elements in the psyche of the child gives us a clear hint of the way the individual mind gradually develops out of the collective mind of early childhood, thus giving rise to the old theory of a state of perfect knowledge before and after individual existence. These mythological references which we find in children are also met with in dementia praecox and in dreams.
>
> (*CW* 4: para. 520)

Childhood is when ego evolves through play with the timeless Self. Self isn't just near to us in childhood, it *is* us. What is time like in childhood when 'later, darling, mummy's got a little bit of a headache . . .' meant inconsolable, endless waiting – when 'this afternoon' is years away and 'next week', distant forever?

Ego emerges slowly into time, slowly develops temporal perception, develops a child's theory of mind. For me watching a snail, wondering what it's thinking, realising, 'I'm thinking . . .' and the snail winked. As it opened and closed, I opened and closed. If 'inner child' is a metaphor for Self, then when scenes of childhood past relive in an analytic now, they do so to allow Self to unfold now. Childhood scenes in analytic sessions are not causal, historical facts. They are mythological narratives, statements about the mental state of the narrator and their feelings towards the analyst as audience. We re-edit old home-movies, adding new scenes (sometimes very small) to change the story – *From Zero to Hero: Childhood, the Directors' Cut* – developmental stories are retold from the Self's point of view, from the vertex of meaning.

This has little to do with 'what really happened', much to do with 'what we really felt'. Tracking the *form* of a childhood story retold in analysis, as Beverley Zabriskie (1997) said, thaws frozen moments of childhood despair by providing validation for an inner, felt experience, then allowing its meaning to change. If the memory *content* is forensically real that's serendipity. The form (myth) is independent of the content, just as how Tom and Huck handle life is real, because they're 'real' boys. Myths help us *solve* reality, by dissolving reality.

We need fairy stories, princesses, dragons and heroes to help us create our story. Tom Sawyer, fantasy hero, pirate, highwayman and Robin Hood is jilted by Becky Thatcher, his first love, for whom he 'took a lickin'. He runs away, fakes drowning. Fortunately, his friends help him through. Then he rescues Becky from a cave, (accidentally) slays the dragon (the villain, Injun Joe) and finds the gold. He becomes a 'for-real' hero. Gold, real or alchemical, is a metaphor for Self, like friendship. The Society of Friends reminds us 'there is that of God in every Man' (Quakers 1995: 32). Self is the source of value, whether moral or material, whether viewed from a developmental or archetypal perspective (Solomon 1991).

Archetypal metaphors describe collective patterns of Self-development, developmental metaphors let us make gold from the leaden times of childhood; times without friends, without collective support. Whatever metaphors we use, it is in the here and now of the session where change begins. For example, Mike, who I discuss later, was born a white African, but grew up to feel neither white nor African. His individuation was a hero-quest: analysis an heroic struggle to deliver himself from the 'terrible witch mother' and learn how to father himself. Whatever theory I used turned into a here-and-now fight. We did not reconstruct childhood with reductive explanations, but relived it until 'meaning *and* feeling' replaced 'feeling *as* meaning'. We went down the developmental spiral so we could come up again, but in a different place. We didn't change what happened, we put a different spin (interpretation) on it.

Wilfred Bion described this as 'condensation of meaning by transformation of beta elements into alpha elements' (Bion 1962: 6–7). If you've studied physics, you'll recall pictures of beta particles crossing a bubble chamber, leaving a vapour trail behind: like a high altitude jet, where the 'plane itself is a barely perceptible bright dot in the sky. 'Particles of feeling' are generated by incoming sensations carving neural pathways through the cerebrum, branching like the Mississippi Delta. These tracks transform sensation from its unconscious perception by the limbic system, turning it into feeling by adding value and connecting it to 'memories' (Carter 1999: 94–5). The feeling value of a particular sensation is given (neuroanatomically) first, by the amygdala assessing whether an event is pleasurable or painful (remembering that fire burns), next by other basal ganglia, particularly connections to the mamillary bodies which link affect to memory, then by associations through the pre-frontal cortex to self-similar patterns (Siegel 1999: 50–66; Walsh 1978).

Memory is a route-map, not a location. It is 'reconstructive imagining'. Like a favourite childhood trail, we don't need to know where a memory is to find it. We just find it. The first feeling values are those of basic survival: we negotiate with real external objects to deal with greed, envy and jealousy. Later the neural pathways laid down early in life which we use habitually become thoughts. We re-cognise when we re-member, that is, we think the object back into being, putting together whole objects from part objects.

As a physicist recognises a particle by its vapour trail through space-time, so analysts recognise particles of feeling: the 'delta blues' of depression, with their characteristic temporal slowing, the 'Latin tempo' of mania or the 'free Jazz' temporal fragmentation of psychosis. When we listen to the rhythm of a person's narrative myth of their childhood, we watch how it forms into discourse, as well as tracking its content. Psychologists explain the importance of separating form from content in the way children learn to name feelings:

> the characteristic point is that one of the conflicting mental states is not given the right name. Happiness is correctly named, but misery is given no name, or is mis-named. The 'right' name here means: use of the name leads to expectations that are fulfilled. As generally, the use of intentional languages is justified by its success in prediction. The child learns that happiness is associated with feelings such as satisfaction and gratitude, and with the natural expressions of

these feelings. But if the word is applied in cases in which the child is neglected, then as far as she is unprepared for her feelings and inclinations; they make no sense. So far the child does not known what she is believing, feeling, or inclined to do. Psychological disorder can result from acquisition of a false or inadequate theory of mind.

(Bolton and Hill 1996: 46–9)

Theory of mind evolves as feelings (values) add to percepts. Initially, a theorising infants' Self might say 'expect mother (other), and seek relationship – use your body to form relationship.' Learning to turn percepts into feeling is done through maternal mirroring. Self realises, 'Hey! When a big sensation fills me, she "digests" it . . .'. Raw sensations come back, named and manageable: 'empty pain in the stomach' becomes signified by the image 'breast', then the sound 'mama', then 'me hungry . . .' metaphors from child development describe Self forming meaning.

Neural pathways are biological correlates of archetypes, which, once installed, can then mesh with numinous cultural myths. An old joke describes how a rich New Yorker, learning her son was in analysis groaned, 'Oedipus, Schmoedipus, as long as he loves his mother . . .'. Child development isn't only a myth about Oedipus (an abused, abandoned child, whose parents pierced his feet), it's about developing a theory of mind, learning to form and use myths, including our own. To study meaning disorders is to reconstruct myths from developmental theory, not to abandon it. Insights from semantics help us ask new questions, to reframe meaning in childhood not only in terms of mother/infant but also in terms of Self.

## Developmental perspective: presence, absence and alterity

As children, we live with too many uncertainties for any grown-up ever to explain everything. We are in *our* time and *their* time: magical time and school time – at about this age we start to seriously question the existence of the tooth fairy. Tom and Huck, inner children, help us make sense of this. Imagine them saying, 'OK. So what is a theory of mind? What has it to do with meaning and purpose?' Kids just don't believe grand narratives, visions of a One God Universe (Burroughs 1987: 119; Chapter 5) They say 'if you say God's in everything, then God's in me . . . then I'm God . . . I'm a child of the universe.' This may bring a deep sense of unity – we may want to fight to save the planet; or we may feel estranged, persecuted, disintegrated by numinous experience.

Secure separation, space to try out our meanings and find our purposes, requires secure attachment. No attachment means no separation. Loss is intrinsic to meaning-making. Play, a creative act using transitional objects (first Teddy bears, then symbols), suspends this sense of loss. As meaning is mutable and always in development so meaning disorders represent developmental delay, arrest, or regression to earlier psychological structures. Meaning-disordered experiences may mirror early loss and impairment of identity (persona) formation. In psychosis and regression, the appearance of infantile meaning-making strategies indicates failure of adult ones. This is not necessarily a jump back to leap forward (*reculer pour mieux sauter*) which, alas, does not happen in degenerative psychoses (like schizophrenia) though it may in self-induced psychotic states of ecstasy, terror and awe.

Functional psychoses don't necessarily have meaning-filled causal connections with very early experience. Infant-like omnipotence fantasies in psychoses and deep regression *may* be uterine memories of the nine months spent dreaming in our own flotation tank, and, as a Buddhist, I've no difficulty believing meaning begins before birth, *between* lives, in the dance of Karma and Time. However, I'm much less sure whether hypnotic regression to 'pre-birth' or 'past lives' is possible, necessary or wise. I find a developmental perspective helps ground my patients and me in now, helps us recognise, accept, hold and contain regression (my own and my patients) within and outside an analytic hour.

We cannot but work within the transference and counter-transference but we don't have to believe its dynamics tell a story of cause and effect. Speculations about initial conditions may let us better imagine present and future patterns of object-relating. How? Infants experiment visually with presence and absence, luminosity (interest) and non-luminosity (lack of interest). Newborn eyes focus at about the distance of nipple to face. For example, as we play 'peep-bo!' the game installs the archetypal percept 'mother' (whose installation begins within a few hours of birth as a newborn can, by then, tell mother's milk from other's milk.) Autistic people can't experiment with presence and absence: they fixate on content, on endless elaboration of detail.

Autistic children feel that their eyes are physical instruments
to control objects, which seem to stab and transfix people, to

'cut them dead', to blank them out of existence, to annihilate them. These are not metaphors to the children; they feel that they actually do such things. Also, if they see something unpleasant, it feels as if their eyes are being struck by a painful object, while a loud noise can be felt as a blow on the ear.

(Tustin 1986: 145)

This is like an experience in disintegrative psychoses when 'the voices', delusions of control (the opposite of omnipotence) and ideas of reference transform content into a closed form, paranoia, being beside the Self. But if, to an observer, an adult psyche appears to undergo dissociative splitting into murderous infant and meaning-disordered adult, this does not prove links to events in infancy, specific failures of early attachment, or the time when identity was defined by alterity; by (m)other. Deintegration and reintegration begin *in utero*, the purple uterine wall is the first *other*. We form meaning through attachment, seeking meaning is primary, derived from an innate theory of mind, as explored in the work of Jean Piaget and Daniel Stern. So, what is attachment and how does it relate to forming a theory of mind?

## Attachment behaviour

Research in progress at the Tavistock Clinic London, the strange object research on attachment behaviour (Patrick *et al.* 1994) studies theories of mind used to attach meaning to objects in a naturalistic experiment. That it can is what I wish to show, to give a flavour of the kind of narrative possible rather than whether it is 'true'. Researchers patiently video thousands of infant and mother interactions through a one-way mirror. Mother leaves the room, the infant feels loss, and reacts. Some infants continue playing, others wail, rock, or nod off. A stranger comes in and sits in mother's chair. The infant may play with them, wail, rock, want to be picked up and comforted, or ignore the stranger altogether. When mother comes back the infant's approach to her is observed.

Analysis of the interactive body-language shows four main forms of attachment : secure, hostile, dependent and anxious – each may be either consistent or inconsistent. Meaning (attachment of significa-tion to body-language) is given by the experimenters in object relations theory, not by the mother. The experimenters suggest per-sonality develops predictably following early attachment – as a result of oft repeated patterns of intersubjective experience. (The same infants may have different attachment to fathers.) The infants are being followed up long-term to see whether these patterns really do predict behaviour mode – (or personality type, in 'Jungian').

The Italian child psychologist, Allesandro Piontelli (1992: 140) suggests it may. She describes twins studied by ultrasound *in utero*. One pair, a boy, Luca and girl, Alice, stroked each other through their amniotic sacs. This continued in the cot, as they put a blanket between them. As toddlers, one hid behind a curtain and stroked the other. We might imagine one as left handed, the other right; one introvert, the other extravert, one sensation type, one intuitive. Which hid, which found? Preconceptions could determine our answer.

Jung suggested our psychological type shapes our preconceptions, as well as our perceptions. Attachment theory might predict secure attachment gives a sensation type, hostile a feeling type, dependent, a thinking type or anxious an intuitive (or it might not). The infant's theories of mind might be, respectively: 'I know my body, that's OK, that's how I make meaning'; 'If I feel, its real'; 'Lets just think about this, then I'll know if its real'; 'I've got to predict where mother is, then I'll know we're both real'. Do not suppose these links between Jungian typology and attachment theory are true or false. In theory building about the mind, what matters for a child (and for an analyst) about a theory is its prediction-generating power and how well it fits the facts together (its efficacy).

Why might we theorise the left handed, introvert, intuitive type hid (and grew up to be a poet) and the right handed, extravert sensation type found, and grew up to play football for Italy? Maybe because these are dominant cultural myths? Whether a narrative link is valid matters less in meaning-making than the concept 'linking'. We may link what Piontelli observed to notions, say, of left versus right cerebral hemispheric function, masculinity and femininity, animus and anima, the balance between dopaminergic and serotoninergic neurones in the proximal limbic system – or yin and yang. Again, what matters about this list of concepts is the form (the dialectic between pairs of opposites) not the content, theories of mind.

Jung suggested that concepts form in opposing pairs, and, over time, one turns into the other (enantiodromia) – a notion he probably derived from Hegel (see Chapter 10). Meaning arises from Self unfolding, deintegrating (object-seeking) and reintegrating (linking to the objects by forming internal images, called imagos). If no objects, then no meaning. There is the object and the shadow of the object: its presence and absence, its luminosity (interest) or lack of luminosity (lack of interest).

### Four states of mind in relation to meaning

$$\frac{\text{Luminous presence}}{\text{Luminous absence}} \text{ is like } \frac{\text{Non-luminous presence}}{\text{Non-luminous absence}}$$

This semantic square derives from the work of the Californian analytical psychologist (and Kabbalah scholar) Stephen Joseph (1997). His theory of mind uses these terms, derived from the symbol of the mirror (as above so below, the microcosm reflects the macrocosm). To determine what kind of object is being observed is like koan practice: objects may be present in the mirror of the mind, or absent. They may be luminous (attracting libido) or non-luminous (negatively cathected). This represents appearance to the infant's emerging mind, as objects appear out of 'the extremity of "what" . . .' (Zohar, prologue 1).

M/other likewise may be luminous or non-luminous, present or absent. The mirror of the mind is a multi-layered truth. For example, whilst on a Cretan beach, struggling to understand these concepts, my mind was noticing the sensation of warm sun on my skin: I free associated . . . the sun is a luminous presence, the sky-father, is the dark moon-mother a non-luminous absence? In Ancient Crete, King Minos, King and God, was a luminous presence, the Minotaur a non-luminous presence, a terrifying monster hidden in his labyrinth, a lurking danger behind dark corners. Attachment styles? Luminous presence might be secure; luminous absence, hostile; non-luminous presence, anxious; non-luminous absence, dependent . . . maybe? . . . what is it like to grow up with parents who are luminously present, or non-luminous absences . . . does the form of attachment reflect the form of this early mirroring?

Self, naturally developing, gradually lets the 'mirroring body of the culture' replace the mirroring body of the mother: different cultures tell different stories. As we tell our stories within them, we appear: luminous, non-luminous, present or absent to our peers. As we play with constructing and deconstructing Self, personality develops. Yet within family and tribal environments there may be little psychological support for our unique way of seeing our world (Quenck and Quenck 1982: 157–73).

If, for example, we're a feeling-type boy born to a thinking-type father in a macho society (like Ben in the previous chapter) or a bisexual child born to straight parents in a homophobic society (like Dekk), then core identity, deep certainty about Self, isn't given validation. Words come to have mirror-meanings. They are reversed. For Tom Sawyer and Huck Finn, separation meant attachment (they ran away): for Mike, whose story I'll now tell, attachment meant separation (he was sent away). As a child, this is like being told black is white.

### Clinical example – Mike

Mike is a strong, intense, athletic artist, born white and raised black. His parents owned a lonely farm in the African bush. He came for analysis as he'd lost purpose and will to live. We met weekly for a year, then twice weekly for six more months till he stormed off slamming my door, yelling over his shoulder, 'You don't care!' Nine months later he stormed back, to come three times a week for a further six years.

Mike breast-fed with his African nanny, ran naked with her children, slept in her hut or under the stars, learnt to hunt with a spear, to fish with his hands, to swim, to fight, to listen to stories round star-lit camp fires. But on Sundays, his black parent scrubbed him, forced him into a shirt and shorts, and handed him to his white parents, for 'afternoon tea'. Mike felt *he* was on the menu every time. Mother took Valium with her tea, saying 'I'm just a little depressed, darling.' She thought Mike was retarded as he spoke poor English (but excellent 'African'). His father was violent. 'Tea' often ended in a belting for having 'native' table manners. Then at puberty, instead of tribal initiation, Mike was sent to a Dickensian African Public School. 'White initiation' meant shoes and school uniform, bullying from other boys and beatings from staff.

Nearby, a civil war raged. Mike volunteered at seventeen to become a commando. Of his platoon of twenty-four, four survived. Like a Vietnam vet., at twenty, on the losing side and feeling a loser, he went to College. Therapy and self-medication with cannabis prevented suicide. Once in the UK, he went on a drug binge. Why? He'd helped 'take out' a native village, and shot an African mother (his 'real' mother). A dream-image provided words:
'I'm in a mud hut and an old woman smears the floor with cow dung' (meaning 'respect'). He said 'mother' in African, crying in shame. He realised he'd seen army service as wish-fulfilling, a way to get revenge on his black family for betraying him to the 'whites' at puberty. Then he dreamed:

'I'm white, yet also a young warrior in tribal dress making my passage to manhood.'

Life-threatening risks may be taken by lads in *rites de passage*. Mike felt he'd missed initiation into two 'tribes', white and black. He wasn't a 'brave'. But, aged twelve, he risked his life to save a friend from drowning; at nineteen, he rescued a younger badly-wounded comrade under heavy machine-gun fire. He had not seen that heroism is heroism, whatever side you're on – winner or loser. His addiction (dependency) was an opposite to an initiation (inter-dependence with the tribe).

Drugs are a self-administered *rite de passage*, equivalent, perhaps, to their use in ancient mystery religions (Zoja 1989: 27–33). Mike then had a series of sacrificial, initiatory dreams, including a descent into the underworld. In the Orphic legend, Dionysus, wild young God of Intoxication, has Hades and Persephone as parents (Cowan 1982: 104–7): a non-luminously present, death-dealing father whose belt left his 'luminous absence' on Mike's back; and a mother who was 'bipolar', all fruit and flowers, luminously present (manic) and non-luminously absent (depressed). Valium intoxication made relating to her like wading through treacle. Being with Mike was like being with a rage-filled infant, stuffed with non-luminous absence. In response, my own 'wild-child' became savage, attacking, competitive, murdering our alliance. Jung described the dynamics like this:

> A mentally unbalanced person tries to defend himself against his own unconscious, that is to say, he fights against his own compensating influences. The man already living in an atmosphere of isolation continues to remove himself further and further from the world of reality, and the ambitious engineer strives, by his more and more pathological and exaggerated interventions, to prove the incorrectness of his compensating powers of self-criticism. This results in a condition of excitation, which produces a great lack of harmony between the conscious and unconscious tendencies. The pairs of opposites are torn asunder, the resultant division leads to disaster, for the unconscious soon begins to obtrude itself violently on the conscious process. Then come often incomprehensible thoughts and moods, and often incipient forms of hallucinations, which plainly bear the stamp of the internal conflict.
>
> (*CW* 3: para. 457)

Mike would sob into analytic silence, ' . . . what am I supposed to do here . . .', as he'd sob on Sunday after tea. 'Suppose there is no suppose . . .', I thought, sadly recognising anything I said would be useless. Father saw Mike as a wild animal, and, beaten like one, he came to behave like one. Being made 'other' (liminal) by difference (alterity), whether from family or society, he learnt to feel his body as 'other', useful when getting beaten (and under gunfire). Now, for a child, ego is a body ego, and 'the ego stands to the Self as the moved to the mover, or as object to subject' (*CW* 11: para. 391). If ego-alienated as the result of physical abuse, then meaning can't be internally validated.

> For consciousness did not exist from the beginning; in every child it has to be formed anew in the first years of life. Consciousness is very weak in this formative period, and the same is true of the psychic history of mankind – the unconscious easily seizes power. The struggles have left their mark. To put it in scientific terms: instinctive defence-mechanisms have been built up which automatically intervene when the danger is greatest, and the coming into action during an emergency is represented in fantasy by helpful images which are irrevocably imprinted on the human psyche.
>
> (*CW* 11: para. 533)

Analytical psychology and object relations theory take development as a play, forming and using objects (presences) and 'not objects' (absences). The theories share semantic ground, holding that patterns of meaning structure closure and opening, as they ask of an object: 'Is it "is", or is it "is not"? If "is not", then, what's needed to complete it? More luminosity, less luminosity? Do I want this object present or absent, to have meaning or not . . . ?' If attachment fails then identity becomes defined by alterity, by others who theorise mind for us. We need to be how they say, believe what we're told to believe, do what we're supposed to in order to make meaning. Mike is an African with a white skin and a black soul. This is alterity.

> The term 'alterity' comes primarily from the psychoanalytic theories of Jacques Lacan and his followers, and refers to what we Jungians might call the archetype of the Opposite or the Other (capitalised throughout to distinguish from the inter-personal other). It recognises the fundamental sense

of otherness that developmentally precedes the notion of sexual otherness. Alterity manifests first in the distinction of Self and other, that begins with the cell mass which grows from conception against the background of otherness, and eventually becomes the contained subjectivity of body-being. Alterity also refers to irreducible otherness that lies outside the subject and is not predicated on projection or identification. This Otherness is awesome in an unimaginable way.

(Young-Eisendrath 1998: 198)

## Meaning and loss

We make meaning from percepts, what is there and what is not (presence and absence) and how significant (luminous/non-luminous) it is. If Self crashes, as it did for Mike, meaning has to form in new ways, or we give up and die. Meaning is a dynamic system (neither open nor closed, both open and closed): it changes. Change means loss – especially change for the better because then we wonder, 'Why didn't we do this before?' Internal representations of external experience are shaped by pre-existing patterns (archetypes), which mediate between Self and (m)other, creating secure boundaries to ensure survival (*CW* 9i: para. 260).

Perception occurs at physical boundaries between 'inside and outside': where skin gives way to mucosa at mouth, anus and genitals; where we literally open and close. Potential for relating is a negotiation of power and love at boundaries: for example, in the {either/ or} of oral sadism, with premature closure (biting) or premature opening (spitting, regurgitating, vomiting). Jung used alchemical metaphors for incorporating and expelling, opening and closing processes (see Whitmont 1969: 176). He described object relating in terms of *coniunctio*, the bringing together of opposites by a process of alchemical change.

Percept and memory together nurture developing Self like milk. Developmental psychology is not just about mothers and babies, it's about cognition and behaviour unfolding through life, as sequential interactions between biological givens and environment. Primary meaning disorders occur if Self's signals to the outside world are mirrored as noise, if in response to our luminous presence, there is non-luminous absence – thousands of tiny failures, till even the expectation of mirroring is too painful. This makes negotiating transitional periods, *rites de passage*, hard. Normally, age-appropriate meanings change to meet new biological possibilities. Clearly, this can't happen if ordinary meaning milestones have not been reached.

Jung's observations on childhood were elaborated by Erich Neumann ('classical school') (1973), countered by Michael Fordham ('developmental school') (1981). Andrew Samuels suggests their opposition arises as they think of Self in different ways (1985a: 155–66). Neumann sees it 'from within', arguing from a 'babies eye view' of the Self unfolding in its 'extra uterine' aqueous merged world with the mother. Fordham sees it 'from without', arguing from a 'mothers eye view' of the infant unfolding in relation to her. The first values the collective, the second the interpersonal relationship as templates for meaning.

I'll contrast these views with child psychology, child analysis, and object relations theorists to show the central place of 'meaning attribution' in development. This begins with luminous presence, the sparkle in the parents' eyes which greet a newborn soul. Neumann understands this as being Self-motivated. Self gradually forms an ego and Self-objects within it, his idea mirrors Fairbairn (1952). Fordham sees value attribution as learnt by millions of deintegrations and reintegrations (openings and closings) of Self both to the inner and the outer world. The American psychologist Erik Erikson (1977: 222–43) suggests Self grows in stable periods, of five to seven years length, when energy goes into work, family, and relating. These intersperse with transitional periods, three to five years long, of assessment and reappraisal.

Like alchemy itself, the meaning of Jung's metaphor has to be distilled from 'the muck in the retort'. Going through black, white, yellow and red, the gold (Self) evaporates, distills and coagulates, as it opens and closes. The gold, the philosopher's stone (Self), is continually shape-shifting. Psychologists use 'opening and closing' to describe how we theorise meaning in childhood. Jean Piaget introduced two key ideas: (1) the difference between psychological and epistemic subject; (2) the processes of assimilation and accommodation. Daniel Stern introduced the idea of invariant properties which determine sense of Self: *origin, motion, time*, and *coherence of intensity* (1985: 85–6). The analytic constructivist perspective suggests the invariants are *agency, coherence, continuity* and *capacity for affective relating* (Young-Eisendrath 1997b), which depend on the former.

## Jean Piaget and Daniel Stern

Piaget's amalgam of biology and logic asks how does our theory of knowing (epistemology) develop? He distinguished between a conscious, experiencing, *psychological* subject (a real child with their own psychology) and an *epistemic* subject (the psychology all children have in common). Piaget states epistemology develops through four overlapping stages. The sensorimotor stage (birth to two years) develops bodily control as we learn about physical objects. The preoperational stage (two to seven) sees verbal skills emerge, we're able to name objects and reason intuitively. The concrete operational stage (seven to twelve) is when we begin to grasp abstract concepts like number and relationship; in the formal operational stage (twelve to fifteen) we start to reason logically and systematically (Boyle 1969).

The goal is development of symbol formation. Piaget held that knowledge *of itself* creates self-regulating (cybernetic) symbol structures, by assimilation/re-integration and accommodation/de-integration (I overlap Fordham's terms, to aid translation not to suggest equivalence). In assimilation new knowledge changes input using existing knowledge. In accommodation old knowledge changes to fit new inputs. We use information feedback loops when we seek objects (secondary process) or objects seek us (primary process, magical thinking), as we open and close to them. Primary process happens first: Self talking to ego. Secondary process happens second: ego talking to Self.

Piaget said concepts we use in later life replace actions in earlier stages. As an example, as a barefoot 'Red Indian' kid I accommodated to Pat the Belfast Cowboy and assimilated his concept {*either* protestant *or* catholic}. In turn, he used my new concept 'Red' {communist, *neither* protestant *nor* catholic}. This let him stop seeing me as a threat (Chapter 2). My adult concept *opening and closing* takes the place of this real event in my past. As kids, we opened our hearts to each other, took a chance and became friends, we accommodated and assimilated, reintegrated and deintegrated. Knowledge grows from thesis, antithesis (its opposite) to synthesis. The London analyst Hester Solomon (1994) shows analytical psychology developed its theory of mind from Jung's notion of enantiodromia, which derives, like the dialectical materialism of Marx, from Hegel.

In Jung's version development is not historically inevitable, it's a spiral – thesis/antithesis/synthesis which, in turn, becomes thesis for the next step – and so on. How the spiral of meaning unfolds depends on the set (individuals) and the setting (culture), which give our actions context (Mike's eating with his hands was in context as a black African boy, not as a white one). Piaget saw children actively adapt to new situations by play. Knowledge acquisition through play is a given for Self, in equilibrium between known and unknown. As in a yin-yang sign, where light (luminosity) and dark (non-luminosity) contains the seed of its opposite, so Piaget places the infant at the centre, creator of its object world. Fordham and developmental theorists sometimes place mother there, as 'good and bad mother', 'oedipal mother', 'castrating mother', or 'terrible witch-mother'. However, an internal mother is mother as constructed by Self, mother as myth and symbol.

Daniel Stern, examining an infant's interpersonal world, reviewed experimental observations on infants and mothers under-pinning (sometimes undermining) favourite analytic theories. Sense of Self depends on origin, motion, time, and coherence of intensity (1985: 85–6) These may be hard to visualise, for, as adults we can't easily vary perceptual features which, for children, define objects. Sense of origin depends on coherent awareness of arriving per-cepts. Once we jumped at twilight shadows. As adults, we may lose origin in liminal (twilight) clouded states of consciousness: exhaus-tion, delirium, sensory deprivation, sleep disturbance, mental ill-ness, or on drugs. Aldous Huxley (1968) gives a good account of this time-space disruption using mescalin. It disrupts the incoming percept stream. Reality becomes *slo-mo* . . . too many frames are missing to make ordinary meaning. First we've an illusion of enhanced perception, and see meaning everywhere . . . but we don't have enough perceptual information to test it. Internal software (which Melanie Klein calls our epistemophilic instinct) makes it up.

We manufacture and export meaning if it goes missing. Later, as the trip deepens, everything refers to us. Time appears to stop as we over-attend to our few remaining percepts. We lose sense of origin, ego dissolves: bliss, if we're lost in Self – hell, if we are simply lost, paranoid, 'beside ourselves', like frightened infants. We lose our meaning-making capacity.

Unity of locus is concerned with agency, says 'I'm me, here in the middle of a percept-field.' Defects here appears as autisms, percepts arrive but have no meaning. For example, in Asperger's syndrome, with poor spatial awareness, severe interpersonal problems result. Self can't spatially locate, or make sense of mother's eye movements

(Carter 1999: 144). Her mirroring signals are noise. Failure of the infant/mother relationship occurs on the infant's side.

Coherence of motion means 'things moving at the same rate are part of the same thing'. This lets us see part-objects sticking together to form whole objects. To newborns, who are all extremely shortsighted, it's not obvious mother's face, hands and breasts connect. Their focal length being about the distance from their eyes to a breast. Further away, mother is a luminous presence. Imagine a dancer in black, with white gloves, face and breasts seen under UV light – only hands, face and breasts are seen – mother, seen by a newborn. It helps to visualise this, otherwise the words part-object whole-object can seem bizarre. Infants don't immediately connect hands-which-pick-up to breast-which-is-hungrily incorporated. Continuous optical transformations of shadowy luminous presences eventually let us detect mother as a constant object, a structural invariant.

Semiotically, structural invariants are syntagms, atoms of meaning. Perception requires positive feedback, sequentially processing atoms of meaning, supporting Freud's assertion that ego is 'body-ego', and our first language body-language. Ego organises time-orientation tasks using body clocks; bio-rhythms synchronised by light and temperature. Coherence of time structure is 'being in one place at a time', this allows affective relationship. Stimuli coming from my body telling me I'm waving my arms. My movements share temporal structure, but stimuli from others may not. In severe meaning disorder (paranoia), or when close to Self it's as if its timeless presence disrupts time-perception.

Piaget and Stern suggest a child's development of meaning comes about by a natural knowledge-seeking (epistemophilic) instinct opening and closing to percepts, making distinctions between Self and other using assimilation and accommodation to adjust to the four specifics of Self: origin, motion, time, and coherence of intensity which permit its four functions agency, coherence, continuity and forming affective relationship.

## Post-Jungian views of development

Jung viewed psyche as a dynamic system. Unlike Freud, Jung didn't hold that feeding (though pleasurable) only equated with sex (Samuels 1985a: 148–62). Influenced by Freud's early hydraulic model where psychic energy (interest, libidinal cathexis, luminosity) flows between opposites (thinking and feeling, sensation and intuition), he believed 'the confrontation of the two positions generates a tension charged with energy and creates a living third thing . . . a living birth that leads to a new level of being, a new situation' (*CW* 8: para. 189) Hegel's influence is clear. Jung named this process enantiodromia (Greek: running counter to). He suggested changes of direction (from opening to closing and vice versa) occur when a concept or direction has reached fullness (*CW* 6: paras 708–9), formed a *gestalt*, or synthesis.

In the to-ing and fro-ing of an infant's relationship to mother, steps forward are accompanied by steps back (*CW* 8: para. 723). Failures in mother–infant relating result from archetypal expectations not being met. We're born expecting maternal support to make meaning from sensation. Archetypal processes require (m)other(s) to humanise them. The 'Catch 22' of a developmental position is the post hoc ergo propter hoc fallacy – after this therefore because of this. 'Because your mother died when you were born Tom Sawyer, you're . . .' or 'because your father beat you Huck, you're . . .' or 'because you killed your black mother Mike, you're . . .' Andrew Samuels, examining the reductionist dilemma in *The Plural Psyche*, spotted a flaw in Fordham's reasoning:

> when the primary self 'unpacks' its archetypal potentials, these are conceived of as emerging in a pure form, untrammelled by external factors, all ready to mate up with environmental correspondences. Little place is made in the theory for the possibility (or probability) that the innate potentials within the primary Self are affected by each other before they unpack. Not only is too sharp a division made between the innate elements and the outer correspondences but it seems to be assumed that the various deintegrates do not interact; succinctly, the model, apparently dynamic, has a hidden static quality. A more dynamic variant would allow for the influence on personality of deintegrates at all stages of their careers – in potentia, in transition, re-integrated – and place greater weight on the interaction of the deintegrates.'
>
> (1989a: 20)

Developmental equations {if a then b} can also be read as {if b subsequently, then a previously}. The teleological perspective fits a view of development as an interlocking matrix, impacting throughout life. Congenital meaning disorders (blindness, Asperger's

Syndrome and Autism) have massive social consequences. Sharing meaning together usually creates a safe space to play in, a transitional space between (m)other and infant. If this fails, a child experiences anomie, unresolvable resentment is carried forward (*Nachtraglicheit*); and, as parents carry the Self of the child, so unfolding of a child's own meaning entangles with parental shadows.

Self begins unpacking *before* (m)other is other and its deintegrating parts continually interact with hers. Analyst Christopher Hauke (1998) suggests a pluralist perspective – using {both/and/either/or} as logical operator – lets us recognise certain problems (like dating the emergence of ego from Self) as insoluble. However, the problems may be named accurately: we accept that as some things are not-Self, we cannot change or be responsible for them. If we do, omnipotence collapses, Self reintegrates, leaving ego in its wake. Mutual envy is inevitable, and necessary, for it facilitates inter-generational separation. However, if the valuable function of envy-as-twoness is not recognised, a child never gets the guidance of its own shadow. Its life fulfills unlived parental shadow (ambitions), not its own. Envy is a source of aspiration. Adult meaning disorders (developmental delay or arrest) indicate lack of space within which archetypal patterns could unpack – here and now, regardless of what happened in the past.

## Imagos

For Jung, complexes contain internalised images of parent figures (imagos) derived from archetypal parents 'the parents are not "the parents" at all but only their imagos; they are representations which have arisen from the conjunction of parental peculiarities with the individual disposition of the child' (*CW* 5: para. 505) Good-enough parents contain a child's sexual fantasies, maintaining them as fantasised, rather than actual, incest. The importance of maintaining a holding space (like clear analytic boundaries) is to allow sharing of meaning, letting Self unfold . . . as:

> it is not the real mother who is symbolised, but the libido of the son whose object was once the mother. We take mythological symbols much too concretely . . . when we read 'his mother was a wicked witch' we must translate it as: the son is unable to detach his libido from the mother-imago, he suffers from resistances because he is tied to his mother.
>
> (*CW* 5: para. 329)

To separate from mother requires attachment to father, father-figures, and a culture. Jung never denied the reality of incest being enacted, of child abuse. He was himself sexually abused as a child by an older man he trusted (Kutek 2000: 26). His life showed it's what we make such experiences mean that counts. This differs from child to child. As trauma re-lives in analysis, we have witnesses: the adult-in-us and the analyst validate an inner child's percept (imago). A chance exists for our adult Self to ally with our child Self; we reinterpret personal history as we rememory it (as described in Toni Morrison's novel *Beloved*, 1987)

If we can't re-interpret we may 'stop trying to make sense of the senseless' – our real parents may not change. Memories of abuse (like Mike's scars) may never disappear but may fade as our relationship to persecuting imagos changes. A different relationship emerges, perhaps agreement to disagree about childhood? Children see parents as archetypal images; this becomes easier to see as we, in turn, notice our own children and grandchildren experience *us* as such images; we realise we've become fat Mum and embarrassing Dad . . .

Alice Miller wrote 'Experience has taught us that we have only one enduring weapon in the struggle against mental illness; the emotional discovery and emotional acceptance in the individual and unique history of our childhood' (1987: 17). But experience is a poor teacher compared to dreams and the collective. Experience easily becomes 'in my opinion . . .', closed system thinking, cut off from culture-wisdom (*weltanschauung*). Inner children need the cunning of Tom Sawyer and Huck Finn to survive. They can act as agents of liberation in close-minded adults, tricksters at best, but, at worst, child-tyrants, like Verruca Salt in *Charlie and the Chocolate Factory*, with paranoid bursts of 'pathological entitlement', with her cry 'Daddy, I want an squirrel! Right now, Daddy . . . !!' (Dahl 1990: 120–1).

Suffering comes from a matrix of physical, physiological, psychological and political causes: greed, envy and jealousy are desires, *dhukka*. As a doctor, 'experience' teaches me the arrogance of grand narratives, everyone dies. This is the 'other end' of a developmental metaphor, the teleological, purpose-driven end. Imagine, at death, our Guardian Angel asks, 'What did you learn, whom did you love?' A teleological approach to development means (from the Greek) a 'knowledge of ends', not 'after this, therefore because of this'.

Childhood suffering is an hero-quest. Tom Sawyer did win the princess and the gold. To understand such suffering as part of a journey to maturity is not to belittle it, nor to seek to give meaning where none exists. Self is *a priori*, a given. All events allow Self to unfold – including the pain of development. If in analysis we relive childhood (and its bewildering, powerful murderous impulses) then idealise the child, we are confusing myth with fact.

Tom and Huck show what I mean. Tom narrates in experience-distant third person, a character in his own fantasy of brave heroes. He is, quintessentially, an 'open child'. To him, 'takin' a lickin' is a chance to show he's a hero. He idealises Huck – 'everything that goes to make life precious, that boy had. So thought every harassed, hampered, respectable boy in St. Petersburg.' But Huck gives us his-story in the experience-near first-person. With his cruel alcoholic father he'd 'taken too many lickin's' to find pain heroic. To Huck, faking his murder and then running away was Self-preserving. Tom's feigned drowning, on the other hand, enacted his wish to sacrifice himself to punish the other, to make *them* be sorry. Tom made a crisis out of a drama. Huck, the realist, helped Jim, a runaway slave, and after Jim's liberty was secure, decided to 'lit out for the Territories'.

Twain made a drama out of the crisis of adolescence, when we live 'The heroes battle for deliverance from the mother' (*CW* 5: paras 419–63). Separation experiences, recapitulating mouth/nipple relations, weaning, 'my first day at school', revise our internal objects. We learn to think symbolically. Symbol formation is a goal in the development of meaning-making. 'There is no such thing as a baby', said Donald Winnicott, an analytic proverb, as is 'there can't be separation without attachment'. I recall an awful joke from my childhood:

*Q:* 'Mummy, mummy why do I keep going round and round in circles?

*A:* 'Shut up, or I'll nail your other foot to the floor!'

Oedipus means 'swollen foot' – a complex, unresolved, a psychological laming leaving us with developmental delay or arrest. Similarly, if we're not attached, we're forever circling a non-luminous, absent mother hoping to do so. The spiral of development becomes a vicious circle, tightening with built-in guilt (Fairbairn 1952: 52): 'as long I'm guilty, then I am responsible, then something I do can make me be what I am supposed to be ... for someone else.' The kicker, as Huck might say, is the 'for someone else'. We can't individuate for someone else.

Developmental perspectives view meaning from time-bound ego, and cannot but see process as linear and time as sequential. That, after all, is what development means. Archetypal perspectives view from the timeless Self, seeing moments in a life as if viewing a wall of TV screens each showing a facet of the same life. Archetypal imagos are like Piaget's notion of schemata: sets of actions designed to perform specific functions, installed by accommodation and assimilation, reintegration and deintegration, closing and opening. Now, let's look at what this means in terms of the development of body-ego.

# 4

# THE BODY AND MEANING DISORDER

i like my body when it is with your
body. It is so quite a new thing.
Muscles better and nerves more.
i like your body. i like what it does,
i like its hows. i like to feel the spine
of your body and its bones,and the trembling
-firm-smooth ness and which i will
again and again and again
kiss,    i like kissing this and that of you,
i like,slowly stroking the,shocking fuzz
of your electric fur,and what-is-it comes
over parting flesh . . . . And eyes big love-crumbs

and possibly i like the thrill

of under me you so quite new
(E. E. Cummings 1962)

## The psychoid

What happens when meaning gets lost in the body, when we can't make sense of sensations? The model we have of the relationship between body, mind and spirit decides whether we construe dis-ease as a natural phenomenon, or believe 'being ill is God's Will' (like 'born-again Christian' Ned Flanders in the American kids' cartoon show, *The Simpsons*). Are body, mind and spirit one, two, or three things? Do they make, as the medieval alchemist Maria Prophetissa suggested, a mystery – three contained in a hidden fourth (*CW* 9i: para. 552)? If so, what is this 'hidden fourth'? Could it be Self?

How do we develop agency, coherence, continuity and an ability to form affective relational bonds – (Self) – and learn to love and make love as whole beings, the most fulfilling thing we do in our bodies: the worst thing to happen if we're sexually abused, if incest fantasies are acted-out rather than symbolised – or, perhaps equally difficult to bear – are neither acted-out nor symbolised? If we never felt loved?

As children, time-free Self and time-bound ego both are 'my body'. In play, we mythologise our body and its suffering; learning to distinguish the symbolic, the real and the imaginary. In the if . . . then world of magical, child-like, primary process thinking, if something is wrong with my body, then something is wrong with *me*. I'll illustrate using a personal myth: when I was seven I had polio. Mind–body separation was real in the physically frozen months . . .

> An eyelid moves, and the figure-in-white, a nurse, moves a finger on the sign-board: up-down, left-right, pointing. Water. My favourite sign is a glass. I'm dry. Am I hot . . . am I alive? As long as the air-pump keeps going and I don't drown in my own saliva . . .

So . . . when I think of signs, signification and representation, I'm in a time when a sign was just a *sign*; when I (and it) could not convey what I meant or felt. Jean-Dominique Bauby (editor of the French magazine *Elle* in the 'seventies) described his experience after a massive stroke, resulting

> in the locked-in syndrome, paralysed from head to toe, the patient, his mind intact, is imprisoned inside his own body, but unable to speak or move. In my case, blinking my left eyelid is my only means of communication.
>
> (Bauby 1997: 12)

I could blink both eyes: left for up-down; right for left-right. Such experiences defy attempts to be made meaningful. Maybe having had one, that's why I'm writing about meaning? Maybe you're reading on to find out more about the meaning of suffering? The word comes from the Latin, *suffere* to sustain; from *sub-* (up from underneath) and *ferre* (to carry). I associate this to visiting the Coliseum in Rome, standing where gladiators came up from the cells under the ring floor to face death. In suffering, then, part of the Self comes up to face death (unknown transformation). Heroic aspects of the psyche surface, asking teleological questions like 'what is the purpose of suffering?' Perhaps, like a Zen koan, the contribution of suffering's purpose to the question of meaning is to challenge the commonly held belief that everything has to have meaning?

Attempts to make sense of the senseless in childhood lead to over-use, or over-early use of defences of the ego, like denial and repression (Freud, A. 1986: 42–3). Later, this causes problems with body-language (gestural praxis). If we do not learn to separate gestures (signifiers) from their meanings (the things signified) if we continue to confuse signified with signifier, this results in mis-communication and anxiety. For example, like most medical students, I'd an imaginary illness during training. An arm-muscle twitched, I stuck out my tongue and noticed it was wriggling in a strange way (fasiculating). I believed this signified Motor Neurone Disease (a rare sequel to polio). Fortunately, my Professor 'cured' me at once, cheerily saying he got inoperable brain cancer annually . . . 'cured' by talking with his friend, a neurosurgeon.

Jung's concept 'the psychoid level of existence' refers to this body–mind amalgam. It is a sort of signifier for it, and we will discuss the psychoid in a moment. Medical students learn about clinical signs to do something about them; perhaps analysts learn about the signifiers of complexes to *be* with them? As a student, I couldn't interpret my own physical signs, emotional involvement altered my perception. This is why doctors say, 'The physician who treats himself is treated by a fool.' Certainly the profession pre-disposes its participants to see particular meanings everywhere: one and one and one . . . made five. This is 'premature closure', like the psychotic man and the ash-tray we met in Chapter 1, or when, as a child I see a shadow move at night and think 'It's a ghost!'

Abused and neglected children use premature closure as a defence: 'father moves, he's going to belt me . . .'. Somatisation, likewise, is premature closure. Fundamentalist thinking, whether the funda-mentalists are religious, political (or analytic) is a response to threats to a meaning system, or indicate a meaning system which is (or has become unstable). How we decide the winner between competing meaning-systems is decided by our theory of mind, and how easily it responds to change: its boundaries, their elasticity and permeability, and what is in the *between* spaces.

This is literally the case: synaptic neuro-transmission occurs when small packets of neurotransmitters (serotonin, nor-adrenalin, dopamine, opiates and so on) are released into a *between*, the syn-aptic cleft. In somatisation disorders neural impulses from above (the cortex) are transmitted to the body below by sub-cortical structures, particularly the limbic system. We shake with fear or rage, we shiver with joy. Jung (following medieval alchemists) believed there were, similarly, permeable boundaries between natural and spiritual worlds.

At twelve Jung himself somatised, having 'fainting-spells' associated with school-refusal. He later said 'this was when I learnt what a neurosis is' (1989: 30–2). Imagine 'impulse transmission' at the spirit–nature interface is mediated by symbols, 'neurotransmitters' for the collective unconscious. The nature of the boundaries across which symbols travel was a living dilemma for Jung and his family. Since early childhood he'd asked, 'How do I put into words experiences beyond words?' Attempting an answer, he invented a language, analytical psychology, to name and describe them.

'Psychoid' is a key word in this language. In late nineteenth-century medicine 'psychoid' was the name for sub-cortical neural processes: activity in the mid- and hind-brain (*CW* 8: para. 368). The network of mid-brain structures called the limbic system (*limbus* is Latin for border), below the cortex and above the medulla, pons and cerebellum monitor vital functions, from cortical glucose and oxygen levels to the complex 'fight-flight-freeze' decisions made in response to threat and emotion. There is a 'slow' meaning-making loop between thalamus, hippocampus, pre-frontal and frontal cortex, which 'names' threats, and a 'fast' loop from the thalamus direct to the amygdala, which readies the body to fight-flee-freeze before the threat has a name (Carter 1999: 90–1).

As a Junior Doctor at the Burgholzli Hospital in Zurich, trying to find the lost meanings of severely psychotic people, Jung, like R. D. Laing (Clay 1996: 46–50) tried to get inside their trapped minds by reading their body-language: the blinks and the grunts of depressive mutism, the frozen postures of catatonia. In a memorable case, a woman with a psychotic breakdown believed she had killed her daughter by not stopping her drinking bathwater she suspected was contaminated with typhus (Jung 1989: 115–17).

Jung uncovered her guilty secret by reading her gestures and using the word association test. Just as reacting to fire by pulling our hand away is a spinal reflex, so is reacting to threatening others by amygdalal triggering of 'fight-flee-submit' body-language *before* the prefrontal lobe has reassembled memories of why this other is threatening or the temporal lobe has found words. This causes the time-delay in the word association test. The body gives the task of facing threat full attention. It releases adrenalin, triggers changes in respiration rate, peripheral blood flow and pupil size. When confronted by a threatening word ('bath', if we believe we threw out our baby with the bathwater) the amygdala circuit engages, producing 'fight-flee-freeze' responses. This causes a brief attention deficit, so we can't produce a response to the cue-word.

The old neuro-anatomical concept (the psychoid) told Jung that the body communicates with mind and mind with body through these sub-cortical structures. When the woman's naming ability was overwhelmed by grief and guilt, renaming her experiences through the word association test re-established links broken by an archetypal response – sub-cortical overactivity, that is, emotion (feeling plus instantaneous bodily reaction).

> Here I will only point out that it is the decisive factors in the unconscious psyche, the archetypes, which constitute the structure of the collective unconscious. The latter represents a psyche that is identical in all individuals. It cannot be directly perceived or 'represented' in contrast to the perceptible psychic phenomena, and on account of its 'irrepresentable' nature I have called it the psychoid.
>
> (*CW* 8: para. 840)

The word 'collective' here implies that sub-cortical processes are common to all of us – mute, submissive stooping is a common primate response to threat. The psychoid is biology and psychology, physical and psychical – yet neither. Near-death and locked-in experiences are also in its realm. Such experiences raise questions about meaning . . . spiritual questions. Whether the emotions we have in such experiences arise from changes in blood-brain biochemistry, proximity to Self (or to Guardian Angels), or all of these doesn't alter their depth, intensity and timeless duration – their numinosity. The numinous is:

> a dynamic agency or effect not caused by an arbitrary act of will. On the contrary, it seizes and controls the human subject, who is always its victim rather than its creator. The numinosum – whatever its cause may be – is an experience of the subject independent of his will . . . the numinosum is either a quality belonging to a visible object or the influence of an invisible presence that causes a peculiar alteration of consciousness.
>
> (*CW* 11: para. 6)

Psychoid processes are unconscious. They cannot be willed into awareness. They appear as feelings – 'I'm thirsty, I need air.' Jung, asked at the first Bailey Island seminar (held in Maine in 1938), 'How do we approach the unconscious?', replied: 'Look! If there were a cave of hungry bears on this Island, how would I tell you to approach it?' (Jung 1938). The psychoid reminds us the 'unconscious is unconscious is unconscious': wild, natural and untamable; a meta-physical common ground which shares with the organic world an ecology, physiology and psychology. However,

> If I make use of the term 'psychoid' I do so with three reservations: firstly, I use it as an adjective, not as a noun; secondly, no psychic quality in the proper sense of the word is implied, but only a 'quasi-psychic' one such as the reflex-process possesses; and thirdly, it is meant to distinguish a category of events from merely vitalistic phenomena on the one hand and specifically psychic processes on the other. The latter distinction obliges us to define more closely the nature and extent of the psyche, and of the unconscious psyche in particular.
>
> (*CW* 8: para. 368)

This level of the mind is bedrock: not *para-* (beside) normal, but *meta-* (beyond) normal: signifying *after*, *later*, *change* (as in meta-morphosis, change of shape). Psychoid experiences are representations of times of *meta*-normal experience (like life-threatening illness), from which we're still trying to make meaning. For example, having had to breathe through a silver tube in my neck, I still find wearing a tie (or tightness round my neck) makes me feel suffocated. This somatic memory has not changed after analysis: but, now I know why it happens, it's not scary anymore – I just don't own a tie.

Near-death experiences are accompanied by strange effects – like seeing a tunnel with a bright figure at the other end who shows us our life and asks 'St. Peter' like questions . . . an experience I have in common with many others (Fenwick 1999: 303–31; Moody 1975: 25–77). Whether temporal lobe anoxia, or sub-liminal perception by sub-cortical brain areas account for these numinous (para-normal) experiences is a side issue. Just because a particular anatomical structure perceives certain stimuli (as the eye perceives light), does not mean it *causes* them.

Jung's life included para-normal experiences from an early age (Kutek 2000: 20–35). After breaking free of Freud he had a vivid spiritual encounter, writing both the *Septem Sermones ad Mortuos* and his seminal essay, 'The Transcendent Function' (*CW* 8: paras 1–160) in a few weeks in 1916 (Hoeller 1987). The first written by 'automatic (sub-cortical?) writing' is mythopoeic, and introduced the idea of transcendence to name meaning-filled links between body, mind and spirit (*CW* 8: paras 188–93). The second, states the same ideas in more 'scientific' language. The first reads like Gnostic poetry:

> And the emptiness of the whole is the Pleroma,
> The activity of the whole is Abraxas; only the unreal opposes
> him
>
> (Fourth Sermon, Hoeller 1982: 53)

Jung took up Gnostic ideas about exchange between the One (the Pleroma, or Self) the Many (the Noumena, sub-personalities or ego-fragments), and Abraxas (the ego-complex). The Pleroma is a symbol for Spirit, the Noumena a symbol for the body-mind. He moved from using the word psychoid simply to refer to sub-cortical brain areas to suggest it is connected to 'spirit'. Richard Noll, who accused Jung of going back to early nineteenth-century 'volkish' science (1996: 269), could also have pointed out that, here, Jung's thinking resembles the medieval idea that the Pineal Gland (part of the sub-cortical brain) was the seat of the soul.

The Gnostic tradition sees body and mind as body-mind, a unity, contained within spirit. If 'psychoid' names where body and mind are inseparable, we could say it is an em-body-ment of the transcendent function; a meta- (beyond) physical concept. The suffering of the body brings about ego–Self separation, helping form the ego–Self axis. Somatisation results if ego–Self separation does not happen enough, if we suffer too much, beyond our capacity to make meaning. If this happens we face a physical and spiritual crisis. If this happens in children (as it did for me) we may develop primary meaning disorders (Chapter 5). The psychoid is an explaining device (an heuristic) as well as a neural structure. As Jung put it:

> It appears that the psychoid is an emancipation of function from its instinctual form and so from the compulsiveness which, as sole determinant of the function, causes it to harden into a mechanism. The psychic condition or quality begins where the function loses its outer and inner determinism and becomes capable of more extensive and freer application, that is, where it begins to show itself accessible to a will motivated from other sources.
>
> (*CW* 8: para. 377)

The 'other sources' are society and the collective unconscious, which, like the psychoid, links physiology, neuro-biology, psychology and para-psychology. I'm concerned here about movement of information in social meaning systems. Individual meaning-systems require affective relating to grow. Illness and illness behaviour represent limit-states of body-mind; as analyst Joyce MacDougall said, '"meaning" is of a pre-symbolic order that circumvents the use of words' (1989: 18). Jung supposed the psychoid accounts for synchronistic, beyond-words events: both body and Self, it is time-free. But if our body isn't a safe place we can't play in a time-free, poetic way with percept and concept, enactment and symbol formation, or use our transcendent function. We can't make a play-space, a third area, a *between* where meaning-conflicts can play out. If we can't form symbols, the body itself is where psychic conflict is acted-out (Redfearn 1994).

## Semantics and body-language

Semiotics, the science of meaning, literally means 'the study of symptoms' (Greek; σεμιος – semios, a symptom or sign). The French semiotician Algericas Greimas called 'gestural praxis' the first step in differentiating (physical, clinical) signs from symbols:

> To determine the signification of the word meaning, all we have to do is consult any dictionary. We can see that this word is always interpreted in two irreducible ways: it is understood either as referencing or as direction. In the first case, it is seen as the super-imposition of two configurations as one code – the code of expression – which refers back to another code, called, perhaps equally arbitrarily, the code of content. In the second case, it appears as intentionality as relation to be established between the itinerary to be covered and its end point.
>
> (Greimas 1987: 27)

The code of expression I'm discussing here is body-language, the code of content is the intention of body-language to convey particular meanings in a given social setting. Analysis, like semiology, asks 'How do signs acquire meaning?' We have few examples from Jung's own work, but in *Association, Dream and an Hysterical Symptom* (*CW* 2: paras 793–862), he described using the word-association test to explore a complex in a 24-year-old girl with 'convulsions'. She began this illness-behaviour before menarche, later replacing her symptom by unbearably painful 'heat in the head'. She was hospitalised by her despairing family, and Jung diagnosed hysteria.

Clinical material and experimental results pointed to an erotic, incestuous transference to him, and strong negative feelings to her mother. Dreams showed incestuous feelings towards her brother. Although Jung's work was pioneering, the patient, on discharge from hospital complained to her GP 'about the hospital and the doctor, with indications that the doctor had only tried to find opportunities to make morally dangerous conversation with her' (*CW* 2: para. 857). Jung continued:

> The complex has an abnormal autonomy in hysteria and the tendency to an active separate existence, which reduces and replaces the constellating power of the ego-complex. In this way a new morbid personality is gradually created, the inclinations, judgements, and resolutions of which move only in the direction of the will to be ill. This second personality devours what is left of the normal ego and forces it into the role of a secondary (oppressed) complex. The purposive treatment of hysteria must therefore strengthen what has remained of the normal ego, and this is best achieved by introducing some new complex that liberates the ego from domination by the complex of the illness.
>
> (*CW* 8: paras 861–2)

Her complex communicated by dream-images and gesture. Gestures (like words) are meaning-atoms (syntagms), fitting together to form a whole meaning. Open mouth, open palm, sticking out the tongue: what does this signify? To my Tibetan friend Aman it signifies 'greetings, friend!' Gestures mean nothing without a social context. Illness is, in a sense, also a social gesture. Contemporary medical sociologists describe 'primary gain' as a direct benefit obtained from illness (getting help) and 'secondary gain' as social benefits derived from illness (victim) behaviour. Jung believed illness could be categorised in four ways: physical, psychological, social or spiritual, and could be both individual and/or cultural. The latter causes greater suffering (see Jung's description of the sickness in the German psyche, possessed by the archetypal war god, Wotan, written in 1936: *CW* 10: paras 371–99).

I'll look at cultural meaning disorders later: now, let's consider the syntagm 'torture' as a signifier of a sick society. Presumably such societies believe torture has a secondary gain, the social benefit to masters of having fearful slaves. Psychosomatic disorders are Self-inflicted torture. Meaningless suffering is inflicted on the body-ego, seemingly, by the Self. Trust in the body is lost or never established. When we somatise we misread physical signs (syntagms) of feeling and read them as physical pain, or do not read them at all. We get exhausted, but we don't know why.

An old name for this is neurasthenia: depression plus denial of depressive symptoms (including mood disorder). This is a *body meaning disorder*. The cause, un-nameable feeling (say, anger after abuse) has no clear meaning for the person in relation to the physical effect (like blushing, but not knowing why). Neurasthenia has parallels with hysteria: physical signs occur in the absence of neurological disorder. For 'illness' to be socially sanctioned the 'sufferer' has to carry signs of disease and produce normal illness behaviour. Semantically, neurasthenia and hysteria represent symbolic failures: the body-language means one thing to the patient but another to physician, family or society.

Such behaviour may simply signify illness behaviour, a wish for secondary gain, enacting the archetype 'the invalid': we have an *ailment* (Main 1957) like the founder of nursing, Florence Nightingale, heroine of the Crimea, who took to her bed and stayed there forty years. Illness relates to illness behaviour like this:

$$\frac{\text{ill}}{\text{not-ill}} \text{ is like } \frac{\text{socially validated (SV)}}{\text{not socially validated (NSV)}}$$

Florence Nightingale was not-ill and socially validated: a successful hypochondriac, like Monsieur Argan, hero of Molière's *La Malade imaginaire* (1959) (assume hypochondria isn't an illness). Four possible states exist: ill, socially validated (e.g. cancer): not-ill, not socially validated as 'ill' (healthy); ill, not socially validated (like addiction, and many mental illnesses); not-ill, socially validated as 'ill'. Miss Nightingale is in the last group. Let's consider Pinochet, the Chilean dictator, whose extradition to face trial for crimes against humanity was revoked as he had 'dementia'. He allegedly 'recovered' on release. Ernest Saunders, director of Guinness, jailed for fraud, also allegedly made an extraordinary 'recovery'. Do they have a hitherto unknown, completely reversible dementia? Or are they doing what a British working-class man would call 'taking a sickie' – malingering?

Their behaviour resembles compensation neurosis, with its

shifting, vague neurological symptoms (often following head-injury), which resolve when the compensation claim is settled advantageously. It means one thing to their supporters, another to their opponents and yet other things to themselves. There is no social consensus: true for psychosomatic disorders. Where do they locate on this grid?

In neurasthenia or chronic fatigue syndrome (ME) there is abnormal illness behaviour (Simpson *et al*. 1997) Some see ME as a contemporary form of dissociative hysteria (Holland 1997), others as a depressive illness lacking depressive symptoms. It is associated with interpersonal problems, violence towards the Self (Bennett 1997), which may arise from attachment failure in the early relationship, preventing separation (Simpson 1997). ME sufferers construe psychic suffering in organic terms, protesting angrily if opposing views are put about their illness (despite the frequent absence of myalgia or encephalitis on physical investigation). There are post-viral syndromes. The issue is not the 'scientific basis' or 'truth' about ME – the syndrome illustrates the power of the name (signifier) of an illness or illness behaviour.

The names hysteric or neurasthenic stigmatise those with body-meaning disorders, suggesting they are 'not-ill, not socially validated' behaviours. Neurasthenia (with its new names, fibromyalgia, chronic fatigue syndrome, myalgic encephalomyelitis or ME) – is this syndrome a 'real' illness, or 'Saunders' syndrome' – a result of confusion between personal and social meanings. Could it be both? The answer depends on the explanatory myths we use.

Several myths about meaning-in-the-body map the mind–body–spirit frontier. Genetics, cell-biology, psycho-pharmacology, neuro-biology, semantics, psychology, politics, religion: each give different, valid levels of meaning. The meaning of illness, of 'meaning-getting-lost-in-the-body', can be examined with each map, and each has a different purpose. The map used depends on the semantic differential: who has the power to give names to symptoms? Do we give suffering a religious meaning, a political meaning – or a medical one? Analytical psychology maps symbolic, imaginary and real worlds, like an illuminated medieval map which says 'here be dragons', or

> as in the case of Newtonian physics, in relation to quantum physics, the limits of our conventional way of thinking are exposed under special conditions. Attempts to explain in causal terms the relationship between the brain and

subjective consciousness create these special conditions. The relationship . . . is one of correlation, not one of cause and effect.

(Solms 1997: 700–1)

If body, mind and spirit don't map together in a person there is a semantic failure between Self and ego, which can't grow through sharing body-meaning. For instance, temporal splits in the psychology of 'somatising' individuals could be read *as if* a fully functioning distressed infant sub-personality is present simultaneously with a disturbed adult sub-personality. Neither can communicate, except by poorly-read body-language . . . tummy rumbles, pains in the neck, cold shivers down the spine.

In analysis, the body used for such communication may belong to patient, analyst, or both. Can we risk learning to speak this language in analysis, while keeping our defences intact? This dilemma arises if our body isn't accessible to our will, or has been over-accessible to the will of another. I'll illustrate with two clinical examples: Maisie, who had epilepsy, and Billie, living with ulcerative colitis. Both suffered developmental delays, had distorted body-Self images and failures of the transcendent function (Sidoli 1993). Body meaning-disorder showed as misinterpretation of body-language (gestural praxis) between us.

### Clinical examples

#### Maisie

Maisie, a veterinary surgeon in her late thirties, came with neurasthenia (somatised depression). Chronic hypochondria took her to her GP two or three times a week. We worked four, then five times a week over eight years. At first, she felt too big for her body, almost too big for my room. She believed she was ugly and dressed dowdily. She'd taken sedating anti-epilepsy drugs from nine to twenty: shame and rage at her ruined childhood recurred. I felt as if it was all my fault. Imagine a typical session. I felt like Richmal Crompton's fictional scruffy schoolboy William, confronted by Violet Elizabeth Bott (the somebody-else's-little-sister-you-love-to-hate) yelling 'I'm going to thcream and thcream 'til I'm thick.'

The urge to say, 'Go on then, scream!', gets stronger . . . I don't like Maisie, she doesn't like me. I'm difficult, I won't tell her to 'do' anything. I leave her feeling bored, and she bores me witless. I feel needy, resentful . . . sexually turned-off. I start to dissociate . . . far away, I imagine Maisie walking round and round in circles. She's moaning about her mother (again . . .) who hated herself for not 'being a mother'. Maisie says she wants to have a baby . . . I can't bring myself to fantasise . . . I just can't imagine having sex with her . . . Umm . . . So, an orgasmic shudder is like . . . having an epileptic fit . . .? Then I notice she's breath-holding. Is her body signifying something? She's blushing. If she has my baby will she have a fit? Will her baby have fits . . . can she give birth to anything but a monster . . .?

Ruminations go in circles, as if mother has nailed our feet to the floor. I feel sedated . . . she's vanished, I can't hear her anymore. Where has she gone? To cope with shame, on sensing my unconscious rejection, she 'vanished'.

*D*: I feel 'not-here'.
*M*: My father was like that. He'd go into a daze near me.
*D*: I wonder whether he couldn't cope with you not being perfect, and you experienced his distance as hostility?

She says this happens with all the men in her life, father, brother, colleagues, boyfriends. Maisie wants to please me, tease me . . . but she doesn't know how . . . I churn out a textbook interpretation about early infant experience, yet feel like an impoverished breast . . . or a limp penis? Whatever I do/she does will never be good enough. She doesn't excite me. So, she didn't 'excite' father?

Maisie worked out she split into two sub-personalities, 'victim-child' and 'punishing-parent'. A persecuting internal object (father-imago) was projectively identified into men . . . next session, she brought a dream: 'My mother (who is invisible) is getting me ready for my wedding. The dress is a big sack. Mother is making black-edged invitations as if for a funeral, not a wedding. Then, on a piece of wasteland, by a bonfire, in my wedding dress, I meet a dirty boy in ragged shorts, "Oh no, not a Buddhist!" I want to spit at the child for spoiling my dress.'

Mother is enviously spoiling, hiding Maisie's body in a sack? The boy could be the child-in-her, a magically thinking child-Self, the body she despises, an internal image of her animus (or her analyst)? All of these? The dream suggested 'mother' (analyst) thought a 'wedding would be her funeral . . .'. Sex equals death. We amplified this using active imagination: Maisie 'became' the boy. At this point she began to feel intensely feminine and realised she needed inner approval from a male (inner) figure (the boy wanted his mother), rather than seeing herself as a 'victim-child' only 'allowed' to relate to other 'victim-children'.

Gradually her appearance changed, she didn't want the 'mother-in-her' (herself as a real mother) to stay invisible. She married, stopped taking the contraceptive pill and began her own symbol formation by writing poetry. Once she saw her capacity to project impotence into others, she stopped projecting it into her body and stunting her own creativity.

### Billie

Billie, an artist in her late twenties, had short hair and a naughty, elfin grin. We worked three times a week for seven years. She came, acutely distressed, after a relapse of ulcerative colitis followed ending a long-term relationship. Sexually, I felt a homoerotic attraction, as if we were both adolescent boys. It was no surprise when she told me she'd been supposed to be a boy 'for my old man'; a tough labourer, a hard-drinking, hard-fighting East Ender. He'd bought her football boots, a cricket bat, and would belt her, 'jus' like wot 'is old man done to 'im – as if I woz 'is son'. She always wore black, her eyes darted hither and thither, checking for threats, as if expecting him to appear at any moment and thrash her.

She couldn't ever be the son he wanted, her body-self was fundamentally wrong. Father's brutal, repeated, rejecting experiences were unbearable to her, and overwhelmed her. She felt intense shame. Billie wasn't recognised as a woman in her family, and was 'treated like shit'. As with Maisie, incest fantasy failed: it became empatterned in sado-masochistic relationships. In ulcerative colitis, the immune system doesn't recognise colon as Self. In analysis she developed two more of the classic 'Chicago Seven' psychosomatic disorders: asthma and neurodermatitis.

Her first episode of colitis occurred after her beloved grandfather died. At the same time she left her first serious boyfriend. She said, 'I blushed away my inside.' She'd had a total colectomy, embodying her Cockney slang metaphor, 'I'm gutted' (mortifyingly upset). Speech says more than language, symbol says more than sign. She told me this as if reciting someone else's story, with no feeling. Imagine a session:

Billie talks about having sex with a boyfriend, but without feeling. I start to feel sexually aroused. She says her problem is working out why she stayed with 'that shit' so long. She stops suddenly, and blushes. Her thinking, and my penis, collapsed. I felt attacked and excluded, as ashamed as if I'd actually shown her my erection. Her burst of blushing was followed by a pain in my guts. I was left dizzy, nauseated and with intense colic.

She put physical sensations into me: sexual pleasure if she's remembering sex, gut pain if she's 'gutted', as if we've just one body between us. Counter-transference fitted the relationships she'd had with boyfriends and her father to her expectation I'd 'belt her' with interpretations, or sexually abuse her. I said so, she yelled, 'You make me dizzy!', then bursts into tears, remembering a time her mother threw her down the hall, leaving her dizzy. Mother laughed.

Billie began to see mother as not just a victim of father's rage, she could abuse too. Mother, it transpired, had had a post-partum psychosis and recurrent depression. Billie's earliest percepts were not modulated, and 'this state of ultra-sharp awareness (is) associated with an abnormal or precocious psychological birth, some children observe objects with astounding accuracy' (Tustin 1986: 143–4). Like an autistic child, Billie produced incredibly intricate, hauntingly beautiful drawings and photographs in which wholes separated into parts.

Separation from mother depends on attachment. If mother is mad, she can't be attached to. Sadly, as Billie's father was so cruel, he couldn't be attached to either. Hence her fear of thinking (animus) and difficulty using it? Signs can't be 'as ifs' – symbols. I kept being unable to symbolise with Billie, and identifying with her as victim. The idea of the Scapegoat complex helped me locate the problem in her, instead of me, then we could both think. In ancient Judaism, two goats were led to the Altar in the Temple on the day of Atonement. One was sacrificed, its entrails (colon) burnt; the other had the people's sins laid on it and was driven out – the (e)'scape Goat.

The complex arises when parents polarise children into evil and good, then play them off against each other. Billie's younger sister was the bad child. When she ran away at fifteen no-one bothered to find her. Billie was the good child, chosen to stay and be sacrificed. This complex constellates the archetype of shadow, often projected into physical illness, as a divine punishment (Morrish 1980: 2–63). 'What have I done to deserve this, what am I guilty of . . .', a question I asked about my own childhood illness, asked by anyone who faces major trauma. Sylvia Pereira (1986: 30–3) says when the patient's shadow appears in analysis, so does the analyst's. My temptation was to give Billie a sadistic 'shake' to start her mind. It happened 'accidentally'. One day, my kids were squabbling, enviously attacking each other outside my consulting room door. Billie turned on me in fury: 'What a shit you are! How could you let them . . . I'll never feel safe here again!'.

'Well,' I think. 'At least you've felt *something*!'

I hinted to her that rage about my noisy children was partly because they were not ours, but mine. She said she felt envious of them, and blushed. She felt envious of my wife, and of her mother, who had had children. Colectomy had changed her body-image, her anus was now beside her belly button, she felt unable to have sex or bear children. I thought of dazzling interpretations about intrusion, incest and so on . . . but they felt cruel. Instead, I fixed more wood to my door before her next session. It made no difference to my kids' noise, but I'd done something constructive, as her father (a carpenter), might have.

Then, that night, I dreamed of being in a collapsing tunnel, pursued by poison gas. Billie's inner world (her lethal colon), was a collapsed poison-filled tube. In analysis our attempts to make symbols collapsed or were poisoned, till gradually, a movement began from identifying her Self almost entirely as body-sensation to mourning 'being gutted'. As she began to recognise her image of herself as 'scapegoated son', she began to stop being a 'tomboy'. My counter-transference felt more hetero-erotic. She dreamed: 'Two men are fighting about me: one is dark and hairy (like my father), the other is blonde (like my analyst). Then a white lady, neither dead nor alive, floats above me – "Mother".'

Is this about intimacy with me, I ask? That I'm willing to fight for you?

She took a big risk and looked at me . . . tearful with relief, 'Yes . . .'

## Illness behaviour

Collective meaning pre-empts how we choose to give meaning to our inner experiences. If as infants our glucose receptors fire 'low', this connects via the psychoid to the cortex, creating a feeling (hunger) which initiates mother-seeking behaviour using born-in software (mother archetype). Persistent mismatching of basic needs in infancy and childhood deforms our ego–Self axis (Edinger 1962). Need becomes stigmatised (a source of shame) and this becomes an internalised negative myth, says social psychology (Frazer, in Gregory 1987: 721–3).

The people I've described had such myths: Maisie had 'not enough' mirroring of incest fantasies, Billie had 'too much'. My counter-transferential, physical responses at crux moments showed my body was used as a 'third-area'. Sharing this awareness began to allow symbols to form. Joseph Redfearn (1992a) suggests somatisation occurs if an infant has difficulty distinguishing its body from the mother. This easily happens if mother can't reality test. Mother's psychosis meant she couldn't test reality for Billie, mothers (natural) anxiety about Maisie had similar consequences. Child analyst Mara Sidoli said 'these patients are emotionally detached observers of their own images . . . their emotional memory has been lost in the archaic somatic memory of the body' (1993).

Analysis (a deconstruction, not a destruction) may not change the underlying illness, but may change the illness behaviour. As Maisie and Billie began to remember their bodies, they could form relationships. Men also trap meaning in their bodies. Ben (Chapter 2) or Storm (who we'll meet in Chapter 5) both slashed their arms. Cultures subtly determine which signifiers are gender-appropriate (bright colours, ear-rings, long hair, tattoos), and similarly, which illness behaviours are acceptable – which are 'fashionable'.

Given the long-time low status of women in patriarchal Western, monotheistic, monogamous societies, the pressures on women to gain status are great. They can become 'honorary boys' – unnaturally thin (Young-Eisendrath 2000: 33–56). Projection of meaning into the body is seen as a valid female illness behaviour, it 'keeps women in their place'. Hysteria, after all, was originally thought (by the male medical profession) to be caused by a wandering womb (Greek: ηψστεροσ, hysteros, uterus).

Somatising is not a common way of handling feeling in men (boys don't cry – they hurt themselves): 'anti-somatising' (denying the body by over-use of sex, drugs, rock 'n roll and addiction to violence) is far commoner. Fewer men seek analysis or become analysts. Do we work-out instead of working it out (like Mike, in Chapter 3 or Yukio, who I'll introduce in Chapter 6)? We need a sense of gender, to form sexual identity. This was lacking in all the patients I've mentioned here. To decide how to express sexuality concerns animus and anima, traditionally (but limitedly) understood as the contra-sexual aspects of our psyche (the 'man' in the woman and the 'woman' in the man; CW 9ii: paras 20–42). Animus and anima are aspects of counter-transferential experience. Contemporary analytical psychologists (Gordon 1993: 365–7; Samuels 1989a: 103–4) use anima and animus to refer to *unexpressed* sexuality . . . my animus represents all the male aspects I could express – all the different forms of straight, gay or bisexual man I could be.

Jung suggested dissociative splitting as a key to understanding abnormal illness behaviour (Kawai 1998: 135–46). In body-meaning disorders, parental complexes tend to replace body-based ones: as the use of dissociative splitting diminished, Maisie and Billie stopped idealising the 'wonderful childhood' they never had. When we could use together the erotic and sexual feelings in the transference and counter-transference, their egos could 'leave off' playing 'invalid' (hurt, damaged, wounded, victim-child) and start playing something else: partner-seeking. They could use their unexpressed sexuality.

Joseph Redfearn developed the concept of dissociative splitting (1992b: 165), suggesting repression of physical pain, numbing of the body-mind with auto-hypnosis, withdraws energy from the body-image into depersonalisation (as happened to Billie when she was beaten). Michael Fordham emphasised the difference between deintegration and this defensive splitting:

> In splitting, the baby's objects are not just good and bad but persistently persecutory. The infant projects bad objects into the caretaker. There is no integration, no depressive position but rather a persecutory depression leading to a sleep which this time was not sign of integration but a defensive cutting off using a splitting defence. Objects take on the characteristic of a fetish rather than a transitional object.
>
> (1985: 100, 122, 60–140. Author's paraphrase)

Illness can itself become a fetish, a sexually-charged behaviour, as in Jung's example of the girl with hysteria, or a magnificent excuse: 'I have invented an invaluable permanent invalid called Bunbury, in order that I may be able to go down to the country whenever I choose,' said Ernest, in Oscar Wilde's play, *The Importance of Being Ernest (1999)*. Ernest had 'hypochondria by proxy' – exploiting an imaginary person's imaginary illness.

Secondary gain from 'illness' may mask depression, like Maisie's hypochondria. They lack a sense of feeling depressed, but if their mood is measured with rating scales, they show depression, which responds to treatment with anti-depressants. They often become indignant on recovery, as they can no longer take 'trips to the country' – their invalidity has become invalid. And, in such circumstances, new 'physical signs' appear (symptom substitution). It is as if these people lack words for feelings, called alexithymia (like Jacques, introduced in Chapter 8). Early affects have not been named.

The psychoanalyst Murray Jackson (1979), paraphrasing Melanie Klein, pointed out that mother's role is to contain the child's thought. When she cannot, primitive, split-off, disorganised parts of the psyche communicate by projective identification into others or parts of others, or into their own bodies. The analyst is left with counter-transferential feelings of shame, hopelessness and bewilderment (my dream of the poison-filled tunnel with Billie). However, Jungian analyst Erich Neumann argued 'When Klein writes, "the mothers' body is therefore a kind of storehouse which contains the gratification of all desires and the appeasement of all fears . . . " she is describing a genuine objective element in the primal situation, not an infantile projection' (1973: 38). He believed Klein took as facts what Jung took as symbols. He suggested, and is supported by Redfearn, that infants cannot separate sense-of-its-Self (experience of its own body and real mother) from the archetypal image of the Great and Terrible Mother without a real human mother to help by mirroring feelings.

Archetypes are patterns, including patterns for experiencing the body. They have to be learnt (installed properly). Deeply embedded instinctual responses, such as suckling (a spontaneous act of the newborn) are triggered by innate releasing mechanisms, like the smell of milk. The experience of fullness, which brings sucking to an end, is in the infant's body, not the mother. The feelings involved are in both, and between both. If the infant has to contain mother's anxiety, it's the reverse of what's needed. The infant's inevitable failure to do so creates depersonalising shame as it leads to rejection. The infant needs to have shaming feelings of hopelessness and bewilderment contained by mother (Sidoli and Davies 1988: 107–28).

Peer Hultberg (1989) connects shame with Self and Self-esteem. Deep shame is a reaction to offences against archetypal patterns, and protection against overwhelming despair. Jung wrote:

> Whoever introverts libido – that is, whoever takes it away from a real object without putting in its place a real compensation – is overtaken by the inevitable results of introversion. Libido is 'psychic energy', directed towards life and wholeness, not just sexual energy.

> (*CW* 8: paras 60–130)

Shame inverts libido. Jung emphasises libido's role in differentiating ego from Self. Introversion of energy is seen in self-destructive illness behaviour and sterile relationships. Attacking projective-identifications get into the analyst's body-mind. Self, body and Great (Terrible) Mother are fused – 'If something is wrong with mother, something is wrong with me . . . something must be wrong with my body.' Hysteria, in the words of the World Health Organisation (WHO), may be a shame-driven abnormal illness behaviour:

> in which motives, of which the patient seems unaware, pro-
> duce either a restriction of the field of consciousness or
> disturbances of motor or sensory function which may seem
> to have psychological advantage or symbolic value.
>
> (WHO 1978: 35)

Recent research shows people with conversion hysteria, who make up 4 per cent of those referred to psychiatrists and neurologists, have functional differences in their anterior cingulate and orbito-frontal cortex, parts of the limbic system involved with reconstructing memory. Halligan *et al.* (2000) showed similar changes occur under hypnosis. We are near to being able to see the effect of difficulties in early relationships at a neuro-anatomical level.

## Body meaning disorders in historical perspective

Jung's notion of feedback failure in body-mind (psychoid) as origin of psychosomatic disorders contrasts with traditional psycho-analytic theory. Psychoanalysis thought certain physical illnesses, the 'Chicago Seven' (Alexander 1952), were psychosomatic responses to bad internal objects. Asthma, eczema, diabetes, ulcerative colitis, neu-rodermatitis, rheumatoid arthritis and duodenal ulcer were thought to result from body-zonal fixations – e.g. asthma from 'oral sadism'.

All these conditions are now known to be allergic immune responses or auto-immune diseases in which we make antibodies to our own tissues. This happens in other diseases too: in multiple sclerosis we make them to myelin, in thyrotoxicosis to the thyroid gland and in colitis to the gut wall. Mood does alter physiology: adrenalin release in response to stress signals the immune system to fire-up and prepare for attack. Adrenal release is controlled by the amygdalo-thalamic circuit. An increase in adrenal steroids stimulates white cells to raise an immune response. The psychoid exists at a neural, hormonal and cellular level.

Whilst the over-exact correlations to early experience suggested by Alexander and others may be wrong, the theoretical principle is sound, part of a long tradition of observing clinical signs and attributing psychological (and spiritual) purpose to physical disorder. Medicine – Western, Chinese, Aryuvedic, Ancient Egyptian, classical African, Greek, Arabic, Tibetan, Siberian and Native American shamanic traditions – involves a healer in trying to find an illness's meaning. Mircea Eliade (1964: 300), historian of religion, describes how a shaman, with a new patient, wonders, 'why this person now, what's going on in their life?' The diagnosis (Greek: δια dia, two; γνοσισ, gnosis, knowledge) is between the patient having taken in a 'disease-causing object' or 'soul-loss'.

The first needs effort to expel the bad object; the second, finding the lost soul and guiding it back into the body. This parallels primary meaning disorder: in 'the borderline', bad objects (bad parental images) are projectively identified into others, in 'the narcissistic' the soul has lost love for the body, hence its infatuation with image. Faced with harmful, magical (internal) objects, the shaman may summon spirit helpers (archetypes, parental imagos, supervisors) to help in a healing ritual (or analytic session – both involve regression). The shaman (analyst) deals with projections and introjections, using skills learnt during their own initiation and vision-quest (training analysis). They may embark on a 'vision quest' (free associate).

A shaman (analyst) does not change the signifier (disease-causing internal object), but its representation, what it *means*. This brings about a paradigm shift from a single, closed meaning (say, my childlessness means I'm not a person) to multiple, open meanings (my childlessness could mean I need selenium, or I'm not in love with my partner, or I hate my Self). Soul-loss is due to meaning following a departing soul (exit life events). Hostile magical internal objects may be due to sorcerers (bad objects), who, in turn, can act for third parties (projecting collective disapproval into the body-mind of another). Both problems respond to collective revalidation. In Celtic tribal magic, the part represented the whole. Wooden, iron or silver models of afflicted body-parts were thrown into a sacred lake to expel the bad object (Delaney 1986: 90–2). In psychosomatic illness, it's as if the unconscious throws back a bad object, afflicting a part, which, if 'spoken to' (by active imagination – 'talk to your cancer') may hold a repressed memory (Redfearn 1992a: 29).

Or, the opposite may happen. The ill themselves may be cast out. A medieval 'ship of fools' enacted driving out the wandering madmen, as French philosopher Michel Foucault made clear in *Madness and Civilisation*:

> Navigation delivers man into the uncertainly of fate; on water each of us is in the hands of his own destiny, every embarkation is, potentially, the last, it is for the other world that the madman sets sail in his fools boat, it is from the other world that he comes when he disembarks.
>
> (1965: 11)

Stigmatising lepers, those possessed by spirits (or with ME, or AIDS) also goes back as far as the history of medicine. The alchemist-physician Paracelsus suggested 'compassion is the physician's schoolmaster'. He held we are intimate mixtures of matter and spirit, representatives of God in His Creation.

> Then the light of nature is the quinta essentia, extracted by God himself from the four elements, and dwelling in our hearts. It is enkindled by the Holy Spirit. The light of nature is an intuitive apprehension of the facts, a kind of illumination. It has two sources: a mortal and an immortal which Paracelsus calls 'angels'. Man, he says is also an angel and has all the latter's qualities. He has a natural light but also a light outside the light of nature by which he can search out supernatural things.
>
> (*CW* 13: para. 145)

Analysts' theories of disease are like the shamans: illness is due to taking in a disease-causing object, or soul-loss. Again, they hark back to medieval times, to the maxim 'as above, so below'. It wasn't till the seventeenth century that Dutch microscopist Van Leeuwenhook discovered bacteria, invading bad-objects. Miasms, bad vapours, spirits of place causing illness, were believed to be equally real. Samuel Hahnemann, founder of homoeopathy, imagined these miasms had resonances with the body, and treatment with minute doses of 'miasmic agents' (disease causing substances) could potentise the body against attack. He inspired English physician Thomas Jenner to begin inoculation against smallpox, using serum from cow-pox.

Jung used the same alchemical idea, that of the *unus mundus*, the oneness of nature and spirit, in his theory of disease. Body, mind and spirit inter-relate, forming an inter-subjective field. Joseph Redfearn, discussing Jung's concept of Self and its origins in his personal development, says Self-images are origin for compensatory symbols which organise consciousness (1985: 29–30). He extends the idea of Self beyond the limits of an individual body-mind, stressing its teleological, forward-looking purpose.

It is an inherent property of Self to attribute meaning to events (Sandner 1986 : 1–17). The implications of illness depend on our theory of illness. The Chicago analyst Murray Stein (1996) emphasised the role of the immune system (a constitutional, therefore archetypal, factor) in recognising Body as Self. Jung's close colleague, C. Meier (1962) suggested that the relationship between psyche and soma may be synchronistic rather than causal or developmental. Unfortunately, insight does not produce change, as:

> Practical experience teaches us as a general rule that a psychic activity can find a substitute only on the basis of equivalence. A pathological interest, for example, an intense attachment to a symptom can be replaced only by an equally intense attachment to another interest, which is why a release of the libido from the symptom never takes place without this substitute. If the substitute is of less inert energic value, we know at once that a part of the energy is to be sought elsewhere – if not in the conscious mind, then in unconscious fantasy formations or in a disturbance of the 'parties superiors' of the psychological functions (to borrow an apt expression of Janet's).
>
> (*CW* 8: para. 139)

Meaning can impact (like a tooth that won't come out) preventing movement from physical to psychological dilemmas, and vice versa. We can't link our over-drinking, over-eating and lack of exercise to why we don't feel good about ourselves . . . because we don't feel good about our Selves. We can't symbolise what is denied.

Joyce McDougall (1989) suggests failure to create and relate to mental representations predisposes to psychosomatic disorders. Intensely painful experiences can't be held in symbols, only in body-mind: in the psychoid. Depth psychologists agree symbols include unconscious process, have an *as if* quality, hint at 'meanings behind meanings behind meanings' (Gordon 1978). Hanna Segal (1975) linked symbol formation to sublimation: symbol formation can happen if there's been a good negotiation of object loss, pain and mourning. Thereafter, symbols may replace lost objects and be used creatively by the Self. (Billie opened up into fine art, Maisie into poetry.)

## Working with body-meaning disorders

When a name becomes negatively connoted – like melancholia or neurasthenia – it's changed: as happened with some congenital meaning disorders – idiots became mentally defective, then mentally handicapped, now they are people with learning difficulties. As the name changes, the meaning (signified) changes too. If symbol formation fails between body and mind, and meaning is trapped at the level of the psychoid, there has to be a payoff. In the classical psychoanalytic view the payoff is allowing sexual fixations to remain in place.

Jung took erotic, transformational language from alchemy to describe the embodied, erotic transferential and counter-transferential feelings around such people (*CW* 16: paras. 457–66). To be aroused (or turned-off) by a patient involves imagining the *coniunctio*. For my purpose here, this symbolises the union of matter and spirit 'a marrying of the opposites in an intercourse which has as its fruition the birth of a new element . . . symbolised by a child that manifests potential for greater wholeness by recombining attributes from both the opposing natures' (Samuels *et al.* 1986: 35–6).

The coniunctio is the 'hidden fourth' of Maria Prophetissa, the capacity for body-mind-spirit to relate affectively to others. Death and loss are as much part of this process as new birth (in Elizabethan English, 'the little death' was slang for orgasm, a source of puns for Shakespeare). The thalamus (Greek, 'bridal chamber', the setting for a coniunctio) is at the centre of the limbic system. Here signals from the body meet the mind, and as mind meets body, feelings are added to percepts. The limbic system is a *between* place, its sub-cortical nerve centres change blood-flow and life-breath. Jung's experimental work measured galvanic skin response (GSR – skin electrical potential, dependent on peripheral blood flow – Billie's blushing), and breath-changes (pneumography – Maisie's breath-holding) (*CW* 2: paras 1036–347). These change if we touch a complex.

Now, applying this: if during a session we notice changes in unconscious gestural praxis – breath-changes as a result of a feeling (we sense a flash of anger and imagine the face of someone we hate) – we're facing a complex, a projection of a symbol in our imagination rather than an out-there reality. Body-language evokes the past. It allows meaning to be found in the body. By imagining different body-language we can affect the future. For example, awareness of breath, of what makes our breathing change, is like using an inbuilt pneumograph.

For example: Storm, the young eco-warrior we'll meet in the next chapter, needed help with anxiety. I asked him to picture a time when he'd felt both scared and confident. He imagined surfing. When he noticed shallow breathing, he learnt to imagine surfing by tapping his wrist (a body-cue). He could accept his fear (and feel confident) as he faced a difficult encounter both by working from body-sensation to feeling his rage (expressed to his analytic father in the transference) and by using active imagination.

Many Eastern and Western medical approaches attempt to change body-meaning: visualising white blood cells destroying a cancer, or imagining pleasurable sex to treat impotence or frigidity. Imagination lets archetypes unfold into physiological changes, as symbols form. Any projective technique can lead to deep regression (like hypnosis), unlocking the 'Spirit Mercurius'. If we can't express 'manifold meanings' an angry genie is trapped in a body-memory. When released, it grants wishes, if we can withstand its murderous rage and trick it back into its bottle before it kills us (CW 13: paras 239–46). Making-meaning develops as we learn (re-learn) body-language. In congenital meaning disorders like autism, parts of the body-mind meaning-system are encapsulated – never open. Reclosure occurs in hysteria and hypochondria – disorders of the meaning of illness, and in primary meaning disorders (Chapter 5). Perhaps the payoff of somatising, rather than maintaining sexual distance, is avoiding the unbearable shame of rejection? Acknowledging the value of Freud's insights, adding Jung's understanding that there is more to body-meaning than sex, by being open about our sexual countertransference, may bridge the split? Or maybe the shame in body-meaning disorders is as great as that in primary meaning disorder, which I discuss next.

# 5

# PRIMARY MEANING DISORDER

Consider the one God universe: OGU. The spirit recoils in horror from such a deadly impasse. He is all powerful and all knowing. Because he can do everything, he can do nothing, since the act of doing demands opposition. He knows everything, so there is nothing for him to learn. He can't go anywhere, since he is already fucking everywhere, like cow shit in Calcutta.

The OGU is a pre-recorded universe of which he is the recorder. It's a flat, thermodynamic universe, since it has no friction by definition. So he invents friction and conflict, pain, fear, sickness, famine, war, old age and death. His OGU is running down like an old clock. Takes more and more to make fewer and fewer energy units of Sek, as we call it in the trade. The magical universe, MU, is a universe of the Gods, often in conflict. So the paradox of an all powerful, all knowing God who permits suffering, evil and death, does not arise.

(William Burroughs, *The Western Lands*, 1987: 113)

## The One God Universe

William Burroughs's picaresque novel describes a soul's journey after death to the Western Land, ruled by Osiris, God of Death-and-Rebirth (Hades) guided by Thoth (Hermes) inventor of language. Egyptian gods, like their Graeco-Roman counterparts, mixed freely with men and could assimilate other gods, or be assimilated, as, in a magical universe the divinities are fluent forms with open boundaries. Problems of a One God Universe (OGU) are common to closed, rigid, over-boundaried systems: whether these are social meaning disorders (politico-religious fundamentalisms), congenital meaning disorders (Kanner's syndrome), body-meaning disorders (somatisation) or primary meaning disorders (borderline/narcissistic sub-personalities).

Complexes are OGUs in the psyche: protective meaning strategies devised to manage unbearable physical or psychological distress and pain which made no meaning to us at the time – and may never do so. When pathologically operating, a complex is a psychological structure encapsulating an internal object (Greenberg and Mitchell 1983). This happens when an archetype has not been humanised (installed properly). Think of a pearl forming round dirt in an oyster – a complex is not necessarily 'bad' of itself, it can be beautiful. In analytical psychology 'ego' is short-hand for 'ego-complex', though the notion of a perfect (or perfectible) ego is non-sense, that is, it has no meaning.

As explored in the previous chapter, after severe trauma the 'fear circuit' in the brain (between the thalamus and amygdala) cuts in before the 'meaning-making circuit' from limbic system via prefrontal cortex to frontal lobes can operate. However, what is severe trauma to one may not be to another. This depends on personality type, differences between the personalities of child and parent, and the social setting.

For example, the two patients I discuss in this chapter are sensation types. Storm, a young eco-warrior, felt his parents were thinkers; Geoff, a rich businessman, felt his father was also a sensation type (both were artists). Storm and his parents had difficulty communicating as sensation types and thinking types explain the world in very different ways. Geoff and his father had similar difficulties because of cultural distance between them caused by father's horrific wartime experiences. For Storm and Geoff the outer world (parents and culture) did not validate inner experience, creating meaning disorder.

I suggest here that 'borderline' and 'narcissistic' sub-personalities are two names for one problem, 'primary meaning disorder'. Personal and social problems arise from inability to create new meaning.

Two-headed Janus, Roman god of doorways, was symbolised by a key to open and close the door and a stick used by doorkeepers to drive away intruders. In primary meaning disorder it's as if we cannot tell whether to use key or stick. We're stuck on a meaning threshold unable to go out into the world, go home to our inner space, or prevent intrusion. These 'strange effects at boundaries' result from problems Self has 'downloading' into reality. For there are two boundaries, not one, between ego and Self. The boundary has an inside and an outside. Like a cell membrane, or a medieval city wall, there is a space, neither in nor out, both in and out – a *between* – a threshold. Borderline trait concerns the boundary between ego and Self; narcissistic trait between Self and other.

Unfortunately, the terms are often used casually, in an impersonal, stigmatising way, rather than naming lost sub-personalities, 'lost Selves'.

Primary meaning disorder is a strange effect at a boundary: neuro-anatomically, this describes events in the limbic system, the threshold between mind and body. Analysis can open up trauma formerly closed-off in complexes, let shadowy split-off parts cross the threshold and find new meaning. Developing the transcendent function allows archetypal patterns to reinstall (Williams 1983). We could imagine new neural pathways forming which bypass the 'fear circuit' as we learn new words for feelings.

For it is *as if* there are two mutually incomprehensible languages on either side of the ego–Self boundary. Suppose Self and ego represent the areas outside and inside a walled city respectively. 'Between' is the space between outer and inner walls (see the 'Gates of Carcassonne' dream in the next chapter). Borderline sub-personalities get stopped at the outer gate of the city, on the Self side. They never enter the city, time-bound experience or shared reality-testing, never get into the ego. Ego remains unformed because it is uninformed by anything outside itself. These marginalised, liminal sub-personalities are the gypsies, refugees and asylum-seekers in our psyche – shadow parts nobody wants.

Narcissistic sub-personalities get (developmentally) arrested at the inner gate (on the ego side), separated from the riches of Self by a 'mine-field' – everything is 'mine, mine, mine'. When borderline sub-personalities lay siege to the ego-complex, they make meaning as if Self's existence is on the line every time, using the stick of projective identification to penetrate the body-mind of others, not trusting that words or gestures will be an adequate key. Narcissistic sub-personalities exist by splitting and denial, using the stick of narcissistic rage to prevent Self getting in and to maintaining their illusion of omnipotence (Jacoby 1989: 150–88). Both are defensive behaviours of the 'One God' in an OGU, as if only *my* body-mind, *my* ego and *my* point of view exist. As this defence costs dearly, people with primary meaning disorders keep running out of psychic energy ('units of Sek', or libido) and end up stealing it from others. Like Oedipus (the young shepherd-thief who stole the kingdom of Thebes, rightfully his) borderline and narcissistic sub-personalities both steal from their Selves.

This simplistic model of complexes-in-action, is, of course, wrong! Add the concept *strange effect at a boundary*. As ego emerges from Self, it struggles to negotiate meaning, by assimilation (reintegration) and accommodation (deintegration). We seek objects and objects seek us as we open and close to them. Primary process happens first, Self talking to ego. Secondary process happens second, ego talking to Self.

Erik Erikson, following Freud, suggested this occurs as ego gradually begins to separate id from superego (1968: 208–12). Analytical psychology, applying Occam's razor (that entities ought not be multiplied beyond necessity), neither has nor uses the concepts id or superego. The ego-complex develops by (and to) holding tensions between primary and secondary process, an essential encapsulation of meaning. It grows between three pairs of opposites: the first pair is fragmentation vs. withdrawal, the second seduction vs. neediness, the third separation anxiety vs. over-attachment.

Faced with a real or imagined threat to their 'comfort zone' of conceptual openness or closedness, borderline sub-personalities fragment (open very fast and can't close – they explode); narcissistic sub-personalities withdraw (close very fast and can't open – they implode). Borderline sub-personalities are terrified of separation. They seductively draw in others, then shame them so as to get their own way. Narcissistic sub-personalities, with their 'cling film' attachment, often use 'guilt trips' to push their needs into the other. Both approaches end up pushing others away, confirming the subjects' feelings of worthlessness and rejection. Both problems arise from not being able to 'change psychological gear' between closing (re-integrating), and opening (de-integrating) – between primary and secondary process thinking, *not* from being too open or too closed. Imagine a car with two speeds, stop and go: the clutch between the engine (Self) and gearbox (ego) is broken. 'The clutch' is being able to grasp changes in meaning.

## Primary meaning disorder and stimulus-meaning

Imagine a little green man in analysis: Zork, the Alien. We'll understand Zork by interpreting his 'stimulus-meanings'. Do we hear the same sound or see the same gesture (signifier) each time we point to an object (referent)? If we say 'Zork' to Zork when we point at ourselves, does Zork grin or frown? Which means yes, which means no? How do we know if Zork is a he or a she if we have no common signifiers?

The concept stimulus-meaning comes from the branch of semiotics studying meaning-attribution (philological semantics). Stimulus-meaning is a signifier of Self in a discourse. Meaning-making originates with Self, expanding into the world through the space-time bound ego-complex. American philosopher Willard Quine suggested that, to grasp this idea, we imagine investigating a totally unknown language. Quine argues that naming processes can't give a one-on-one map of any investigator (subject's) language, or meaning system, that can be transferred on to another's (an object's). It may give a 'good-enough' fit, enabling us to share signs (Cohen 1962: 88–9).

Sharing signifiers requires recognition of intersubjectivity between Self and other, which requires recognition of signifiers of Self. The psychoanalytic researcher into childhood Daniel Stern specified signifiers of Self as origin, motion, time, and coherence of intensity (1985: 85–6), as discussed in Chapter 3. In the developmental metaphor, a mother's reliable presence has an origin (her physical body), which usually moves coherently through time. However her psychological, meaning-making body may not if she's drunk, drugged, psychotic or an ever-changing substitute mother (Stevens 1982, 85–104). In meaning-making, a vital quality is coherence of intensity, as measured by an object's luminosity and presence. Mother has to mirror the infant's expectation of being a 'bright, shining object'.

Recognition of intersubjectivity relies on our being able to use Jean Piaget's idea of separation between 'psychological subject' (a real child's unique personal understanding of psychology – 'me as me') and 'epistemic subject' (the psychology all children understand in common – 'me and my mates'). This depends on children gradually learning the difference between mother as 'my mother', and 'all mothers' (the archetype of the Great/Terrible Witch mother), between 'mother-as-an-internal-object', mother-as-a-social-construct' and 'mother-as-collective', 'motherland', 'the Mother of God' and so on – that is, on being able to personalise their experience of the mother archetype, then other archetypes in an appropriate sequence. The diversity of meanings in an archetype lets us develop groups of stimulus-meanings, a unique signifying system of gestures and words. We learn our first signifying system the same way we'd learn Alien, by having objects named consistently. A sense of Self – origin, motion, time, and coherence of intensity – allows experiences of agency, coherence, continuity and affective relating. These, with object-constancy, develop ego. However, if we receive inconsistent stimulus-meanings, we never learn words-for-feelings, or how to form symbols. We have to name percepts and have the names validated before we can form stable internal objects (images) from in-born archetypes. Such images provide a basis for meaningful, ethical negotiations between Selves.

To illustrate: imagine an infant's cry has four stimulus-meanings – feed me, pick me up, change me, put me to sleep. Mother has to guess (value) which needs doing. Baby has to guess (value) what her approach gestures mean: 'Are you going to meet my need?' In anxious attachment, 'Are we going to get it right for each other?' In hostile attachment, 'You never get it right, here we go again . . .' and so on. Imagine a fully-formed Self in an infant body, able to make value-judgements about its inner world, dreaming and reflecting, finding its signals treated as noise:

> 'I cry, nothing consistent happens. My Self is not recognised. When I look out through my ego, all I see is my shadow . . . I expect a sparkle in mother's eye [luminous presence], I get fearful darkness [non-luminous absence]. When I'm anxious, I get met with anxiety. When I'm hungry, I get met with hostility . . . when I want to go to sleep, I get woken up . . . when I want to wake up, they want me to go to sleep . . .'

Piaget supposed infants learn self-value and experience ethical success or failure in such negotiations, the origin of a child's natural sense of justice. When mother and child get it right for each other often enough, 'mother-as-person-out-there' is incorporated as a 'good-enough internal object'. When (m)other is there to be projectively-identified into, this humanises an archetype, which continues installing the transcendent function. The transcendent function links Self to ego and Self to (m)other and begins installing as ego starts bridging the gulf between conscious and unconscious *in utero*.

Touching the uterine wall, hearing mother's heart are our first experiences of other – 'the symbol is born in the gap between the two realities, inner and outer, where the baby is getting to know about a two-person relationship' (Moore 1975). Ultrasound studies show purposive movement appears at as early as six weeks post-conception (Piontelli 1993: 238–9). We're just sentient . . . we can thumb-suck as soon as we have thumbs: presumably, to install suckling reflexes (and security?). Babies and mothers nearly always bond, given favourable initial conditions, by learning each other's stimulus-meanings through sharing body-language (gestural praxis). Archetypal images of mother (and/or our own body) may not form a 'motherboard' if the hardware is damaged (say, by intra-uterine hypoxia, infection or the foetal alcohol syndrome) or the software can't run – there is no consistent mother-figure. In primary meaning disorder, the body-reference system is insecure.

Primary meaning disorder represents a failure of the transcendent function, but only by implication a failure of initial conditions (Balint 1968: 20–3). Whether we say failure to interpret stimulus-meaning is pre-verbal, or pre-symbolic, failure on the infant's part or lack of empathy on the mother's part, the result is chaos in the meaning system. Self-to-ego meaning failure arises if mother gets the infants four meanings wrong with *in*consistent inconsistency: ' . . . sometimes I can predict, sometimes I can't, but I never know which'. Then, like a dog in a behaviourist's cage given random electric shocks, the infant gives up. Mother becomes an internal confusional object, as for Geoff in the following clinical example. Having two mothers, he had no mother. As he said: 'So, maybe, one of them understood sometimes . . . I just never knew which.'

Borderline sub-personalities are like Johnnie, the tough bike-gang leader Marlon Brando played in *The Wild Ones* (Benedek 1953). When asked, 'What are you rebelling against?', Johnnie replied, chewing gum. 'What've you got?' His inner dialogue might be: 'Whatever I do's gonna be wrong . . . may as well jus' be wrong, and get it over with . . .' In counter-transference: 'whatever I do is wrong – interpret, don't interpret'. With luck, I notice how these aspects of a person absorb my own shadow projections *so* easily' (like Geoff).

A patient's Self mirrors the analyst's shadow (and vice versa). Both need to learn to accept being human and fallible, to make a time-bound ego-founded relationship by working through omnipotence fantasies – 'divine rescuer' or 'divine victim'; omnipotent patient, omniscient analyst. If empathy fails, somewhere, someone isn't seen as human. Suddenly an all-seeing eye accuses, deep inside our Self, and, with terrifying accuracy, finds our shadow, our weakness, and mirrors it back, ruthlessly.

It's like being seen by Sauron, the evil *Lord of the Rings* whose lidless eye follows the heroes, Frodo and his servant Sam, on the quest to destroy his One Ring, with which he hoped to become the One God (OG) of his own OGU (Tolkien 1954: 421). Tolkien, a Professor of Anglo-Saxon, used traditional Western mythological images to explore the dilemma of good and evil. As in a fairy-story, the evil sorcerer is defeated by a child-like, innocent trick. Sauron can't believe anyone would be stupid enough to send his precious treasure and symbol of his power to destruction. An impotent act by which the loser wins, is non-sense (meaningless) to a potential OG.

Persecutory projective-identifications, like Sauron's eye, create a twilight state of inattentive drowsiness in me, accompanied by intense feelings of hatred, sometimes of paranoia, sometimes with nascent sexual fantasy or arousal (Winnicott 1984: 194–204). I take this as a shadow/trickster quality. The patient has tricked themselves over my meaning-threshold, out of my free-floating attention, out of mutually satisfying intercourse. The Winnebago folk-hero, Trickster (also known as Coyote) carried his penis in a box on his back. This real part-object was projected across a lake into the body of the Chief's beautiful daughter (Radin 1972: 19–20).

The penis makes animus/anima connection, as a living bridge (Gordon 1993: 69–85; Jung, *CW* 9ii: paras 20–42) , across which *coniunctio* occurs – a union of spirit and matter. Projective-identification is like being a part-object (I feel as if I'm only stiff penis or sexually-aroused feeding nipple). This inattentive, drowsy, fey quality happens when I'm possessed by other archetypal processes. My humanity feels inconsistently present, like a flickering flame. I'm not sure if I am in the room with an angel, or a devil: I know I'm in the room with a 'borderline aspect' of Self, because I feel my Self on the line. My memories and free associations surface, rather than the patient's . . . I've 'gone'. But, with other patients, there is a flash, then they're 'gone' – light's on, nobody home.

In primary meaning disorder, it's almost impossible for both analyst and patient to be in the same room and both remain human. It's like being in the room with a robot, or being turned into one (Ledermann 1981). Ridley Scott's classic sci-fi film *Blade Runner* questioned what it means to be human and what it means to be free (Scott 1992, based on *Do Androids Dream of Electric Sheep*? Dick 1968). Roy (Rutger Hauer), leads a rogue gang of replicants (genetically-engineered humanoids), who escape from deep-space slavery. A shadowy/trickstery anti-hero, Roy had his life-history supplied by his creator, so he can 'feel like a human'. However, to prevent the Creation replacing the Creator, replicants live only four years.

To be near-perfect, yet so mortal, is anguish. As children, we are near Self. We feel immortal. We have little sense of chronological, Chronos-time. We live in near timeless Kairos-time (Chapter 7). If possessed by the archetype of eternal youth (puer or puella), we believe we can play around forever (Hillman 1979: 23–30). Such sub-personalities are good at starting things, but rarely finish. Fear of success is common, the fear of one's meaning being lost, unvalued, enviously attacked, castrated, blocks creativity.

This is the tragedy of the puer, Narcissus. Echo, the invisible nymph, is sick with love for the beautiful shepherd-boy. She calls him, till her voice fades away. The gods punish Narcissus by having him fall in love with the first thing he sees, his reflection. He loves no one but his Self-image (not his Self) till he fades away (Schwartz-Salant 1982: 83–6). Narcissistic traits are naturally strong in adolescence. Endless hours are spent studying our appearance, trying on personae. We play precocious grown-up, like a little girl in mummy's high-heeled shoes.

Borderline traits retain magical meaning-making ability (primary process thinking) as dominant meaning-making mode through adolescence into adulthood. Such traits are often intensely self-destructive, like the Beast, in Beauty and the Beast. In the story, the young prince is cursed for refusing hospitality to an old crone – a fairy princess in disguise. Unless the lad can find someone to love his shadow-side, he is fated to remain forever trapped in his animal nature. Narcissus was trapped in his reflection: the 'Beast' is trapped in his shadow. As Nathan Schwartz-Salant explains:

> the reflection or shadow is an object of mana, power that is transpersonal, the god-like or soul-like quality of a person. When Narcissus sees his reflection, he is looking at his soul, his vital centre. An important example of the identity between the mirror image and the Self is found in the early Greek Dionysian mysteries.
>
> (1982: 89)

. . . in which the initiate was being prepared for their encounter with the God whilst looking in a mirror, seeing their suffering and death approaching:

> psychologically, the shadow or reflection carries the image of the Self, not the ego. It is interesting and even psychotherapeutically useful to have a person suffering from narcissistic character disorders study their face in a mirror.
>
> (ibid: 90)

Lack of ability to recast, to have different sub-personalities centre-stage or working together, leads to ritualised defences of an 'egg-shell fragile ego', with a false smile, and an 'I'm alright' attitude (like Maisie in the last chapter). We become like the Queen in Snow White, always asking the mirror for reassurance, murderously envious of the beautiful (inner) child (Andersen, ed. Ehrlich 1986: 58–73), but with little sense of Self, or Self-worth.

Using the international border analogy, 'borderline' frontiers hardly contain an overcrowded, starving population. Narcissistic frontiers resemble an armed camp, highly defended, always expecting attack. Jacques, a young French journalist (whom we will meet further in Chapter 8) said, 'It's like having the Maginot Line inside.' (This defensive fortification was built to prevent German invasion of France after World War One. When World War Two began, the Germans, knowing exactly where it was, just drove right round it.) A sense of being invasive or invaded results from lack or loss of confidence in meaning-making, symbol forming and reality testing. If borderline sub-personalities hardly keep boundaries at all, narcissistic ones keep them too tightly.

Permanently hungry for affection, borderline sub-personalities, like Frankenstein's monster, feel as if made of fragments of the dead (bad internal objects). They lurch from one failed relationship to the next, unable to make human contact. The latter, like Count Dracula, are the un-dead, vampires sucking life from their victims, themselves once victims of vampires. Narcissistic over-achievement is an example of ego trying to be Self, instead of simply being with Self. If ego is flooded by Self then ego is maddened in the process. If, however, ego assumes it *is* Self, this is like the inmates taking over the asylum (see *CW* 9ii: para. 45). We no longer value the dreamy, crazy, mad parts of our psyche, creative manias and depressions, schizoid poetry, *between* experiences – uncertain, numinous, timeless moments essential to any creative act (Koestler 1969: 327).

When we are uncertain we approach a meaning limit-state. Facing change, we face uncertainty. Analysis, like Shamanism, uses clear boundaries to contain uncertainty, to permit new meaning to form within these new limits, the analytic frame (Langs 1979). Certainties about place and time (sweat lodge at dawn, morning session on the couch), holidays (Summer Solstice, half-term), fees (two goats, forty pounds), and recommendations about how to communicate about analysis, to decide whether it's worth the goats/money, require continual attention. In primary meaning disorder, failure of the transcendent function is seen in those areas requiring reality-testing, including creativity and humour. Others either have too much reality, or not enough, but it always feels like the joke is on us.

### *Clinical examples*

## *Storm*

Storm, a young eco-warrior and a keen rave-dancer, feels reality-testing is a concrete function of words. He uses words like he uses his flick-knife, to fight with. Between us, negotiation required precise agreement on the meaning of words. Like Ged (the sorcerer's apprentice in Ursula Le Guin's *A Wizard of Earthsea*, 1968, whom we'll meet in Chapter 12) Storm uses magical thinking. Words have only one enchanted meaning at a time. I upset him by saying grown-up instead of 'adult': to him, the first is 'parents', the second, 'men in suits'. He saw little value in either.

He came as a few days earlier he'd slashed his arms with a razor, and cut a pentagram over his pierced left nipple, above his heart. Within minutes of our first meeting, he stripped off his tattered T-shirt and showed me. I said something like:

*D:* 'Hmm . . . a Pentagram. Symbol of the Pagan Religion, isn't it? You're a Pagan, huh?'
He peers up from under matted dread-locks, astonished. A huge grin broke on his dirty tear-stained face.
*D:* 'What is it, then . . . an initiation thing?'
He nods, very shy, wipes his hands on his torn cut-down combat pants, and asks, 'How d' you know . . . ?'
*D:* 'I recognise your symbol,'
Storm proudly touches his heavy-duty tribal tattoo and shows me his knife-fight scars, saying, 'Yeah. My chi was blocked. I had to let blood flow.'

Storm has problems at both frontiers of *between*. He hurt himself rather than his family. He was flooded with archaic images, close to the Earth, seductive, anxious, withdrawn, with an overpowering sense of guilt. He experienced cruel parents inside, forever bullying his 'nature-child', and acted out his battle for deliverance from the mother (*CW* 5: paras 419–63). He felt defeated as he'd gone back to live with her as he couldn't cope on the road as a 'New Age' traveller.

Born and raised on a beach in California till his artist parents' marriage failed, he moved to the UK at ten and went to a tough inner city school. American beach-boy met tough street-kid reality. Rather than be bullied every day, he imitated his persecutors. He bullied, stole, truanted, fought, and started using cannabis heavily.

Storm's acts appear, to him, to leave him at others' mercy. He bullies himself into action, or gets others to do so. In his words, blocked Chi – hence his need to dance, to let his body express his turmoil. He used primary-process thinking, and as a Pagan, invoked the shaman within.

Developmental delay left the bridges between percept and concept as tenuous for a ten year old, the age his idyllic childhood ended. His bloody pentagram is a numinous symbol: for a Pagan, as potent in meaning as the Cross for 'born-again' Christians, a signifier of a spiritual impulse, a mark of initiation. Storm's body-markings are meaning-atoms (syntagma), identifications with Earth-Mother and Sky-Father.

Recognition and acceptance of his meaning-system created trust, as did positively connoting his 'self-medication' with cannabis and giving him the paradoxical injunction that he must under no circumstances reduce his consumption. I used the archetype of trickster with a trickster (knowing its efficacy from past experience working with addictive behaviours and researching cannabis psychosis: Mathers and Ghodse 1992) – and knowing it was a contributing cause to his disturbance. Within two months he was using hardly any, had a job as a labourer and began actively resisting interpretations. He felt able to validate his own meanings, and 'fight me' when the ten-year-old in him stopped being drugged and despised.

### Geoff

Geoff felt he'd two mothers, but no father. He came as his wife 'told him to' – his marriage was threatened. A small, intense, powerfully-built man with a room-filling personality, he'd come in on the ground floor of his father's firm, raced cars, had 'countless' girlfriends – but no children. His father was torpedoed twice in the Navy during World War Two, drank heavily, and divorced when Geoff was twelve. Mother was rivalled by her own mother, who lived with them. 'Mum was dad, gran was mum', was Geoff's formula. I asked:

> *D:* 'If you've two mothers, have you no mother? If you have two wives, have you no wife? And if you have no wife, have you no mother . . . ?'
> 'No, you don't understand!', was his angry response.

I felt concerned about his unacknowledged depression and suicidal impulses. He refused 'pills', saying he'd see his doctor for that, (forgetting I'm a psychiatrist, making me into an impotent father . . .) till one night he sleepwalked to the roof of his ten-floor apartment block. He woke, about to jump. From then, instead of denigrating me as a 'useless waste of money', I was idealised. Bringing idealisation and denigration together was hard.

For Geoff, in the Oedipal drama, father was both 'too easy' to defeat and too hard: first, because he was absent, then, after the War, father couldn't forgive himself for not being able to save his best friend from drowning when their ship was torpedoed. Though he was seen as a hero for trying, he didn't give that meaning to his actions. Geoffrey continually needed to do heroic things to rival his hero father, even though father felt a failure. His competitiveness appeared in his trying to be on the couch and in my chair at the same time.

Outwardly, a classic 'over-achiever', I disliked him at first: perhaps my liberal with his conservative, or my 'puer' in competition? Perhaps, like his mother, I worried about him, saw him as a boy-nuisance to be kept in order? Initially, 'defeating depression' meant 'defeating me' – particularly in the harrowing weeks up to his suicide attempt. When his denial diminished he began taking medication (and sleeping). He dreamed of fearful wartime scenes of flying bombs devastating the countryside. He associated to his dread/hope his father might or might not come home, his own fear of 'bombing' (slang for failure), and of impotence. Gradually, the dreams became more 'here and now':

> A jumbo jet crashes on his West End tailor's, he's outside with a group of men in new green and brown striped suits . . .
> Geoff starts to laugh.
> *G:* 'What's brown with green stripes . . . ?'
> *D:* 'I don't know . . .'
> *G:* 'A humbug . . . just like me . . .'

As he laughed, he cried. He read the dream image – being a humbug (dishonest) was self-castrating. His moment of recognition broke through his need to control: he took a holiday, cut down on work and resumed his sex-life. Celebrating his sixtieth birthday, he retired, started fundraising for a children's charity . . . and practising his favourite 'profession' – as a children's conjurer.

These two people may appear opposite: one, a boy trying to be a man, the other a man trying to stay a boy. In archetypal terms, they are puer (the eternal youth) and senex (the wise old man). Both were 'sensation types' who deeply loved nature, had a strong aesthetic sense, and were children at heart: but children whose worlds fell apart, who had to be precociously adult, (had to install 'hero' too early) whose primary meaning function did not work well enough to form symbols. Both acted out their boundary disturbances by pushing others beyond their limits.

'Borderline' is ego-Self boundary disturbance, on the Self side. Ego is invaded: life is lived in hostile compliance, or rebellious schizoid compromise. Like Storm, we 'self-marginalise', becoming liminal even in our own life. Narcissism is ego-Self boundary disturbance, on the ego side. Like Geoff, ego 'assumes command', others obey or risk being torpedoed and sunk. I was struck by how their strongly developed sensation-function led to increased sensitive skin: Storm had as little as possible between skin and Father-Sun; he lived, worked and came to sessions in shorts and sneakers. Geoff, with two mothers, had a passion for designer silk shirts and suits.

Too open, too closed – primary meaning disorder can reside in not enough or in too much meaning. Self-side constrictions produce 'meaning hypertrophy', over-determined, as in Storm's self-cutting (the symbol meant too much): ego-side constrictions produce 'meaning hypotonia', Geoffrey's power-dressing said *look at me, look at me* – but when seen, it was never enough.

## Clinical presentation

Primary meaning disorders are sometimes only discovered after much analytic work; arguably, techniques producing deep regression create meaning disorder by challenging the boundary between ego and Self (opening the gates) as much as they recall meaning-disordered events in childhood. There is a difference between a condition as a *state*, the only behavioural option open (one sub-personality has control of the ego-complex), and a *trait* (one sub-personality amongst a cast of personae).

In appearance, borderline state may be ordinary or unusual – 'rebel without a cause' – whatever the dress code, borderliners break it. Narcissistic state, by contrast, wrote the dress code. In behaviour, borderline are chaotic: they may have little sense of identity, lack a sense of gender, have no clearly defined sexual orientation, multiple sexual relations, (sometimes perversions), frequent job changes, academic under-achievement (perhaps with a history of childhood conduct disorder); brushes with the law or involvement of multiple social agencies. They tend to be brought to therapy, rather than 'volunteer' – unless *in extremis*.

Narcissistic state gets 'nagged' into therapy, fearing they'll 'lose face' in the eyes of a valued other by not going. They over-achieve but find success meaningless (Geoff's sleepwalking suicide attempt occurred the night he received an award). Borderliners may speak in timeless, archetypal language: long, discursive Self-justifications tumble out, interspersed with genuine remorse. Narcissistic speech may be over-precise, the content says 'look what a nice X I've got' – it's another *mine*field.

There are crucial differences in form of thought. Borderline thought tends to over-open chaos: loose associations and flights of ideas, endless creative schemes which never go anywhere (which may lead to confusion with mania). However, there are usually no signs of 'formal thought disorder' (i.e. delusions), though ideas of reference may reach delusional intensity (Gunderson and Singer 1975; Shapiro 1975). Narcissistic thought tends to premature closure, often into ruminations on past or present slights, real or imagined (negative past temporal perspective), and preoccupying fears of not being loved.

Temporal orientation with borderliners tends to future conditional – *if* I . . . *then* tomorrow. Narcissists are time-bound, trapped by concrete meaning-making strategies. Borderliners find meaning 'by magic' (Self-ish, primary process). I discuss this again in Chapter 7, looking at the high frequency of synchronistic events when near to Self (a borderline state) and in Chapters 8 and 9, when I compare time-bound versus time-free language and myth.

Making myth when faced by a cultural catastrophe is universal in societies, family systems and individuals. It signifies a changing meaning-system, 'a meaning-system at a boundary'. Change is loss, met with by mourning. We go through denial, isolation, anger, guilt and sadness repeatedly as we bargain for new meaning (Kubler-Ross 1970: 34–122; Murray Parkes 1966: 29–46). Sometimes, meaning gets lost in the body, in bereavement, meaning getting lost in between, a disorder of the ego-Self axis.

What is the purpose of meaning disorder? Is it to meet the needs of internal or external objects, depending on where the locus of control is? If the purpose of an object is believed to be only for *itself*, never for *us both*, there is little or no intersubjectivity, or empathy. Suppose the goal of meaning-disordered sub-personalities, personality traits or complexes is paradoxical: not to make meaning, not to take responsibility for the subject. Their purpose (teleology) is denied, split off or projected.

Philosophers distinguish *external* teleology (the purpose for which an object is made) from *internal* teleology – the purpose which an object has for itself. When 'borderline' we're externally teleologically driven, meaning and purpose seem only to come from without. When 'narcissistic' we're internally teleologically driven, meaning and purpose seem only to come from within. To clarify the idea of *loci of control*, recall in discussing *The Tempest*, (Chapter 2) that we saw how the shipwrecked lad Ferdinand (Puer) could be understood as the object of Prospero (Senex, as a wise old magician), his external locus of control. First Ferdinand has a sacrificial, initiatory, borderline experience as Caliban's hard-used slave then, a narcissistically rewarding experience as lover of the beautiful Miranda.

Purpose, for a person (or object) depends on locus of control and fitness to function, determined by the cybernetics of the eco-system they inhabit. Purpose, for our species, is determined by fitness to function *vis à vis* our planet – by ecology. This is why I chose a young conservationist and an older conservative as clinical examples. Suffering, personal and political, arises from boundary disturbances: cybernetic and ecological failure. Inability to negotiate for meaning means we can't tell Self from other; we tend to psychic fusion, or its opposite – fragmentation. If we can't tell timeless Self from time-bound ego we tend to inflation (grandiosity) or its opposite – implosion (like former Yugoslavia).

I'll amplify this using Hermann Hesse's story, 'Inside and Outside' (1974: 258–71). Two friends fall out over the meaning of a little green idol. The first, an idealist, believes the idol is magic. The other, an empiricist, says 'There's no such thing!' Their friendship is ended. But the image of the idol becomes a strange attractor in the empiricist's psyche; his thoughts keep returning to it. After many years he revisits his old friend. The idol breaks. He realises its existence continues – it's become a symbol, a magical internal object with a multiplicity of meanings. A Kleinian analyst might say this is about the ability to sustain ambivalence (two opposite meanings at the same time); a Jungian analyst might say it represents the operation of the transcendent function, to hold and contain opposites, allowing archetypes to install with a multiplicity of meanings.

## Working with primary meaning disorder

Medicine thinks of illness in terms of aetiology, diagnosis, prognosis and 'cure' – treatment or management. Acute conditions (like trauma or a heart attack) need vigorous treatment. Chronic conditions (like most psychiatric illnesses and meaning disorders) require persevering management, aimed at alleviating suffering, both personal and social. Which raises a question: is the diagnosis 'meaning disorder' decided by society or by the individual? If we decide someone is 'borderline' (as Storm's family did), or 'narcissistic' (as Geoff's women did) who has to agree?

Treatment outcome in meaning disorder depends, as for any medical condition, on substance (the illness), set (who has it) and setting (where, in which culture). Storm would see Geoff's values as 'meaning-disordered' and vice versa. Meaning disorders impair individuation because if the relation between Self and ego is disturbed, then so is the relation Self to other.

I suggest we need to approach the treatment of meaning disorder from the social and cultural perspective as much as from the individual and interpersonal. We need to consider its epidemiology.

In the famous nineteenth-century case of Dr. John Snow and the handle of the Broad Street pump, the good Doctor traced the epidemiology of a cholera epidemic to one specific water-pump in central London. On removing its handle, the epidemic stopped. The treatment for primary meaning disorder begins with the removal of the pump handle: an internal mechanism which creates negative meanings (Bion's concept of 'minus K' – anti-knowledge, 1962: 47–9) and an external mechanism – a social setting in which physical and emotional trauma can't be acknowledged.

> In psychoanalysis, one does encounter individuals who have been so traumatised that they cannot take in anything from others that they have not already thought of themselves. If in order to preserve the coherence of the self one must exclude other versions of reality, ones ability to learn from others will be impaired.
>
> (Modell 1993: 179)

Social 'treatment' involves recognising social meaning-gradients: again, an argument about locus of control. In *One Hundred and Twenty Days of Sodom* (1989), written whilst imprisoned in the Bastille for revolutionary activity, the Marquis de Sade distills his political philosophy – primary meaning disorder initiates in the organs of the State, with those who take meaning-as-order, and perpetuate closed, static social systems. His astute social commentary advocates anarchy (Greek, 'no-law'), a harmonious condition in society which makes government unnecessary, rather than social chaos (de Beauvoir, 1989: 3–64). Gaoled, he continued to criticise the Revolutionary leadership. When they won, they refused to free him.

In de Sade's polemical novel his four protagonists – the Church (Bishop of X), the Merchant class (Ducret), the Law (President de Curval) and the plutocratic Aristocrat (the Duc de Blangis) secure a remote chateau, four old whores and a bunch of children for a nightmarish orgy. The children are sexually abused, tortured and die. The Chateau of de Sade's imagination resembles an isolated ego. When ego thinks it is Self it creates a 'lie barrier', instead of a semi-permeable membrane between its functions and the Self. If this barrier exists, then as de Sade (himself savagely abused as a child) showed, power takes the place of love, creating a sado-masochistic pattern of relationships, giving pseudo-individuation. Reality is excluded: a masochistic, auto-devaluing child-like ego is tortured by an omnipotent Self. There is no 'as-if' – messages can't get across unless acted out. Opposites war and combine, in unstable alliances of meaning.

An example of a cultural meaning-conflict along Sadean lines is given by the Rainbow coalition ('green grannies', eco-warriors, bikers, the old, the black, the dispossessed and the native American indigenous poor) who protested together at the World Trade Organisation's recent meeting in Seattle. As with the peace protestors in Miami and Chicago (Mailer 1968) the response of the plutocracy was to unleash the police. How do we read these acts? Who had primary meaning disorder – those in favour of the capitalist (ego) economy, or those on the streets favouring the gift (Self) economy?

I develop the notion of meaning-based economics in Chapter 11. It turns on the valuation of symbols rather than currency. In our personal micro-economy, symbols are units of 'emotional currency'. The value of symbolisation or enactment depends, like currency, on what it purchases. For example, when admitting 'Jesus' (found wandering naked on a London common one freezing winter night) to hospital, I wondered if his act symbolised anything. How should I weigh his meaning-system (a 'Messiah complex') against social criteria? What would his act purchase?

The English Mental Health Act (1981) allows people to be taken to, and detained in, a safe place if their behaviour is likely to endanger themselves or others. The legal signifier is Self. Was 'Jesus' a risk to himself, or others? Frances Tustin (1981: 123–34) suggests the asymbolic nature of autistic states is part of their function as a protective shell. If the shell is too tight, the Self never emerges: if it is too weak the Self emerges prematurely, like a limp butterfly from its (maternal) cocoon. 'Jesus', a Self in psychotic process (Perry 1953), enacted his need to emerge by wandering naked. Is it dangerous for 'Jesus' to do this in mid-winter? Probably. Is it dangerous to have a primary meaning disorder?

Damage to meaning-making in childhood as a result of trauma (abuse or neglect, social deprivation or exclusion) is associated with lasting neurological changes, particularly in the amygdala and hypo-thalamus, parts of the brain responsible for fear. Overstimulation damages the hardware: like playing a vinyl record till the groove wears out, there is no signal, only noise. As mentioned in the last chapter, such changes appear on brain scans (Siegel 1999: 42–53).

Such people are prone to depressive illness in adulthood as well as developing both 'borderline' and 'narcissistic' personality states or traits. Gathering evidence shows not only that these problems respond to pharmacology, but also to behavioural interventions. The experiment of doing a functional scan of the brain before and after analysis has not yet been done, perhaps because there is not yet enough shared meaning between analysts and neuroscientists. It will be interesting to see whether it can be shown that not only do com-plexes produce psycho-physiological changes, but whether analysis can create visible changes in neural functioning. Theoretically, we can suppose alternative neural nets are formed as a result of develop-ing alternative meaning-making strategies – as happens when learning a new language.

Cognitively, being unable to engage or disengage the 'fear circuit' predisposes us to believe our percepts (and our Self) have no value – whatever meaning we make has no value either. This accompanies profound loss of hope, social isolation, and difficulty in symbolising. Splitting, denial and projective identification are defences of a Self whose meaning can't be heard (Gordon 1978: 105–20). There are repetition compulsions, tendencies to broken patterns of object relat-ing and failures of archetypal installation. We repeat, hoping for a different outcome with a different (m)other, then punish the (m)other for its failure to create the magically-hoped-for repair.

Mervyn Glasser (1986) and Steven Joseph (1997) suggest this reflects a failure of early mirroring. If the inner world is mirrored back so that an infant's luminous presence (ability to create a twinkle in mother's eye) creates a hollow empty place inside, we're in danger of implosion. With no sense of body, primary objects can't be internalised: there is no 'outside', there can't be an 'inside'. Each meeting is a new, uncertain, start. We're born-again in every moment, or, dying in every moment, experiencing the luminous presence of others as a threat.

The strange effect at a boundary in primary meaning disorder is either a very rigid and limited construction of meaning (funda-mentalism), or an extremely loose construing (anarchy). Many meaning-based approaches to treatment use positive connotation and paradoxical injunction to change the purpose of a behaviour (teleological tricks). If we say 'whatever happens is in the service of the Self', then it can be positively connoted (valued): *provided that* the connotation is true, and has a negotiable name; provided it can be played with symbolically.

Positive connotation can address projective identification as an attempt to take away the analyst's capacity to think, contain, or make a space in which meaning can develop. For instance, I said to Geoff: 'Isn't it useful how you create emptiness inside me by rub-bishing everything I suggest about you being depressed, as this way you can really know I know how bad you feel . . . ?' Or, to Storm: 'Hmm . . . it's really good you use so much cannabis, otherwise you might be overwhelmed by feelings you can't handle . . .'

Self operates by paradox: the worse the inner emptiness, the more Self is experienced in projection. Patient and analyst work through a shared fantasy – 'the inside is empty' – accepting instead it's full of chaos. This is created and mirrored within and without the analytic hour. Initially, the consequence is more chaos, more meaning dis-order. It is a kindness to explain an analytic honeymoon rarely lasts more than three months. Everyone gets worse before they get better.

Clear boundaries help both people in an analysis distinguish between real and unreal. Paradox increases freedom of choice, creat-ing win–win situations, which build trust and reconnect ego to Self. For example, by telling Storm his 'self-medication' with cannabis was the best thing he could think of at age ten to deal with his problem (positive connotation) and that he must on no account change his drug use (paradoxical injunction), first, his level of guilt and masochistic self-attack by spending all his money on drugs became clear to him, then, to make me (a bad father) wrong, he cut down and stopped using. He later said if I'd told him to stop he would simply have used more heavily: as I 'forbade him', he had to stop.

Paradoxical injunction works by returning responsibility for meaning-making to the patient. Another paradox: insisting on seeing Storm on time (which, at first, he took as a signifier of my bourgeois contempt for his free spirit), he began to see his time was valuable too (mirroring). He could then accept his first paid job. We can also positively connote the problem 'ego experiences Self as loss'. By pointing out to Geoff what a good idea of his ego it was to try to sleepwalk him off the tenth floor, Geoff could see what happened as a 'wake up call'. His Self did over-ride his destructive ego-impulse.

When Self is strongly projected on to the analyst, there is envy of the analyst if they're right, rage if they're wrong: it's a lose–lose situation. With Storm and Geoff: 'It's really useful you can make everything I say wrong, so I know how you felt when you failed to get your father's attention . . .' We change when we can recognise and accept that redundant survival mechanisms are explaining devices (heuristics), rather than truths about the universe.

For example, working through Geoff's overwhelming fear of abandonment (deintegrative decompensation before holiday breaks) was followed by reintegration (I'd survived his murderous rage). Severe bonding difficulties, inconsistently inconsistent attachments and infantile paranoid anxieties not allayed by mother, preserved in him a necessary illusion of omnipotence, and allowed in the transference and counter-transference a projection of his Self on to me, letting Self unfold into ego.

If a subject hides inside an object by projective-identification, meaning and purpose are located in the other. In countertransference, we feel our Self is held by the patient, we lose 'as if'. Primary meaning disorder is a defence against individuation, an avoidance of shadow. It is a state in which everything (inside and outside) has one meaning – 'they're out to get me': paranoia, being beside the Self. If Self is trying to manifest without a space to get into, we do everything we can to get inside the other and be 're-memoried'. An old joke says analysts put the *fun* back into dys-*fun*-ctional. Dysfunction in finding purpose may become bearable as meaning shifts. There may be a 'healing' of 'the wounded inner child'; but many 'wounded inner children' (including my own), if told we need 'healing' take this as a threat to Self, and (like Storm and Geoff) refuse to co–operate.

Paradoxically, abused and neglected children, if not living under threat, lack purpose. Purpose became a closed system and meant one thing – survival. For example, when working with a child of

Holocaust survivors (Jacques, in Chapter 8), he and his family knew how to survive – but not how to live. Jacques' shame at fathering a child linked to his families' survival guilt. He'd internalised the Nazi myth 'all Jews must die', so, to father another Jew was a social crime. We reached a point at which he felt he had to reconnect with his culture, and began seeing a Rabbi – discovering the Jewish community as a living social reality, rather than a smoky cloud over Auschwitz.

Trust, the basis of an analytic alliance, arises from shared naming – not blaming. For Storm, Geoff and Jacques, once trust in the naming-process was established, changes in internal object relations *could* occur: renarration of their personal history inevitably occurs, which allowed reconnection to living culture (Storm went protesting again, Geoff began entertaining children). This is like learning to see in colour instead of black and white.

# 6

# DREAMS AND MEANING

'What did he call it?' she whispered.
'An alethiometer.'
There was no point in asking what that meant. It lay heavily
in her hands, the crystal face gleaming, the brass body
exquisitely machined. It was very like a clock, or a compass,
for there were hands pointing to places around the dial, but
instead of the hours or the points of the compass there were
several little pictures, each of them painted with extraordinary precision, as if on ivory with the finest and slenderest
sable brush. She turned the dial around to look at them all.
There was an anchor; an hourglass surmounted by a skull; a
bull, a beehive ... thirty six altogether, and she couldn't
even guess what they meant.

(Philip Pullman, *Northern Lights*, 1998: 79)

Now, Kitty, let's consider who it was that dreamed it all.
This is a serious question, my dear, and you should not go
on licking your paw like that – as if Dinah hadn't washed
you this morning! You see, Kitty, it must have been either me
or the Red King. He was part of my dream, of course – but
then I was part of his dream, too!

(Lewis Carroll, *Alice Through the Looking Glass*, 1965: 343–4)

## What is an alethiometer?

Dreams are 'a spontaneous self-portrayal, in symbolic form, of the
actual situation in the unconscious' (*CW* 8: para. 505). Liminal,
*between* phenomena occurring on the threshold of consciousness
(like 'Freudian slips', memory lapses and synchronistic events)
dreams talk in symbols: meaning-rich fluent forms. Like a waterfall
or a candle's flame, the parts change but the whole remains forever
itself. From Jung's concept, 'Self is multiplicity', symbols, as communications from Self, have multiplicities of meaning. They always
contain an *unknowable X*, and hint at a future perspective.

Analysis takes as long as it does because it is about learning to

116

translate between the languages of symbol, image and reality; realising, as Lacan said, these constitute three overlapping perceptual modes, three languages. We need to approach dreams with a child-like spirit, being-in-the-moment; ready, as when listening to a fairy-story, to wonder 'what happens next?' as our dream-ego lives out the narrative. I'll examine here the meaning and purpose of the language 'dream', rather than its grammar, syntax and vocabulary, to which there are excellent guides (Stevens 1995; Whitmont and Pereira, 1989). To put the semiotics of dreams in context, I'll briefly describe their physiology and psychiatry. My clinical examples show the utility of separating form from content, structure from function, to emphasise how symbolic messages move into the time-stream of waking 'reality'.

Jung emphasises dreams are not the unconscious, which cannot be made conscious, no matter how much we interpret dream-poetry. The psychic structure, 'dream', is separable from its meaning. The structure has a time-orientating function, connecting daily events to past and future purposes. Neuro-biological ideas from the Theory of Neuronal Group Selection (TNGS) suggest dream structures are psychological imaging mechanisms produced by competing neural networks. What we recall on waking depends on a neuronal 'survival of the fittest'.

Dreams are natural phantasies, spontaneous re-edits of Self's documentary film of our lives; a normal integrative process. Meaning-making enhances survival, as we are, above all, meaning-making mammals, living in a complex eco-system of social networks. The functions of Self (agency, coherence, continuity and affective relating) depend on being continually able to retune meaning-making to link with new meaning-patterns in these ever-changing relational networks. Dreams have that function, as seen by the way they change an analysis: the form of the whole session in which a dream is brought says as much about the dream as its 'manifest' content.

As Michael Fordham emphasised, all events around a dream reflect the dynamics between the dreamer-who-dreams-the-dream and the dreamer-who-tells-the-dream (1978: 21–35). Dream symbols orientate us to shifts in meaning. So, is a dream an alethiometer? In Philip Pullman's Carnegie Medal winning book, Lyra, a thirteen-year-old runaway tomboy meets a wise old man, Farder Coram:

> He called it an alethiometer. 'What's that mean?' said John
> Faa, turning to his companion.

'That's a Greek word. I reckon it's from Alethea, which means truth. It's a truth measure. And have you worked out how to use it?' he said to her. . . . 'All those pictures around the rim,' said Coram, holding it delicately toward John Faa's blunt strong gaze, 'they're symbols, and each one stands for a whole series of things. Take the anchor, there. The first meaning of that is hope, because hope holds you fast like an anchor so you don't give way. The second meaning is steadfastness. The third meaning is snag, or prevention. The fourth meaning is the sea. And so on, down to ten, twelve, maybe a never-ending series of meanings.'

(Pullman 1998: 126–7)

An alethiometer, like a dream, is a truth measure, a symbol-compass. It is concerned with signification: the way signs (objects) change meaning depending on the mood and depth of Self, and which archetype is seeking humanisation. An opposite to projective-identification, dream images are introjective-identification – projection on to waking-ego by dreaming-Self (in symbols) to change our personae.

In *Northern Lights*, Philip Pullman conjures up a parallel-world. Each human is accompanied by their daemon: a being which reflects its human's persona by its physical form. Like personae, daemons shape-change in childhood and adolescence, settling to their preferred form by adulthood. (Pan, Lyra's daemon is by turns a moth, a leopard and an eagle.) Daemons are like dream-ego: ego as Self wishes us to see it (Whitmont and Pereira 1989: 17–25). Dream-ego protects and guards Self as it prepares personae for change. Later, we'll see how my patient Yukio's dreams helped him change his congenitally damaged face with plastic surgery. Inner confirmation that his ego was strong enough to face having a new face (and persona) came in a dream in which, in a Polynesian *rite de passage*, a new face was tattooed over his old one.

## Symbolic ambiguity

What dreaming tells us about meaning is not the same as what a dream means. Meaning can be given to dream images in many ways in the special setting of analysis. However, dream images don't differ from any other symbolising system, whether film, myth or fairy-story. Dream images are culturally dependent – dogs dream of bones, fishermen of fish. As prototypical creative acts, critical, interpretative aesthetics applied to any narrative (poetry, music, drama, dance or cinema) apply to dreams. 'Aptness' of interpretation is an aesthetic, rather than a moral or scientific judgement. Dreams grip nations and shape cultures. The 'American Dream' of plenty and wish-fulfilment has its shadow: slavery, dispossessing native Americans, stealing their hopes. Dreams can be terrifying dragons, like the Japanese nationalistic dream of honour leading to horrific humiliation at Hiroshima. In Ursula Le Guin's *Wizard of Earthsea* (1968: 89–107) dragons speak the language of 'making', the words which brought the world out of chaos. Dragons never lie – but nor do they tell the truth. Their speech is true/false, its logical operator {neither-nor-both-and}. The use of pluralistic narrative reflects a dragon's magical being: discursive, self-reflexive – a cunning, punning, symbolic language.

If dreaming is 'dragon talk' providing words for complexes, then if we can interpret it, we do not have to run from dragons by playing hero-prince or little lost princess in an archetypal version of the 'persecutor-rescuer-victim' co-dependency game – 'Alcoholic' is a classic example (Berne 1964: 64). Trapped in someone else's living nightmare, the children of alcoholics both over-attend to and deny reality (like Huck Finn, Chapter 9). Attending to compensating messages from internal reality is very hard for an abused child. They may need refuge in fantasy worlds, dreams or drugs. If a parent is an alcoholic, at least we know something is the matter. Yet we often have 'forgotten' how we lost our ability to define meaning our way.

Alice, back from the looking glass world, engages with this – *who is the dreamer? who is the dreamed?* – a theme explored in a contemporary movie, *The Matrix* (Wachowsky and Wachowsky 1999). In it, Keanu Reeves plays Neo, 'The One' – a cyberpunk pirate hacker by night and a corporate computer programmer by day who suddenly discovers everything he thinks is real, isn't. He's been living in 'virtual reality' controlled by ruthless machines which feed on human energy. But as reality is a machine construct, Neo can change 'reality' to be any way he wants . . . 'Dodge bullets? There! Move from one reality to another without doing any more than pick up the phone? At once!'

The film is like a cartoon, Zen as an Arcade Game, a shoot 'em up for the psyche. The logical operator {neither-nor-both-and} is crucial to the film and Zen dialogue. We construct our reality, we're neither Self nor Not-Self, both Self and Not-Self (Abe, 1992: 128–42) Dreams, like Koans, shift reality. To shift 'reality' fluently is an aim of analysis. As in Zen, it isn't 'solving the koan' that takes time (it solves in an instant), it's waiting for the instant and then translating into action words from a language in which every single word is ambiguous – harder than translating between English and Japanese. The ambiguity of a dream's symbols, like a Japanese symbol, mirrors their function. In *form*, they trans*form*: and, form defines function. I'll illustrate what I mean with one of my dreams.

### The Gate dream: intramural language and creativity

The Albigensian Crusades, late thirteenth century: I'm thirteen, a scruffy blonde kid with a lute, hesitating at dawn on a hot, dusty summer's day at the gates of the walled City of Carcassonne. Standing in the shadow, looking at the huge Gate, I wonder how to enter with a secret message for other Cathars in the City, held by the French invaders. I'm scared. If the Guards catch me it's certain death. No way in except the Gate. To my surprise, the red uniformed guard on the Outer Gate whispers to me in Oc, my language! 'The men in blue on the Inner Gate are French.' Occitaines usually don't speak French (and vice versa). Between Outer Gate and Inner Gate go messengers in red (Oc), white (Latin) and blue (French). They speak French and Oc at the Gates, but Latin to each other – translating between Inside and Outside.

Carcassonne has Oc outside and French inside: mutually incomprehensible. Latin, spoken between the walls, intramural language, translates both. Oc (Jungian), French (object relations theory) and Latin (psychiatry) can all translate meaning in dreams. My dream came when my (French-speaking) analyst felt invasive. I didn't want to hear her 'analytic language'. An adolescent sub-personality resisted her 'French Crusade', and (I guess) wished, stealthily, to 'invade her' (Oedipus being a thief, as well as loving his mother).

I free associate: thirteen? I'm a blonde scruff at Rugby School, exploring my emerging sexuality. Carcassonne's gate resembled the Main gate to the Old Quad, where I learnt French and Latin. My classmates spoke 'public school slang', not my Scots-Irish accent (like Oc, a rustic dialect). I connect: *then* I was joining an academic setting, making friends; *now* I'm leaving one (at the time I was leaving academia). With my analyst, I felt like a stroppy, scared teenager, afraid to arrive or leave. I couldn't ignore my dream-ego –

or her interpreting my dream as from Self about how Self communicates.

She pointed out that dream language is intramural, between ego and Self, and its symbols are (like adolescence) meaning-filled transitions. My difficulties in the analysis (whether internal or external, past or present, real or imagined), appeared as a hesitant kid from the backwoods of Self coming to the small, closed inward-looking walled-city of my over-defended ego. The message pointed to belonging with gnostics, 'Cathars' (the Jungian community), rather than the walled city of academia.

The message was not the lyrics of the troubadour boy, the *content* of his song, but his *form*. The meaning *is* the messenger. I asked myself 'what did I want then, when I was thirteen? What do I want now, what am I here for anyway?' A symbol is a re-entrant signal: in information technology, a 're-entrant signal' is an extremely fast feedback loop, as exists between a dream-percept and the dreamer's perceptual apparatus. Dream associations are symbols acting as 're-entrant signals'. My dream-ego, the scruff, symbolised links between present and past to suggest a future. As with real percepts, dream percepts are concept driven: we conceptualise faster during sleep, as vigilance is taken care of subliminally and attention is free for psychological work.

If the brain were a computer, dreams are like 'timed-backup', file checking and sorting, whilst not using processor power on vigilance. When doing their own diagnostics, computers compare what's in active memory with templates . . . what's supposed to be there, the computer's 'concepts' about itself. Kant said, 'Percepts without concepts are blind.' This is experimentally validated by research on those born blind who gain 'sight' – like American polymath Buckminster Fuller, inventor of the geodesic Dome.

Born extremely myopic, Fuller couldn't 'see' more than a blur till he was four and a half: ' . . . It gave me two kinds of ways of looking at things and therefore two different ways of thinking about my experience: in the hazy coloured way and in the detailed way' (Fuller 1983: 12). The contrast produced, for him, a strong sense of the relationship between intuition and aesthetics. Balancing these two perceptual modes is vital for work with dreams. Analysts can get 'lost in the detail': like film buffs watching Orson Welles' classic *Citizen Kane* (1931) for the lighting effects who miss the message – Charlie Kane inherited a gold mine and was sent away by his mother. A millionaire press-baron's lifetime later reporters want to know who 'Rosebud' is. Did he name a mystery lover in his last breath? We find out in the last scene, when, clearing the wreckage from Xanadu, his grandiose dream-home, his child's sledge (Rosebud) is thrown on to the fire.

Was Rosebud a transitional object, a signifier of mother when mother was 'good enough', the last thing he had to remember the good times of childhood? Giving him the locus of control of his life prematurely, she gifts him a life of empty narcissism. Dreaming, an intuitive process, functions to fill such emptiness. Dream-symbols are transitional objects, and transitional objects become dream images. In my dream, I re-became my thirteen year old self, and my guitar (a transitional object) became a lute. I wonder what that self is telling me. I also wonder how he might play. I try new licks on my guitar – letting psychic energy flow *both* ways through the dream gate is the origin of creativity.

> Ordered, disciplined thought is a skill governed by set rules of the game, some of which are explicitly stated, others implied and hidden in the code. The creative act, insofar as it depends on unconscious resources, presupposes a relaxing of the controls and a regression to modes of ideation which are indifferent to the rules of verbal logic, unperturbed by contradiction, untouched by the dogmas and taboos of so-called common sense. At the decisive stage of discovery the codes of disciplined reasoning are suspended – as they are in the dream, the reverie, the manic flight of thought, when the stream of ideation is free to drift, by its own emotional gravity, as it were, in an apparently 'lawless' fashion.
>
> (Koestler 1969: 178–213)

Dreams occurring between the threshold of conscious and unconscious open doors. They actively select symbols we need to attend to, matching them to one another through neural maps as carefully as a film director and his cutting editor match different 'takes'. Meaning is continuously updated in the process.

## The psycho-biology of dreams

Dreaming (D-sleep) occurs when brain waves return to low voltage; de-synchronised activity from periods of deep, high voltage syn-chronised brain activity (S-sleep). In S-sleep hormones for growth and body-repair are released. D-sleep begins about 70 minutes into sleep, a cyclical event occurring roughly every 90 minutes, closer nearer waking. In D-sleep the autonomic nervous system is activated, rapid eye movements occur (hence its name, REM sleep) with loss of reflexes and muscle twitching (if you've a cat, you'll see its whiskers twitch as it dreams), often with penile or vaginal engorgement, occasionally orgasm.

Neuro-physiologists speculate that millions of inter-hemispheric information exchanges take place between the linear clock-time abstract thinking (analytical) left-brain and the non-linear eternally present, holistic (magical) right-brain during dreams (Lambert 1981: 171–2). Adults have four or five D-sleeps a night, lasting a total of about 90 minutes; a quarter of sleep. Young people sleep longer and dream proportionally more than older ones. *In utero*, we dream nearly 50 per cent of our time, like other mammals (Dawes *et al*. 1972; Jones 1978). The role of dream-sleep in pre-natal life is to develop the central nervous system (Roffwarg *et al*. 1966). Foetal dreaming is 'installing the software', and adult dreaming is 'maintaining the programme'.

Starting from the premise 'memory is reconstructive imagination' (a phrase used by the psychoanalyst Charles Rycroft, 1981: 38–70), when we're 'awake' in dreams as dream-ego, every aspect of the landscape speaks for us. Anthony Stevens (1995: 180–91) links this to pioneering work by Frederick Bartlett, of 'twenties Cambridge and Gerald Edelman from Harvard in the 'eighties. Bartlett said we create mental schema in dreams. Edelman suggests these schema exist as neuronal nets. 'Neural Darwinism' (TNGS) suggests these nets develop by natural selection. Neural-nets fittest to enhance survival develop more rapidly and are better maintained than those which don't: the latter are complexes – stuck information. It's like growing more phone lines into your Website depending on how successful it is – more hits, more lines. Or, like the interlocking tree roots in a vast forest, inseparably meshing together with symbiotic fungi as they meander under the forest floor.

As a forest is one huge organism (an ecosystem) so are neural nets, the hardware which creates and re-creates symbols. Neural nets map archetypal patterns: brain areas related to sex (for example) clearly must map areas related to touch, sound, sight and smell as well as to sex. And like sexual arousal, the topography that 'turns on' any neural net differs from person to person. Continuous interaction between the nets occurs by re-entrant signalling as very fast neurons link together in multiple feedback loops (Edelman 1989): an organic information superhighway. In dreams this neural activity is de-synchronised, producing characteristic EEG changes.

TNGS says D-sleep is a time for integrating and problem solving activity. The neural nets are mended, especially those concerned with attention, recall, secondary process thinking and self-guidance. Ego-function reorganises in this play with the somatic Self. Post-Jungians assume we are innately interested in Self (in object relations language, we Self-cathect). Essentially, the psychological function of dreams is to do this, to reality test, to orient us in time, connecting today's events to past and future, giving space for the unconscious to suggest new adaptive strategies. For most of us, most of the time, this happens without waking consciousness being more than minimally aware. Dreams do not normally require interpretation.

If we're 'on course' we don't need to check our alethiometer all the time. We don't need to use secondary process ego-consciousness continuously. Primary process (Self) consciousness is the set of fast feedback loops combining together sense-experiences at a threshold which attaches feeling values to them. Neuro-anatomically, this happens in the limbic system (Chapter 4). Unlike waking consciousness, dreams have no sense of 'time', they are 'here and now', with free-floating attention (like the meditative 'awareness' in an analytic attitude). In Vipassana meditation we're conscious of the meditation object (say, the breath), of sensations, mental images and affects which arise, and we note them: we do not have to interpret them (Mahasi Sayadaw 1971).

Dream images form an 'internal present-time' as a dream is in progress. They may incorporate environmental stimuli (external sounds). Day-residues assimilate, dreams connect what had value and meaning before to what has value and meaning now. D-sleep protects S-sleep, in which somatic repair and physical growth take place. Psychological growth takes place in D-Sleep. TNGS says survival depends on recognising, categorising and integrating such new information (Edelman 1989).

Dreams use parallel process, like viewing several TV channels at once. This loosens up meanings fixed to one construct and lets it transfer to others. Everything becomes incredibly meaningful, which means everything has the same nominative power. No part of a dream is of more significance than another. Dreams ought to be unmemorable – most are. However, symbols, sometimes whole dreams, become significant if they transfer to consciousness but images which survive don't do so by acts of will – *lucid dreaming* is a rare gift. Ordinarily, the affective fabric of the dream gives the dream-ego the illusion of 'locus of control'. If we lose that, then dreams become nightmares.

The verbal and visual puns of dream-language, displacement, concretisation, condensation, hidden analogy, impersonations and double identities, reversal of causation – every trick of any sci-fi movie – are deconstructions of daytime reality. We can have any meaning disorder in dreams. Neuro-psychologically, then, it's not as Freud said, 'dreams are guardians of sleep', rather, S-sleep is the guardian of dreams and dreams are the unconscious guarding of waking consciousness. Dream-ego guards day-ego by maintaining reality testing.

The purpose of dreaming – reality testing – is fulfilled by playing serial and parallel time-narratives against each other. Remember outside 'Oc', inside 'French' and intramural 'Latin'. This biologically essential restoration and integration of psychological creative processes is disordered in mental illness and by acute stress: a clinical sign, a physical warning of the dangers of ignoring the unconscious, of ego being cut off from Self (Storm and Geoff in the previous chapter were hardly aware of dreaming before analysis).

## Dreams and mental disorder

A psychiatrist's routine mental state examination includes questions about the form of dreaming, rather than the content: 'how many dreams', 'what did they feel like', rather than 'what did you dream?' Dream and sleep patterns reflect underlying meaning disorders. Symbol-formation is a dialectic between ego and Self; if either is threatened, dreams may spill over into consciousness. In severe depression there is circular thinking (ruminations on object loss, real or imagined) and disturbed temporal perspective (concentrating on past events and an inability to future). This is reflected in dreams: in mine, the boy from Oc couldn't see a way ahead, just as (at that time) I was lying awake at night trying to do so.

If sleep is disturbed, the ego–Self axis is stressed. Sleep-deprivation rapidly creates psychotic states (failure of reality testing) in days, quicker in children, even quicker in the newborn. This is why sleep deprivation makes children 'get beside themselves' and why it is used in 'brain washing'. Laboratory research suggests the characteristic depressive symptom of early morning wakening is linked to failure to process dreams. Normally, bursts of D-sleep are followed by brief spells of alertness, in which the conscious attends to the dream before drifting back to S-sleep. In depression, the dream (REM) happens, we 'wake' to attend to it, but can't recall its images, then wake fully, lying in the dark searching for a vanished meaning –

a psychic experience of loss 'here and now' that mirrors the losses (exit life events) precipitating depression (Brown and Harris 1978; Paykel *et al.* 1969)

In schizophrenia (and psychotic states), floods of dream-images invade consciousness, reflected in the old name for that illness, *oneirophrenia* – dream minded. People with such severe boundary problems between ego and Self/Self and other, do dream but can't tell 'asleep' from 'awake'. If nightmares interchange with waking, it feels the same as if the nightmare is real. There's no *as if*. This explains their state of fear, worst in the over-arousal of catatonia which is like 'dream paralysis' occurring whilst awake. As Wilfred Bion observed:

> I had noticed that much work was needed before a psychotic patient reported a dream at all, and that when he did so he seemed to feel that he had said all that was necessary in reporting the fact that he had dreamt . . . I was not clear why the patient called his experience a dream, and in what way he distinguished it from other experiences which, though variously described by him to me, seemed to be hallucinations.
>
> (1993: 77–8)

Similar difficulties occur when consciousness is clouded by drugs, fever or delirium. For example, an LSD 'trip' need not be interrupted by falling asleep. If trips last more than 24 hours, 'dream time' and 'real time' become interchangeable. Cannabis slows perception of time, in high doses it has a similar effect. Though it appears to enhance concentration, in fact the effect is like watching a film with frames missing – we over-attend to the remaining signal to get any information at all. The signal-to-noise ratio changes, the sound (or any other percept) goes fuzzy.

Psychomimetics (drugs mimicking psychosis, like LSD, mescaline and peyote), unlike alcohol, do not suppress D-sleep. Increased alcohol consumption is associated with depression: there's no dreaming, no connection of present events to past experience. Fever often produces 'fire dreams' – one of the few instances when dream images relate directly to somatic states. I'd such dreams regularly as a child, processing experiences of high fever, in which boundaries of consciousness were blurred (delirium). I could say 'I was recalling a past life experience of being burnt at the stake' or, 'the flames represent uncathected oedipal libidinal energy' or they 'symbolise heat under the alchemical container of the developing psyche'.

This is the problem with dream-language; it's both all-but-impossible and far too easy to translate. Any of those interpretative myths could be true. But, as a patient who spoke Japanese fluently explained (Jacques, Chapter 8) when amplifying his dream 'the cat in the bottle' with me, Japanese characters don't translate into simple English; they're polyphonic, having multiple meanings. In neurotic dreaming translation of images gets stuck, signs remain signs. For example, patients with obsessions and addictions dream about their particular locus of loss of control (like Dekk and Ben, Chapter 2), and as shown in the following account by Jung of his clinical work. In 1906 he used the word-association test to treat a girl with hysterical convulsions (discussed in Chapter 4, and cited in $CW$ 2: 793–862). Her associations pointed to a complex around emerging sexuality and her relationship to mother. She could neither talk nor associate to this, so Jung asked her about her dreams:

> Nature has an apparatus that makes an extract of the complexes and brings them to consciousness in an unrecognisable and therefore harmless form: this is the dream.

She had repetitive dreams of blood and fire. Jung linked them to a popular song of the time, 'No fire, no coal can burn as hot . . . (as love)'; though his argument convinced him she wished for an incestuous relationship with her brother, it did not convince her. Simplistically, in depression the problem is too little dreaming; in schizophrenia, too much and/or at the wrong time; in neuroses, not enough variety or 'the wrong sort of dreams'. In all instances, there are failures in automatic translation of internal language. Dream interpretation helps the psyche perform the dream's task 'manually', and is dependent on . . .

## Theories of dream meaning

Freudian and Jungian views of signification differ. A semiotic approach treats dreams as natural, spontaneous symbolisations. Freud said that in sleep there is less inhibition of primitive (id) impulses, controlled by primary process (magical) thinking. Dreams keep these impulses from causing waking by expressing them as images. Unconscious material projects on to a dream screen between conscious and unconscious, like the objects in Plato's Cave metaphor (Chapters 9 and 10). Jung and post-Jungians do not have the concept 'id': they see dream-images as Self-projection.

Freud distinguished between the latent content of a dream, the underlying drive (sexual wishes) and its manifest content, the actual images. I'll invent a dream to illustrate: 'a flame under a waterfall'. Flame and waterfall are signs (manifest content); sexual intercourse could be the latent content, the thing symbolised. How I interpret the image depends on which part I identify with, and what kind of a whole I make of the parts. The psychoanalyst James Grotstein (1979) (analysand of Wilfred Bion) distinguishes between the dreamer-who-dreams-the-dream and the dreamer-who-understands-the-dream.

To answer Alice's question, 'who dreamed the dream?' first, part of the psyche projects primary process (magical thinking), creating a dream image; second, another part of the psyche (the abstractly thinking conscious mind) finds the meaning. Grotstein supports Jung's view; dreams are communications from Self. As Self is multiplicity (crowds are often images for Self), the multiplicity of a dream-image's meanings reflects the nature of the artist creating them: a Multiplicity. Fellow psychoanalyst Thomas Ogden (1990: 234–8) describes dream images as products of the unconscious which transform in a 'dream space'. He believes dreams result from the play of imagination during sleep on internal objects. They are

> an internal communication involving a primary process construction generated by one aspect of the self that must be perceived, understood and experienced by another part of the self.

The parallels to Jung's formulation – 'a spontaneous self-portrayal' – are clear (*CW* 8 : para. 505).

Jung saw dreams as more than repressed sexuality (*CW* 8: paras 443 ff.); as products of Self, they directly access consciousness. Self writes the script, directs, is all actors, all locations and, when we wake, ego is critic, press and public. Jung took dream-narrative as an honest account:

> What Freud calls the 'dream facade' is the dream's obscurity, and this is really only a projection of our own lack of understanding. We say that the dream has false front only because we fail to see into it. We would do better to say that we are dealing with something like a text that is unintelligible not because it has a facade – a text has no facade – but simply because we cannot read it. We do

not have to get behind such a text, but must first learn to read it.

(CW 16: para. 319)

Jung emphasised no dreams have full interpretations. As creative illusions, they need context – the dreamer's life. For example in his 'autobiography', his 'earliest remembered dream', the underground phallus (Jung 1989: 25) provided a symbol for a lifetime's work on parallels in meaning between sexual and sacred – whether this is 'true' or not, that's how he wanted the story told. That was his context. In the dream, young Carl went underground into a sacred space and saw, hidden behind a curtain, an enthroned living pink pillar with an eye at the top. It was terrifying, and he heard his mother say 'Yes, just look at him. That is the man-eater!' Jung later felt the dream phallus symbolised a connection between sexual and religious longing (1989: 11–13).

Michael Fordham (1976: 26–7) suggests this dream gives a Jungian image of a part object, a 'breast-penis'. Again, whether it does or not, that's how *he* wants the story told. That has to do with his context, a wish to be seen as 'respectable' by his psychoanalytic buddies. Jung argued strongly against such developmental, reductive interpretations. In early infancy dream images *may* represent body-parts and functions. Making meaning continues, but does not begin, as infants gradually recognise their body and needs as separate from mother. In Jung's dream it was mother who said 'this is the man eater' – which separates boy from mother, and, in incest fantasy, potentially reunites them.

However, as Jung pointed out 'the penis is just a phallic symbol' (*CW* 16: 340). It represents the 'Man Tribe' which draws a boy to it, just as the 'Woman Tribe' traditionally pushes him away. Post-Jungians divide into two positions on dream images. Andrew Samuels names them the symbolic/archetypal and the historical/personal (1985a: 239–40). Murray Stein suggests both shape personal narrative: the symbolic/archetypal view emphasises dreams are fleeting experiences of image, metaphor and symbol; intensely private, difficult to communicate acts of poetic imagination (1996: 114–32). Commenting on this, James Hillman said:

> The datum with which archetypal psychology begins is the image. The image was identified with the psyche by Jung (*CW* 13: para. 75) a maxim which archetypal psychology has elaborated to mean that the soul is constituted of

129

images, that the soul is primarily an imagining activity most natively and paradigmatically presented by the dream. For it is in the dream that the dreamer himself performs as one image among others and where it can legitimately be shown that the dreamer is in the image, rather than the image in the dreamer.

(Hillman 1983: 6)

Hillman argues, given the biological necessity of dreaming, what matters is not frame-by-frame analysis but encouragement to play in the dream stream: write the images down, use them in stories, poetry, drawings. Dream the dream on – ask what happens next. As Louis Zinkin (1987) suggested, if a dream is a hologram, then any and all parts contain the meaning of the whole. Any image can be amplified. Michael Fordham, in the historical/personal developmental tradition emphasises the dream's utility in understanding transference. He felt many of Jung's patients had either lost contact with Self, or never adequately established it (1985: 26). In place of 'self-assurance' they had a complex. Dreams let the synthetic processes of Self operate. Fordham believed Jung (like Winnicott) treated dream images as *transitional objects*. As such, explaining what they mean with elaborate amplification changes their value, risks depersonalising their content and losing their bridging function between 'I' and other.

However, dreaming begins before there is experience of 'other'. As embryos we dream from about the twenty-eighth week (Piontelli 1992: 33). Embryo dreaming, we guess, digests day residues, and rehearses motor experience – say, learning where our fingers are. Developing brains have to learn to grasp, swallow and so on. In childhood, dreams have a similar psycho-physiological practice function. Unfolding archetypes create plots for dream movies, to install new patterns of behaviour, for instance, for many boys sexuality starts in wet dreams. The Berlin Jungian Gustav Bovensiepen points out how dreams change in adolescence:

in puberty, when the ego is highly labile, it seems reasonable to get in touch with conflicts, repressed feelings, and impulses first through the ego experience in dreams ... Whether the dreams are interpreted or only listened to seems to be less important than observing modifications in the relationship between ego experience in the dream and ego experience in the waking state.

(1988: 245–64)

Notice the emphasis on form over content. Marie Louise von Franz, studying dreams of those near death, discovered the unconscious treats dying as a form (transition), rather than an end (1987). Up till the moment of death, dialogue between Self and ego continues. Her text beautifully illustrates the opposite of a reductive approach: end-less seas of association, amplification and alchemy until personal context is completely washed away and only 'golden meaning' is left. Over-interpretation in a developmental direction risks becom-ing narrowly reductive, over-interpretation in an archetypal direc-tion risks becoming over-inclusive – everything means everything else. The first is like having only brown in a childhood paintbox, the second is like mixing all the colours together – it all ends up brown.

Dream images are a multicoloured paradigm for an open system, their symbols can't have a lexicon. There can't be a Dream diction-ary *(clef du rêves)*. When Nerys Dee, (dream interpreter for *Predic-tion* magazines) says, for example 'Ocean means vast emotional potential reflected as shallow, deep, turbulent or calm feelings' (1989: 222) this could be true – or not.

Dream interpretation has a particular logical operator {both/and/ neither/nor}. Like an alethiometer, a dream's meaning depends on the mental state of the interpretant and interpreter. Lacking closed interpretations, they help us handle uncertainty. I agree with James Hillman that the content of a dream is far less important than engaging with the act of dreaming. For dreams, if they are anything, are liminal experience, *between*.

### Yukio's dreams

Yukio, a lad I've worked with four times a week for nearly ten years, had a crucial dream sequence at a crux point in his life. He led a liminal life, abandoned as a baby by his parents and brought up by his traditional Buddhist family in rural Japan. At ten, his parents reappeared, took him to Africa, then sent him to school in the UK. He believed all his problems were due to being ugly. Born with a bilateral cleft palate, this led him to believe he was morally bad. Dreams helped him ask, 'Does my life reflect my belief?', and let him establish links to collective images. Analysis did not erase his pain; it allowed new meaning to flow into old experiences. Dream interpret-ation and 'dreaming the dream on' through active imagination let a mute part of his psyche talk.

First, he dreamed he was naked on a beach on a Polynesian island, at puberty, being held down whilst the men of the tribe tattooed on a new face. Second, naked on my couch, whilst I buggered him. Third, on a hot summer afternoon, again naked, on a London pavement with his closest male friend, having sex. The dreams explore his complex. The first dream is the past, his wish for a new face and, with it, initiation into manhood. The second is a 'here and now' fear: if he's attached to me, an idealised father-analyst, then I'll rape him. A karmic pattern will repeat (he was raped by his father). The third is his 'current relationship', his hope/fear that he's gay.

Yukio was scared by his strong homosexual feelings. A homo-erotic phase is normal in development: being able to love another has to start with loving one's Self, exploring one's own body – and bodies like one's own. In cultures like Polynesia *rites de passage* humanise these feelings, often in a group event. Maleness (animus) is a shared, collective experience. Animus often appears in dreams as a group or crowd (Emma Jung 1978: 1–43) Lads need to group and secure identification with other lads before seeking partners of the opposite sex. Yukio then dreamed of being an eco-warrior fighting to save a forest. In real life he increasingly shared this value system, opposed to both capitalist and collective social order. He hung out with such a group, restarted karate and got a tattoo – enacting his dream.

A new face given by a 'group of men' is an image for a new persona, as well as a thing in itself. Yukio realised he'd never go through the pain involved until he knew he 'was worth it'. He inquired about surgery. But to accept he was 'worth it' felt like betraying his karma. At this point came a powerful dream in which his sister (an anima figure) tried to seduce him. But he didn't want her. While telling me this he rocked to and fro like a baby. I felt intensely maternal and said, 'You're rocking like an abandoned infant.' I said his sister stood for his mother, and found myself suggesting he tell me how he felt in his mother tongue:

Y: 'But you don't speak Japanese!'
'No, but you do,' I agreed, 'maybe you need to tell you what you feel like?
The atmosphere changed. Time stopped. He took a huge breath, and began, with the voice of a frightened little boy, weeping as he told me (in Japanese) of being ten, sent alone on a long flight to parents he didn't know in a country he'd never visited, and a culture and language he didn't understand. As he

wept, I gently said, 'Now you are crying like a baby, like a baby who chokes on mother's milk, a boy nobody wants.'

Y: 'I want him.'

D: 'Yes, you do. That's new, you didn't want him before.'

## Dream images: symbol, signifier and signified

Dream interpretation is a dialectical process between an analysing couple, concerning the meaning and semantics of symbols. The word symbol comes from Greek: σψμ (sym), same; βολον (bolon), to throw. A σψμβολον was a stick or clay tablet broken in half then 'thrown together again' to prove a messenger's identity to its recipient (Stein 1957). The aim of a symbol is to bring unity (not fusion) not to find the truth – there may not be one to find.

Symbols are a subset of information. Like a cassette or CD, they can only be played with the right equipment. Dreams are members of the set {ambiguous information carriers}, like optical illusions. In mathematics, there's a similar set, {indeterminate numbers}, numbers which really exist, have value, but cannot be known in an equation without the equation collapsing. Equations containing such numbers are fundamental to quantum mechanics and chaos theory: part of probability functions. Dreams (like alethiometers) describe probabilities.

Yukio's 'face' dream could have meant 'gaining face' – the opposite of his shameful experiences of 'losing face' (being shamed) as a child. Interpretation depends on the emotional, intellectual and spiritual technology available, and has infinite variety. To deal with the risk of getting lost in detail, useful dream interpretations concentrate on form over content; pointing to how information is held in symbols, increasing the dreamer's understanding of mythopoesis (Siegelman 1990: 13–16). Dream symbols originate from day residues, unconscious infantile objects (for example, memories of the breast), interplay between inner figures (from internalised parents to chance daytime acquaintances), the relationship between a patient and analyst (transference and counter-transference), between dream ego and archetypal images, and between dreamer and the collective unconscious.

The difficulty of giving meaning to the images (signs) in dreams is obvious. Any given image can mean any of the things listed, one after the other and/or all at the same time. Interpretation of dreams is the semiotic handling of a text in which multiplicities of meaning overlap. There are signs, the signifiers (objects in the dream), and symbols, the signified (multiple meanings). Patients of Jungian analysts expect to bring dreams, hoping 'we know' what they mean. Sometimes no dreams come. A patient of mine used TV, film and theatre as culturally provided 'ready-made' dreams. By my handling them as if they were dreams he gradually admitted he did dream. The problem was not a lack of dreams, but shame at sharing their disturbing sexual content.

What a dream means is different to the information it contains. My Carcassonne dream (p. 120) contains information drawn from reading, travel and personal history. What it means is more than the sum of the information – no matter how much it is amplified. In analysis the presence of symbolic material changes the tone of the session, regardless of the information (facts) around and within the session. Dreams may tiptoe in at the start, or flood a session so there's no room for interpretation. In my first analysis, I brought dream after dream, each so full of associations that it became completely impossible to work on them (or anything else). Like Mickey Mouse in *Fantasia*, I was a Sorcerer's Apprentice who wanted to do all the magic myself (an omnipotence fantasy). Each time Mickey cut the water-carrying broom in half, the halves grew legs. As splitting continued, each part grew, fetched water and split again, until the cave was awash. Or I'd do the opposite, withhold dreams till the last minute, and leave with fury at the door that there has been no 'answer'.

Jung felt it is what the complex says in the dream that's important. When in a consulting room, whether brought by the patient or the analyst, dreams can be as much a hindrance as a help. We need to assess their ecology: not only 'what is the function of this dream to the dreamer' (whether dreamer be patient or analyst), but also 'what is this doing in here between us, right now?' The shape and feel of a session and the strange effects at boundaries around it (from how the front door is opened to how it closes) amplify the dream, no matter where the dream itself is placed in the session. For example, the 'Cat in the bottle' dream (Chapter 8) was preceded by Jacques meeting my cat on the stairs to my consulting room.

Jung recommended we look at each image, not as signs needing interpretation but as symbols, to be explored in a cultural context. Jacques meeting my cat was synchronicity, 'cat' for him meant 'jazz cat' (father hated jazz, I love it). Then he dreamed of being a red balloon floating over the ocean. I asked him how he felt. 'Lonely,' he replied, adding, 'If a balloon is punctured by a needle then the balloon is likely to say it's the needle's fault.' That I'd spoken meant I'd burst his balloon – I was a little prick. Anne, an artist in her mid-seventies, brought to her first session a dream about walking along the seashore near her home, but the beach was covered in a labyrinth of tank-traps: concrete blocks. She was, at the time, thinking concretely about the blocks and obstacles in her life. Her inner defences resembled the wartime sea defences along the coast where she lives and paints. Naming her problem 'unnecessary defences' gave it new meaning. The dream showed her, as it showed me, the personal value of unconscious, symbolic material transferring to everyday life, which we can learn to handle as if it were dream material.

Ann had 'blocked off' memories of being sent to boarding school in England before the war, away from her beloved Kenya, where her parents were missionaries 'doing holy things for God . . .', as she put it. She found walking around the ruined shore defences (which she did for hours during the course of a four year twice-weekly analysis) was the best place to re-memory her childhood, reconnecting to events many years earlier. There is reversibility in the analytic approach, everything reported in a session could be dream. Self doesn't speak in its own voice, but through projected voices: actions. Ego projects its experiences on to others, Self projects on to the dream-ego: using the same symbolic language for both processes provides a context and structure for analysis. In a long analysis, dream-symbols recur again and again, becoming words in a narrative system of 'ambiguous signs', a term proposed by the Italian semiotician Umberto Eco (1976: 271). He suggests:

1   Many messages on different levels are ambiguously organised
2   The ambiguities follow a precise design
3   Both the normal and the ambiguous devices in any one message exert a contextual pressure on the normal and ambiguous devices in all the others
4   The way the rules of one system are violated by one message is the same as that in which the rules of other systems are violated by their messages

Over time, ambiguous dream-symbols become mythological signifiers. Anne's dream of *The Concrete Blocks*, Yukio's dream *The New Tattooed Face*, Jacques' dream *The Cat in the Bottle* became, in the myth-stream of their analyses, metaphors for complexes constellating new purposes. Changes from signifier to symbol occur when the properties of the dream-image and its interpretation are neither reiterating nor moralising if they respect the compensatory function of the dream; if they account for the personal context of the dreamer's life, psycho-biography, and social milieu; and essentially, if they connect the dreamers to the cultural and mythological time-stream at an archetypal level. This cannot occur if the dream-symbol is reduced, boiled down or subsumed by the analyst's theoretical myths.

Interpretation (making clear in one language what has been said in another) is translation: from Latin *latus*, supine of *ferro*, (to bear, bring or carry). Do the images and their meanings connect to and/or translate (move forward) the day-to-day reality of the dreamer? Sometimes if no dreams are reported then practising dreaming during consciousness (using guided imagery and active imagination) can help, teaching people to see their life story as a myth.

I used this approach with Emily: in her early forties she was in a therapeutic community with intractable depression. She also had drugs, ECT, art, dance, group and individual therapy. Guided imagery evoked her ability to dream: a small part in her cure, but one which reconnected her to purpose. She brought images of being a small black crab on an infinite shore, afraid to move. Gradually she linked this to the death of her father from cancer when she was a little girl, and her terror of forming relationships with men (including me). Transference phenomena were given sea-shore imagery, reflected boundary phenomena. Ocean appeared in Anne's, Jacques' and Yukio's dreams: ocean as a collective symbol for Self?

## Dream: sacred space or field of healing?

To show what I mean about interplay between dream and reality, here's a 'lived dream'. As a hippie-kid at Glastonbury Festival, 'by chance' I stumbled into the Sacred Space, a new-made stone circle (a Temenos). Folk sat in almost-silence, danced or drummed quietly. We shared deep respect, smiles, sunshine, innocent nakedness – nothing had to be said, no words – then, 'by chance', I found the Field of Healing: booths, hucksters, palm readers, tarot cards, astrologers, snake-oil salesmen (even psycho-therapists). People with something to sell waited for people wanting something to buy: bargains, negotiations, shouting – too many words.

The previous term, at medical school, I'd been wondering whether the sacred was healing or healing was sacred? Without ego-purpose, on a wander led by Self, untroubled, not searching for meaning, it found me. Sacred Space was like Self: Healing Field, like ego. My Self created a meaning from 'found objects', as Michael Eavis, the

Festival organiser, had created potentials for meaning by sticking signs up in his fields. The signs became symbols as I unconsciously projected an inner dilemma on to the environment, 'now on to now', creating a symbolic switch in my time-stream – a numinous, timeless moment when meaning reorganised.

A symbolic switch uses a pluralistic logical operator {both/and/neither/nor}, to deconstruct meaning, like this: Self showed me 'Medicine is {both/and/neither/nor} a Field of Healing {both/and/neither/nor} a Sacred Space.' My 'chance wander' was {both/and/neither/nor} a real event {both/and/neither/nor} a dream. Sculpting meaning with symbols isn't about historical truth (signification in an objective world), but subjective truth: true for dream material, and for numinous events (like the one I've described). Causal approaches to meaning have real limitations: uniformity of meaning implies a system tending to close, {<}, rather than tending to open, {>}.

Self's multiplicity of images can turn fragmentation into creativity. The physicist Wolfgang Pauli's dream of the World Clock (*CW* 11: paras 111, 128, 138, 158, 164) shows a moment in his analysis (which Jung supervised) when parts became wholes. Pauli used his dream creatively: from it came 'Pauli's exclusion principle' – that electrons in an atom exist in certain mutually exclusive energy states, quanta apart. This allowed chemistry (contemporary alchemy) to describe 'the why and how' of molecular structure – and, coincidentally, to discover a way to turn base metal (copper and tin) into gold (Roob 1997: 96).

Similarly, cultures contain 'meaning structures', irreducible molecular meaning-patterns underpinning them (Henderson 1984). We can have the idea of 'sacred space' whether or not we enact it by positioning stones or concrete blocks: it gives me freedom when I imagine analytic theorists with stalls in the Field of Healing. I don't have to 'buy' them. Their goods don't help me make a space sacred with an other, though they do help me recognise when an other is trying to 'set up their stall' in my consulting room.

Sharing dream images in a social dream matrix (Lawrence 1991) is a group experience of dream amplification. The large group recount their dreams, without amplification. As the image of a crowd represents Self, then 'free market economics' applies. What do the economics of the Self look like? Symbols are its currency. 'Supply and demand' and 'diminishing returns' apply to dream images.

In a social dream matrix there tends to be amplification by repetition of symbols: if one person dreams about an ox, another may have dreamed about bullfighting, or a herd of cows. If too many dream images are put into the matrix they lose value: if too few, they can be over-valued. If too much 'effort after meaning' is made, then the experience is that of a procession of amplificatory gems – gold is turned into lead. Dreams retold in a group tend to spontaneous amplification.

For example, in a group supervision of humanistic psychotherapists we used the social dream matrix. Each therapist brought a difficult dream from one of their clients. No biographical details were given. The dreams were spoken into a meditative silence, reflected on, then group members wrote down the strongest symbols: parents and family, vehicles, houses, nudity, telephones and numbers, falling and flying, cross-dressing, changing sex, having sex, water and drowning, coming of age, being at a funeral or ones own funeral, executions, punishment and sado-masochistic fantasies, being in a group or a crowd (particularly male), birds and animals, windows . . . doors.

Distilling, common themes are: life, death and rebirth/ transformation/gifts/precognition/bridges, – archetypal themes. We found, too, that sharing dreams in a group validated our inner experience of them in our counter-transferences. Relativising symbols like this is an ordinary making of meaning, an archetypally humanising function. In the group, the symbols functioned as a psychic regulator, restoring a balance between our conscious and unconscious urges to make meaning, addressing our group dynamics and inner feelings. We noticed we brought dreams of food at lunchtime!

We felt glad to discover we're all psychotic in dreams, know what it is to be out of touch with consensual reality, and appreciated the value of dreams in reconnecting us to that reality. Sharing dreams in such a setting was therapy for therapists, sharpened our diagnostic tools, and elucidated and illuminated links to collective experience. And it demonstrated meaning-filled coincidences, as dream-events projected into the time-stream, which I discuss in the next chapter.

# 7

# TIME AND MEANING

Here the Dormouse shook itself, and began singing in its
sleep 'Twinkle twinkle twinkle twinkle,' and went on so long
that they had to pinch it to make it stop.
'Well, I'd hardly finished the first verse,' said the Hatter,
'when the Queen bawled out ' "He's murdering the time! Off
with his head!" '
'How dreadfully savage!' exclaimed Alice.
'And ever since that', the Hatter went on in a mournful tone,
'he won't do a thing I ask! It's always six o'clock now.'
(Lewis Carroll, *Alice in Wonderland*, 1965: 97–8)

## Meaningful coincidence?

This chapter looks at the role of time in the meaning-making process. I'll suggest Jung's concepts – synchronicity, acausal connection
and meaning-filled coincidence – encourage us to ask how does 'time
fill with meaning' rather than 'show meaning-filled time' exists. Further, his use of 'scientific' language, I believe, says more about a wish
to reframe his own mystical experiences in terms of a dominant
cultural myth than about the nature of being and time.

Suppose there are time-free and time-bound parts of the psyche:
call the first 'Self' and the second 'ego'. Both meaning and problems
in meaning attribution arise between them. For instance, if Self
rushes in to defend a besieged ego, but 'floods it' with meaning, we
have a 'too much' meaning disorder (borderline – 'rain is a deliberate
persecution'). If ego makes a wall against Self and time-free, numinous experience ('I'm too busy to notice raindrops') then we have a
'too little' meaning disorder (narcissism). These primary meaning
disorders Melanie Klein describes as 'positions' (life positions),
the first is 'paranoid/schizoid', the second 'depressive' (Segal 1975:
24–38, 67–81).

Like the Mad Hatter, March Hare and Dormouse, when we're
trapped in a frozen moment (stuck in a life position, held by a complex) a closed system exists in 'no-time', in the numinous world of

Self. If time does not flow, there can be no new meaning: if time flows too fast, we can't reflect on new meanings, or validate them with the collective. Synchronicity describes meaning raining all around us – irrigating, rather than flooding. In a *between* experience, Self links inner and outer time with common meaning, allowing new acts of closure by the ego. I described this in the previous chapter when my dilemma about medicine resolved through the 'sacred space/field of healing' contrast at Glastonbury which juxtaposed spiritual and material value-systems.

Jung's concepts hark back to the alchemists, whose maxim, 'as above, so below', reflected his belief in meaning-filled links between matter and spirit, man (microcosm) and God (macrocosm). In the Gnostic idea of the Pleroma (the infinite) and the Noumena (the now), Jung found a reassuring precursor to his ideas of a time-free Self interacting with a time-bound ego. Could these concepts prove the existence of meaning as a thing-in-itself (*ding an sich*) in a time-free non-relativistic world, given that we live in a time-bound relativistic world? What would be necessary and sufficient to support his proposition of an acausal ordering principle in the universe, which offers a neat intellectually symmetrical opposite to causality?

We'd need to compare metaphysical theories of meaning with lived, daily experiences of meaning-making; just as when evaluating a religion (or an analysis) we'd look at correlations between belief and practice. We could look at parallels between parapsychology, new physics and mystical experience, ably done by, amongst many others, Lawrence Le Shan (1974) and Victor Mansfield (1995). But parallels are argument by analogy, not proof. Further arguments might have to cover the same ground as those attempting to prove the existence of God, or by tracing the development of the interrelation of concepts of time and of meaning through culture-myths (religion and politics). Such accounts are set in archetypal, collective time: before the world began, 'once-upon-a-time' time, the time Jung had in mind when he wrote about the 'two million year old man' in us all.

We could argue backwards to synchronicity as demonstrating meaning-filled time from the concept 'archetypal experience', or forwards to the concept of archetype from experiences of time-free reality, but not, as Jung did, argue both ways at once – if archetypes are acausal then acausality proves the existence of archetypes is a definition, not a proof (Main 1997: 35). Time and meaning are natural phenomena, as well as metaphysical themes. Beliefs about the nature of time and the nature of meaning shape perception of both.

I suggest a parsimonious explanation: we see meaning-filled 'coincidences' because we are meaning-making beings. Like Dorothy in *The Wizard of Oz*, we see the Emerald City as green because we're wearing green spectacles (Chapter 10).

## What is time?

In man's original view of the world, as we find it among the primitives, space and time have a very precarious existence. They become 'fixed' concepts only in the course of his mental development, thanks largely to the introduction of measurement. In themselves, space and time consist of nothing. They are hypostatized concepts born of the discriminating activity of the conscious mind and they form the indispensable co-ordinates for describing of the behaviour of bodies in motion. They are, therefore, essentially psychic in origin, which is probably the reason that impelled Kant to regard them as *a priori* categories.

(*CW* 8 : paras 833–841)

Time perception is a function of consciousness. To understand time, its perception and role in meaning, we have to say what time is. I'll review ideas from philosophy, physics, psychology and parapsychology then look at the value of these ideas in clinical work.

### Philosophy, natural philosophy and time

In Western philosophy time is traditionally viewed as either static or dynamic. The static view, attributed to Greek philosophers Zeno and Parmenides, sees time as 'change' (rather than a fourth dimension of space). They held that change is an illusion: there's 'no such thing' as time, it is a mental construct. Some philosophers argue this denies the existence of 'an absolute now' as distinctions between past, present and future become subjective (experiential) rather than a property of pure being (ontological). The dynamic view of Aristotle and Heraclitus said the future isn't a thing-in-itself. It's constructed (and grows) as a sequence extends: more events, more possible futures.

The problem of time being relative is overcome by defining 'present time' as including events not causally connectable by physical means. For example, events on planets in a far-away galaxy, happening now, are forever unknowable. They exist. They're not unknown due to lack of trying to know, but because we know no means by which information from such solar systems can reach us. Like space, dynamic time is inherently asymmetric, moving from known towards an unknowable limit – setting a natural limit on causality.

Causality, in contemporary usage, means cause and effect, a temporal sequence – if A then B. However, for Aristotle, temporal causality was but one feature of an event. He argued persuasively that simultaneous and backward causation (events preceding causes) are conceptually possible. Further, it's not enough for there to be a sequential time relation between two events (A and B) to prove A *caused* B: 'all babies drink milk, all criminals were babies, therefore milk causes crime' – the *post hoc ergo propter hoc* fallacy. Causality has to be necessary and sufficient for order to emerge from chaos.

Chaos theory is a mathematically-based discipline, derived from observation of changes in oscillating systems (Stewart 1989: 5–22). It shows how self-similar patterns arise in the natural world: think of trees, flowers or the shapes of snow crystals – each is unique, yet each has a self-similar fronded structure (all oak trees look like oak trees). Individual variations in pattern are due to exquisite sensitivity to initial conditions, 'the butterfly effect'. The name derives from Edward Lorenz's studies of weather-modelling. He noticed that accidental, tiny differences in initial variables in a pattern-generating program produce, over time, widely different pictures, as if 'a butterfly stirring the air today in Beijing can transform storm systems next month in New York' (Gleick 1987: 8, 11–31).

Suppose the same is true for archetypal patterns, genetic tendencies to certain behaviours. Now, if synchronicity is an asynchronous meaning-generating event outside time, is it outside exquisite sensitivity to initial conditions? An answer depends on whether we take a meaning-filled-moment as static (closed) or dynamic (open), or (as I think Jung supposed) both at once. It also depends on which moment, which meaning is taken as the initial condition, and by whom – who is observer, who and what is observed? (The 'sacred space/field of healing' coincidence was only meaningfully coincident for me, as observer.)

Time perception involves recognising collectively meaningful sequential arrangements of information. Meaning-giving information has to be simultaneously present both in observer and observed events for synchronicity to occur. We don't know if time is made of anything other than oscillating information – if there are 'fundamental particles' of time. As light, a ripple in space-time has variables (intensity, luminosity, perspective), so has time. Unlike light, it's not sensed by a specific organ. As a sequence of information, time can have a particle or wave nature (Meredith, in Frazer 1972: 259–73). It is perceived in two different modes, by conscious and unconscious mind; ego (chronos) time is linear, serial, particulate, and *now* – something happens out there, something happens in here. Self (kairos) time is cyclical, parallel, wave, and *eternal*. Out there stimuli from the present interact with data gathered in the past, to allow prediction of possible futures.

Physicists know that while we can make statistical predictions about atomic behaviour, we can't make predictions about individual atoms. Analytical psychology applies the same principle to human behaviour, especially to our dominant culture-myths – religion and politics. In those modes the observer (believer or voter) also changes the experiment (belief or government). These cultural-myth systems are designed to deal with incomplete knowledge and, again, the information required is not attainable. Werner Heisenberg said, 'Incomplete knowledge is an essential part of every formulation in quantum theory,' and this is equally true of analytic theory. Culture-myths (beliefs/theories) measure what is meaningful to a culture at a given moment. The meaning exists in the culture, not the event. To test this out, consider any headline in any newspaper and ask, 'Why this story now?'

### Parapsychology

This delicate interface between individual and cultural myth is clearly seen in parapsychology. Certain observers (mediums) seem to perceive atemporal events. Past vice-president of the Society for Psychical Research Arthur Ellison takes up physicist David Bohm's analogy of a holographic universe, suggesting information about the whole is contained in all of the parts. Psychologist Karl Pribram developed this position, suggesting the brain stores information as an interference pattern between competing neural informational nets, as a hologram. Apparent movement through time is illusory. Events emerge from a primal enfolded reality, called the implicate order by biologist Rupert Sheldrake (1981: 153–8).

Quantum physics and parapsychology, natural philosophies, are efforts after meaning, knowledge-making (epistemophilic) activities. Parapsychology studies how knowledge-making occurs other than in time-process: mediumship, spiritual healing, telepathy and tele-kinesis. Good reviews of the field are given by Ellison (1988) and American parapsychologist Dean Radin (1997). Their subject became fashionable at the end of the nineteenth century, and was studied by physicists Sir Oliver Lodge and Sir Henry Crookes, and Nobel Prize winning biologist Charles Richet. For many today, 'psychic research' associates with cults begun at the same time: the Theosophical Society with colourful Madame Helena Blavatsky; the Anthroposophists, with dour Rudolf Steiner; the 'wild sex magick', of Aleister Crowley (1979) and the madcap antics of the Hermetic Order of the Golden Dawn (Howe 1972). Jung's interest in time arose from paranormal experiences: ghosts, seances, dialogues with inner figures. These

> seemed to occur at critical junctures in his life: paranormal events accompanied his decision to make a career of psychiatry, his conflict and eventual breach with Freud, his relationship with his 'ghostly guru' Philemon, the writing of Septem Sermones ad Mortuos in which he adumbrated much of his later psychology, his formulation of the concept of the Self as the centre of psychic totality, and his heart attack and transformative near-death experience of 1944.
>
> (Main 1997: 7)

Such events happened round him, in meaning-filled 'coincidences' between daily events, his dreams and his patients' problems. This led him to suppose time had a qualitative dimension. He knew clinically (and personally) how near-delusional moods may accompany deep psychological changes, threatening to overwhelm the conscious mind. He felt synchronicity counterbalanced and compensated for this by showing that meaning is everywhere, if only we choose to see it (Aziz 1990: 66–90).

For example, frequently noticed constellations of similar meaning toned events can occur within a few days. I once came to a session knowing my analyst was about to tell me she was going to India (where I'd lived for a year as a lad with Tibetans – I'd had a letter from Tibet that morning). She said, 'Before you say anything, yes, I am going to India.' On another occasion, a healing group I belonged to were asked to dowse for a missing parrot. At the right space and time there was indeed a parrot matching exactly the description we'd been given – alas, it was the wrong parrot.

Arthur Ellison suggests such events may, in part, be acts of closure on meaning, occurring at moments of extreme awareness in sensitive individuals: a response to 'threat'. 'Apparitions' are an enduring psychic charge, perhaps the result of strong emotion, a 'frozen moment' (Ellison 1988: 24) – not necessarily the medium's own

(Tyrrell 1943: 42–3). The 'sensitivity' need not be to 'spiritual reality', rather to Self. In trance states there is, typically, *abaissment du niveau mental* (deep relaxation and letting go of ego constraints, with reduced attention and concentration – a dream-like state). The ego, temporarily, loses reality-testing ability. It is as if we're awake and dreaming at the same time.

You're a child, in a dark house, at night, alone, half-awake. You see a vague shape. You can't name it accurately. But you're threatened. The shape appears to move. So, it's a ghost! (technically, it's a misperception). As children, we continually attempt to make sense of the unknown. So many possible explanations, wind, the shadow of a tree . . . Aliens, pixies or ghosts. Anxiety, apprehension and panic cause premature closure, naming the percept before relevant information is gathered.

Threatened systems close, stop collecting data and start acting: attempting to make time stand still. Here is a collective example:

> The era that saw the first flowering of psychical research coincided with the end of Western imperialism. A time of collective threat culminated in the 'War to end Wars'. Aged twelve, in the Memorial Chapel at Rugby School, I realised seven hundred boys from the school died then – a school full. Bereaved parents seeing mediums was, temporarily and collectively, 'normal'. Such losses, repeated across Europe, define the Twentieth Century as the century of the absent father, hence perhaps its need for gurus, 'Great Leaders' and urgent need to understand the problem of meaning.

Place 'synchronicity' in historical context: 'belief in spirits' threatened the dominant myth of the twentieth century – the myth of scientific materialism, perverted into the myth of the military-industrial complex. Given the desperate need to make meaning out of useless sacrifice, and the intellectual climate, it's no surprise Jung's work as an experimental psychologist grew from psychic research (as did that of William James), nor that he wanted to meet the cultural desire for an explanation of mass slaughter. If there is a 'scientifically proven acausal connecting principle' guiding even the smallest event – such as the flight path of a bullet – then there is a God in the Universe, a ghost in the machine: material evidence of the Spirit World. The sacrifice of young heroes was not in vain. Given the response the word 'spirit' arouses (fear of the unknown, of death) and its challenge to conventional meaning systems, there's no surprise Jung is denigrated for his theories by some and idealised by others.

## *Psychology*

From origins in parapsychology and spiritualism, the emerging science of psychology underwent a materialist reaction (behaviourism) before settling down to its long-term project of correlating human cognition with neuro-biology. From the perspective of cognitive psychology, normal time perception requires us to be able to:

1   recognise incoming stimuli – sense
2   value the stimuli in survival terms – feel
3   connect the feeling to concepts – think
4   predict the consequences – intuit

All of these depend on perception of 'now', a function of a 'good-enough' ego (summarising Von Franz, in Frazer 1981: 218–34).

In loss, feeling overwhelms sensation. Neuro-anatomically, if the amygdala interrupts the formation of meaning by the prefrontal cortex then time-orientation tasks can't be performed (see Chapter 5). We can't perceive anything new in pathological mourning (like Queen Victoria for Prince Albert). Survival is threatened when we can't *as if* – if we can't imagine a future, we become depressed: submissive, rather than fighting or fleeing.

In fact, time perception is a parallel-process, all four functions occur simultaneously, feeding back to each other. As heat triggers 'withdraw hand' before we yell 'fire!' through a spinal reflex, so in circuits between amygdala, thalamus and prefrontal cortex if early interactions produce fear – say, fear of men as a result of being beaten by father, like Mike (Chapter 3), Billie (Chapter 4) or Yukio, (Chapter 6) we'll see father-figures as a threat. Sensation is driven as much by inner, unconscious needs as by percepts – except when overwhelmed by loss.

When the need to seek others is paramount, Self 'breaks through' ego-barriers to create meaning. Meaning-filled coincidence (synchronicity) arises from within not without. It is purposive. A hazard of this teleological view, as London analytical psychologist Helen Morgan points out, is turning thoughts into things (reification):

> The keyword here is meaning. When discussing his thoughts
> on synchronicity, Jung stressed the a-causal nature of the

relationship between the inner psychic state and the external events which seem connected when these events are experienced as mere coincidences. It is not that the inner state causes the events to occur, or vice versa; rather, it is the meaning that consciousness finds in these occurrences that gives significance. It is what 'fixes' the event.

(Morgan 2000: 124–5)

The connections exist in the neuro-biology of time perception. Memory, or reconstructive imagination, is remade by feeling tones – particularly fear. Memory of sequence (of time as sequence) isn't stored in discrete digital chunks (like a CD). It's made anew in each moment from components scattered across our brain. For example, hypothalamic-reticular activating system connections synchronise sleep and waking (Fenwick and Fenwick 1999): changes in this system initiate dreaming. Neural networks which orient us in time are maintained during D-sleep (in dreams) as day residues 'upload' from limbic system stores in symbols through hippocampal-frontal connections (Carter 1999: 160–4). The unconscious selects suitable dream-images from a reference system (library) of internal objects/ humanised archetypes.

Serial (Self) and parallel (ego) time have order, sequence (like making a word) generation (making sentences), depth (awareness of infinite possible sentences), and intensity – the felt-experience of time (the meaning of sentences) (Ornstein 1969: 15–24). Self and ego can treat each variable separately. Pattern recognition, essential to differentiate sequential events, requires differentiation of figure from ground (Corcoran 1971: 59–93). In adults, this is usually 'seamless'. We don't notice the semantic leaps made from moment to moment, idea to idea. When time is suspended in an eternal now, it's a primordial 'booming, buzzing confusion'. In such states there can be no purpose (desire). We need time to have purpose.

Purpose is defined as 'prospect, direction, design, aspiration, end'; movement through time. It has no meaning without future time. Hope is positive future perspective; despair, negative future perspective. Severe depression with psychomotor retardation has no time perspective – perhaps a re-living of the frozen moments of childhood?

## Child development

Developmentally, learning to perceive sequential time is hard. It may begin as we notice uterine bio-rhythms (mother's heartbeat). At birth, to survive, we rapidly learn temporal co-ordination (not to mix breathing and swallowing). Long-term sequencing is initially disorganised in a new-born infant's 'free running' wake-sleep cycle. It takes months for mother-time and infant-time to synchronise and create meaning-filled coincidence, as feeling spontaneously collides with gesture.

Donald Winnicott guessed internalising a 'good–enough mother' provided an internal time-referent – infants fit their sleep-wake cycle to mother's, not vice versa. Jung believed our internal time-referent is Self, which fills 'coincidence' with meaning – an idea he took from the philosopher Arthur Schopenhauer, who took it from Buddhism (*CW* 8: paras 828–30). In Schopenhauer's view time-free moments are Self-recognitions which change knowledge, open us to new meaning and increase our capacity to manage uncertainty.

As we develop wider temporal perspective, we move from concrete to formal operational thinking, losing infant-like omnipotent needs to control objects. We learn to make open rather than closed meanings – symbols. We can act-in-imagination, as well as act-out. We begin to see life as an open system. Daily events occur in serial-time, *chronos* time. Events are sequential {A, B, C}. Moving through time requires learning temporal orientation. 'I'm bored', from a child means 'I've time I don't know how to fill.' Neglect (never valuing a child's time by playing with them, for example) produces meaning-disorder as effectively as abuse. Both create a strong negative past temporal perspective (guilt is the expectation of blame projected forward in time). This predisposes to depression, in which time does not seem to move at all.

Imagine 'guilt' as a temporal meaning-disorder. Ego takes responsibility for actions of Self. But to suppose the time-bound can be responsible for the time-free is an omnipotence fantasy. Imagine 'shame' as a temporal discontinuity disorder. Ego imagines it can cause Self's annihilation, which wipes out shame. Guilt and shame, for a child, are ego-forming events because in them time itself seems to stop. We wonder, 'How did I create that illusion of meaning? . . . If so, why did Self create this illusion for me right now? Why is what I did bad news?'

Suppose 'bored' from a child means, 'I've lost future perspective.' Children easily slip into eternal moments of reverie, through the looking glass and down the rabbit hole, or, (like Tom Sawyer in Chapter 3) into moments of existential despair. If under-stimulation (neglect) or negative stimulation (abuse) form too much of a repeating pattern, we do not form a stable sense of time. Melanie Klein described this in her analysis of 'Fritz', a depressed, inhibited seven year old. Of his inability to organise time she wrote:

> The conscious equation of sleep, death and intra-uterine existence was evident in many of his sayings and fantasies, and connected with this was his curiosity as to the duration of these states and their succession in time. It would appear that the change from intra-uterine to extra-uterine existence, as the prototype of all a-periodicity, is one of the roots of the concept of time and of orientation in time.
>
> (Klein 1985: 99)

Jung devoted his youthful research career to measuring such temporal disruptions:

> As I have shown in my association experiments, the intensity of these phenomena can be directed determined by daytime record, and the same thing is possible also in the case of an unrestricted psychological procedure, when, watch in hand, we can easily determine the value intensity from the time taken by the patients to speak about certain things.
>
> (*CW* 8: para. 22)

Unlike Klein, Jung did not attribute this to 'castration anxiety' – he didn't buy Freudian theory. Like her, he saw the complexes which cause temporal disruptions as due to psychic energy fixation. If we close on one meaning (usually negative, like shame) time stops. Any meaning my Self makes is wrong. Guilt stops ego-time, any meaning I make, I'm *to blame for*.

### Depth psychology

Reflections on meaning and purpose tend to support one or both of our experiential theories of time: linear or cyclical. People may appear to themselves to be moving through a linear sequence of events (such as childhood, youth, and maturity) or through a cycle of integration (such as repeated encounters with attachment, separation, and loss). They

> may appear to themselves to be in a combination of these
> two experiences of time, in a 'spiral' of repeating patterns
> that moves in an irreversible direction.
>
> (Hall and Young-Eisendrath 1991: 5)

We live in a temporal field. The contribution to this field from the patient in analysis is the transference, their constructions about the past in the now. This evokes a mirroring unconscious response in the analyst, counter-transference. Harvard psychoanalyst Arnold Modell cites psycho-biological explanations given by Gerald Edelman (1987) for the repetition compulsions underlying these phenomena. Edelman proposed memory is not a permanent neural record, linked with past experience, rather, memory is a dynamic reconstruction that is context bound and established by means of categories. This description is consistent with and provides a neuro-biological backing for Freud's concept of *Nachtraglichkeit*.

> In this theory the motoric system plays a vital part in per-
> ception, from which it can be inferred that repetitive effects
> of transference function similarly to categorical memories.
> Transference affects are motoric in that they actively scan
> the human environment in order to refind an affect
> category . . .
>
> (Modell 1990: 60)

Modell is pointing out how body-language, an internally-driven motoric response, creates external, felt reality.

> This scanning, as we know, not only may be a refinding but
> also may lead to a self-fulfilling prophecy to the extent
> that transference affects induce a complementary counter-
> transference response. Thus, the repetition of painful affect
> categories is an essential mode of cognition. In this process,
> the patient's motor apparatus (affects) evoke the therapist's
> affective responses to find a perceptual 'fit', to establish an
> affect category.
>
> (ibid.: 61)

Intersubjective fields arise from mutual projections into shared space-time. Transference repetition drives change, in an attempt to gain control, to do what Winnicott called 'bringing trauma within the orbit of omnipotence' by re-placing a timeless event back into the linear time-stream, hoping it will 'wash away'. Freud's idea of *Nachtraglicheit* is that traumatic memories, resentments carried forward, are amenable to change – the way the memory is put together can be changed in the neural record. The memory is not erased, its meaning is changed.

Time is a percept, given and generated. Perceiving systems are driven externally by percepts, and percepts themselves are selected by the internal perceiving system. This feedback loop creates 'intersubjectivity' by shaping boundaries between Self and self-object (Atwood 1984: 71–5), results from projective identification into 'a third area' (Schwartz-Salant 1989: 131) and reflects the timeless quality described by Jung as 'perambulation about the Self', within a Temenos – in a sacred space (*CW* 12: para. 170) (not a field of healing).

A strong transference/counter-transference moment is an intersubjective event. Two timeless areas intersect, allowing redefining by both patient and analyst of lost internal objects. Modell says repetition compulsion represents a search for perceptual identity between present and past objects. The analytic time-frame is set up with clear boundaries to accentuate this interplay of different times.

Temporal discontinuities provide a way of understanding transferential phenomena, movingly recounted in an infant observation by London analyst Marilyn Mathew, who said, 'Could it be that my adult intellectual strivings for structure and sense are obscuring an inner vision where the archetypal qualities of experiencing and encountering a crystallising personality can perhaps be better hinted at in the language of poetry, music and art?' (1992). Awareness of temporal discontinuities provide an aesthetic, a way of understanding transferential phenomena as those of an emerging, timeless, Self.

### Neurobiology

Experiencing synchronicity is a natural, constructive property of an ordinary human mind, a response to information moving through our prefrontal cortex. It assigns meaning-filled connections, adding 'feeling-as-meaning' through feedback via the hippocampus, to iconic stores in the temporal, occipital and visual cortex. This arranges patterns, neural networks, which compete on evolutionary lines: those carrying signals (memories) best adapted to survival are faster. We could, like the author Alan Garner, call these engrams: 'In neuro-physiology the engram is a term for a hypothetical change in the protoplasm of the neural issue which is thought by some to account for the working of memory . . .' (Garner 1997: 112).

What is the neuro-anatomy of an engram, a syntagm, an 'atom of meaning'? Until recently, the brain was difficult to study. Knowledge came from lesion studies, defects seen in the dissecting room. Contemporary neuro-anatomical studies using magnetic resonance imaging (MRI scans) and positron emission tomography (PET scans) show people with schizophrenia have defects in frontal and prefrontal lobe function, which correlate with cognitive changes: passivity phenomena (thought insertion, withdrawal and broadcast, 'made' actions), perceptual delusions, auditory hallucinations, (third-person commentary on actions or thoughts) and delusional perceptions.

> The last is a two stage process, involving perception of a normal object followed by sudden intense delusional insight into the object's new, strange, and personally significant meaning. Often preceded by delusional mood, i.e. altered affect (fear, foreboding, ecstasy).
>
> (Bird and Harrison 1982: 21)

Innate body-language (involuntary pupillary dilation when emotionally aroused, increased capillary skin blood flow, altered cardiovascular function) is common to all mammals. We respond to environmental change by 'down-loading' these archetypal body-patterns. The amygdala has a central role in triggering these responses, but doing so interrupts the giving of meaning to events. The limbic system (and body-maintenance circuits below it in the hind-brain) are 'the two million year old' man. Living in an unconscious eternal present, this creates emotions, feeling-plus-instantaneous-bodily-response. Expression of affect is modulated by the frontal lobe (Le Doux 1998: 138–78) to which the limbic system connects by two routes – a 'quick and dirty' one from thalamus to amygdala, and a 'slow way' via the hippocampus and prefrontal cortex (Carter 1998: 81–105).

The amygdala's role as threat-perceiver alters time perception and creates atemporal experience. If you have been in a life-threatening situation you know that in the moment – 'when the car went out of control, when we saw the gun aimed at us, when Dad came in drunk with his belt raised', time stops. Meaning-making stops. Research shows beyond doubt that early childhood trauma scars the hippocampus, the part of the brain which attaches feeling to memory, causing post-traumatic stress disorder (PTSD) (Siegel 1999: 40–53).

Complexes, moments of frozen time, are tiny, chronic PTSDs. Synchronistic events are Self-referential ego-constructions, attempts (by the prefrontal cortex) to reconnect us to the external world's time-stream, and to move on. We have to bypass over-determined amygdala-hippocampus-thalamus connections, the body-based meaning system. In psychotic states we are unable to do this: it's not clear yet whether this is cause or effect. Maybe the constant and consistent containing repetition of the analytic experience allows new meaning-filled connections to form? Maybe 're-memorying' is a function of synchronicity?

As Jung noted, the interesting fact is not that such events occur, but that we pay so little attention to them in contemporary Western culture. The time-free has been forgotten along with the sacred. Eastern cultures retain a closeness to atemporal experience: religious ritual is part of daily life in the streets of Kyoto and Bangkok. Numinous experiences are embedded in culture to hold societies together. They express politico-religious archetypes (Chapter 11), which have a similar function in individuals – to hold the psyche together.

> I am therefore using the general concept of synchronicity in the special sense of a coincidence in time of two or more causally unrelated events which have the same or a similar meaning ... synchronicity therefore means the simultaneous occurrence of a certain psychic state with one or more external events which appear as meaningful parallels to the momentary subjective state – and in certain cases, vice versa.
>
> (*CW* 8: 849–50)

Moments when we are 'near' Self and enmeshed in its timeless quality are triggered as a normal instinctual response to threat. Similarly, in *satori* states (deep meditation) there is *no-time*, as there is focused body-ego consciousness. In *satori*, there is no synchronicity, as there is no time: we could say ego is inside Self (held by the Self). The opposite, a state of continuous synchronicity could be called paranoia (being beside the Self), or 'temporal meaning disorder, time sickness'. Storm (Chapter 5) experienced this on Ecstacy (MDMA).

## Neuropharmacology

Psychomimetic drugs interfere with patterns of time perception. Brought to a standstill by LSD (Huxley 1968) misperceived on cannabis (Mathers and Ghodse 1992), accelerated on amphetamine, slowed by barbiturates and benzodiazepines or made 'uninteresting' by opiates. Drugs act at neuro-receptors changing how neural impulses are received by affecting ionic movement between inside and outside of a nerve cell, disrupting sequential recognition of stimuli (Carter 1999: 64; Ornstein 1968: 46–8). Over-attention to inconsequential detail increases with increasing intoxication. With less information on which to make repeatable, reliable and valid judgements, our 'ego-boundary' feels more fragile, until, when we can no longer form meaningful gestalts, we 'make them up'. Each ' . . . word teems with hidden meaning, like Basingstoke' (Gilbert, W. S. in *Ruddigore*, Act 1, 1997).

Natural neurotransmitter fluctuations create differences between pleasure and pain, sanity and insanity. In depression, with depleted levels of serotonin and noradrenaline, time is subjectively slow (Kitamura and Kumar 1982). For example, Jay, a young lawyer with whom I worked analytically three times a week for five years, had bipolar affective disorder. He struggled to accept his episodes of low mood (which lasted 'forever') alternated with states of excitement when 'anything is possible' – roughly every six months. When his neurotransmitter levels were low, his temporal perception lost *order* (daily routine falls apart, sleep breaks up with early morning wakening), *sequence* (he can't remember what to do next or when things happened), *generation* (he can't plan the future), *depth* (can't anticipate), and *intensity* (loss of arousal).

Mania differs from depression only in loss of intensity. A result of analysis was acceptance that his illness had a strong physical component as well as a relation to traumatic childhood experiences and adjusting to being gay. As a result, he took Lithium, a drug which stabilises ionic movement across nerve cell membranes and stabilises mood. He complained this took the edge off living, as do some patients taking serotonin-increasing drugs – an important neurotransmitter in the amygdala-hippocampus-temporal lobe circuit.

Serotonin is released at peak experiences, switching on prefrontal cortical centres specifically concerned with meaning, interrelatedness and affection. LSD is mediated by similar neural pathways. These anti-depressants act 'homoeopathically' – as if taking a minute amount of LSD, which usually causes an atemporal (time-free) meaning disorder. In such states we lose self-synchrony, that is, our consistent sense of being-in-time.

Self-synchrony (Condon and Ogston 1967) is also disrupted in Parkinson's Disease and depression, severe temporal meaning disorders. In the first, we can't detect meaning in sequential signals from our own motor system and co-ordinate them. In the second, we can't orient in time, and are stuck in the past. Everything has the same, grey, temporal intensity. (Temporal intensity is the value attached to a temporal percept, such as 'a moment with mummy'. It can be assessed by how long a percept remains luminously present after it has vanished, the 'after-image'.)

The opposite, temporal intensity overload, is like being dazzled by time, for example, if high on Ecstacy. A bad come-down is caused by disordered serotonin activity in the thalamus-amygdala circuit. We lose control of sleep, sexual behaviour and mood as amygdalal functions are disinhibited. When alcohol disinhibits our frontal lobe, we lose control of emotion; when our amygdala relaxes, we can't differentiate between dreaming and waking, between enemy and friend, sexual arousal or non-arousal, Self and Other. Rave-goer's call this being 'loved-up'. Storm said, ' . . . I get all empathic and affectionate an' everything's, like, meaningful? A finger-flick from another dancer, an' we share the secrets of the Universe? Music is our bodies. It's telepathy on the dance-floor. I'm Us . . . everyone is Us . . . but if I start hearin' Pixies and Aliens, then I know I'm wrecked.'

Meaning may shipwreck due to over-attentiveness to incoming signals. Why? The answer concerns meaning-attribution. The amygdala searches for subliminal perceptions of 'fear'. When the thalamus perceives a threat, it triggers the amygdala to initiate fight, flight or appeasement gestures *before* the prefrontal cortex has evaluated the stimuli (felt it) or the frontal cortex 'thought' about it. As discussed in Chapter 4, these conditioned fear reflexes determine body-language in phobic avoidance and complexes. When we feel less threatened, this also shows in body-language.

As the amygdala relaxes in meditative states (or on psychotomimetics), we pick up subtle body cues far more easily (Carter 1999: 90–5). However, as amygdalal disinhibition deepens, these cues become increasingly self-referential. As we lose information we need to make meaning and attribute what we are talking to 'Aliens' or 'Pixies' (London street-names for LSD). We identify with symbols from the collective unconscious – like my patient 'Jesus' (Chapter 5). This *abaissment du niveau mental* also occurs when Self is in the presence of thousands of other Selves in a crowd: one joy of live sport (raves or rock festivals) is to join a 'belonging' crowd.

In such states it is easy to commune with spirits. We feel Shamanic, as described by anthropologist Carlos Castaneda, who had such experiences on Mescalin (1968). Colorado analyst Don Lee Williams points out (1981: 12–13) it doesn't matter if the story is objectively true or not, it is a valid, self-consistent myth. Mythologising experience regenerates meaning between a culture and an individual and between a Self and an ego. When a larger system makes an open space, meaning forms in it. If our sense of difference between Self and object diminishes, we can find meaning anywhere. This happens in delirium, in near-death experiences, in acute pain, in religious ecstasy and, as described, on Ecstasy (MDMA): it's the hallmark of a time-free state.

Moments of high arousal (closeness to Self) are moments of change, and loss. Natural, linear movement through chronological time causes identity crises: we don't want to grow old or die, we want now to be forever, 'this loss now' never to happen. Loss occurs when 'feeling *as* meaning' replaces 'meaning *and* feeling'. We can't relate to new events with new meanings. Time perception slows dramatically: in depression, minutes seem like hours (Tysk 1984). When time goes in circles, we're at the Mad Hatter's tea party.

## Clinical synchronicities

Storm, after attending a Rave (a modern Mad Hatter's tea party) had a persistent delusional mood. This preceded his self-harm – an intense spell of fear and foreboding alternated with meaning-rich moments – temporal meaning disorder is common in borderline states. For Mike (Chapter 3), such a moment happened when he found a blue golf tee on my doorstep. He'd dreamed the night before I was an African Witch Doctor sucking poison out of his heart with a small blue blowpipe. And, when he showed me the tee, 'at that moment he knew' . . . he could trust me. Psychiatrically, this is a brief delusional perception: ' . . . a two stage process involving perceiving a normal object followed by a sudden intense (and delusional) insight into the object's new, strange and personally significant meaning' (Bird and Harrison 1982: 21).

Yukio (Chapter 6), brought a recurring dream in which he was a child, being chased by an unknown group of men. We worked with the dream using active imagination, and, as he dreamed the dream on, he realised part of him always felt it had to flee persecution. This part deeply resented attempts made by the 'adult' in him or by me as analyst to change it – to have change demanded felt like persecution. The day after, he was doing voluntary play-leader work with a group of young kids. One, an autistic boy, kept putting stones in his mouth, risking choking. When Yukio took a stone from the boy's mouth, the boy bit him very hard.

It was a moment of satori – like a Zen story of a student achieving enlightenment when the teacher hits them in the face. At the moment of biting, Yukio felt panic, rage at being intruded on, and unbearable anxiety about not being able to breathe. These are his counter-transferential responses to the autistic boy *in the room* and *the autistic boy in himself* (who, as an infant with a malformed palate, choked on his first feed). Later, whilst meditating in the Zendo he found it almost impossible to sit. He was flooded by early memories of not being able to breathe, of choking on his own saliva. As he spoke to me, I noticed changes in his body language. His respiration rate slowed and he blushed deeply. I told him about this. That he connected what his body was doing in the room to his sense of shame, his sense, as an infant, and later as a badly abused child, that his body was not a safe place. That, like the autistic boy, he would 'bite' anyone who invaded his inner space, including me. Here we have a synchronistic series: a dream, worked on in a session, acted out in the afternoon, meditated on in the evening, dreamed about again (another chasing dream followed) and re-explored in the next session. Again, the synchrony exists in our interpretation, rather than any event-in-itself. How did Jung reach the idea of acausal connectedness from similar events with his own patients?

His clinical background was as a member of the team that defined the functional psychoses. Bleuler, his Chief, named schizophrenia; Jung helped clarify the definition and differentiate it from mania, as described in *The Psychogenesis of Mental Disease* (*CW* 3). Time perception forms part of this distinction, an ego effect (*CW* 3: para. 84). Temporal acceleration and deceleration occur in Bipolar Affective Disorder, and atemporality in schizophrenia 'the wrong time' vs. 'no time'. Time perception is assessed in mental state examination: related to level of consciousness, whether traumatic, psychotic or neurotic. His experimental studies, the association test experiments, show time delays between stimulus and response indicate the presence of a complex. Similarly, *between* experiences are accompanied by time distortions: in play, dreams and active imagination; in clouded consciousness, during hallucinations and delusional states; in meditation, paranormal phenomena and peak experiences.

However, when ego-constructed distinctions between different parts of the time-stream are, temporarily, lost, the events following may well be what psychiatrists call 'effort after meaning': attempts to make sense of the senseless. These occur when Self is under threat. They may point to mental disorder or developmental delay. Whilst we can't necessarily distinguish between synchronistic events occurring around people with acute functional psychoses or 'spiritual emergencies', we can say that if such events are occurring to the exclusion of most other events, a person may be acutely psychotic, out of touch with time-bound reality.

Imagine for a moment you're a liminal, out-of-time figure pushing a pram-full of what others call 'junk'. But, *you* know . . . ! Each scrap holds meaning. (This is the Diogenes syndrome, a symptom of end-stage schizophrenia, named after the grubby Greek philosopher who lived in a barrel.) We hear 'The Voices . . . are they . . . inside or outside? God or the Devil? Is the fate of the world in my hands? Is this my thought being echoed, or is it someone else's put into my head?' We're driven, like my patients, to attribute meaning. We have ideas of reference, assume everything happening around us is about us, like the patient with the ashtray, who we met in Chapter 1.

Jung believed synchronicity was an *a priori* experience – in the moment, we know. I suggest 'synchronicity' signifies a changing meaning system, a meaning system at a boundary. Change signifies loss. It's met with by mourning, an attempt to redefine meanings, a between activity. Synchronicities, between events, are extremely common in bereavement. Many people sense the presence of the departed. Whether this is strong projective-identification, a psychological defence or a psychic phenomenon matters less to my argument than that effort after meaning occurs. Bereaved people make new meaning from such experiences, opening closed-down, grief-stricken meaning systems.

Ego relates to an experience of Self, and unconsciously projects meaning into seemingly random events, creating meaning-filled 'coincidence'. It fills up the gaps. This is a therapeutic function of altered states of consciousness, sleep, dreams, hypnagogic and hypnopompic hallucinations. It can be facilitated psychologically, pharmacologically and by environmental manipulation – as in the sensory deprivation of a floatation tank. As Schopenhauer remarked:

> The imagination is, consequently, the more active the fewer perceptions from without are transmitted to us by the

senses. Protracted solitude, in prison or in a sick-bed, silence, at twilight, darkness are conductive to it: under their influence it comes into play without being summoned.

(1970: 177)

Perhaps such moments of solitude are also possible in the analytic space, in reverie on the couch? By allowing the mind a 'holiday' from effort after meaning new meaning can arrive without effort.

## Conclusion

The I-Ching and other mantic techniques work, Jung supposed, as the moment the question is asked contains the answer. The assumption is Self 'knows' which archetypal pattern may help in any given moment. The questioner's psyche focuses through time-free ritual when consulting a mantic system: tarot cards or astrology, medium or analyst. Synchronistic events occur around Shamen and analysts, as in the famous story of Jung amplifying a patient's dream about a scarab, when a cockchafer beetle (the European equivalent) landed on the windowsill – the experience shocked the patient out of her complex. She had a meaning epiphany (*CW* 8: paras 840–5). Jung says:

> The archetypes are formal factors responsible for the organisation of unconscious psychic processes: they are 'patterns of behaviour'. At the same time they have a specific charge, and develop numinous affects. The affect produces an *abaissment au niveau mental*, for although it raises a particular content to a supernormal degree of luminosity, it does so by withdrawing so much energy from other possible contents of consciousness that they become darker and eventually unconscious.
>
> (*CW* 8: para. 841)

The concepts of luminosity and presence, developed by Stephen Joseph (1997) relate to meaning – things which mean a lot shine brightly, become luminously present as we polish them with attention, like the scarab in this myth about a patient. In describing the event, Jung later said,

> synchronistic events rest on the simultaneous occurrence of two different psychic states. One of them is the normal,

probable state, (i.e. the one that is causally explicable), and the other, the critical experience, is the one that cannot be derived causally from the first.

(Jung, in Hannah 1991: 306)

When ego finds its existence threatened, it suddenly and deeply attunes to Self and opens to find meaning. This has nothing to do with a quality of the moment *qua* moment: it *has* to do with the way Self makes meaning under threat. We live in our theories of meaning, and of person. We express them in our language, which I will discuss in the next chapter.

# 8

# LANGUAGE AND THE
# STRUCTURE OF MYTH

'But "Glory" doesn't mean a "nice knock-down argument",'
Alice objected.

'When I use a word,' Humpty Dumpty said, in a rather
scornful tone, 'It means just what I choose it to mean –
neither more nor less.'

'The question is,' said Alice, 'whether you can make words
mean so many different things.'

'The question is,' said Humpty Dumpty, 'which is to be
Master – that's all.'

(Lewis Carroll, *Alice Through the Looking Glass*, 1965: 269)

## A nice knock-down argument?

As Humpty Dumpty makes clear, meaning is power. Meanings exist
in a language, a signifying system with intrinsic power dynamics.
Humpty, with his inflated pseudo-adult ego, is on top of the wall:
Alice, the child, is at the bottom. Negotiation is impossible. Any
language (verbal, gestural or figurative) has grammatical boundaries
and semantic differentials. Semantics is a part of natural philosophy
which studies meaning and its attribution. A 'semantic differential' is
the difference in understanding of structural linguistics between two
people, and shapes power dynamics between them. It includes the
right to give names, and a set of agreements over grammar. For
example, in his speech of surrender at the end of the Second World
War, Emperor Hirohito of Japan broadcast to the nation in court
Japanese, a language unchanged since the middle ages (imagine King
George VI of England making his victory speech in Chaucerian
English). Not surprisingly, Hirohito's listeners had no idea what he
was saying. The Emperor thus maintained an illusion of power.

Or, think of semantic differential as potential difference ('volts') in
the current of meaning ('amps') flowing between two signifying
systems. In electronics, volts (potential difference) divided by amps

(current) equals resistance: true in analysis, when there are differences naming objects. Who gives the names? I'll use semantics to examine the language of analysis, and language in analysis to see how meaning is attributed in analytic dialogue and how we can use these tools in reconstructing personal mythology.

## The language of analysis

Nominative power, ability to name, to form the language in and of a narrative, may lie with patient, analyst, both or neither; for, though each has equal value they do not start with the same nominative power. Acquiring fluency in symbolic translation is a two-way process. Analysts have spent longer developing their theory of mind, and speaking 'analytic language'.

Analytic languages can build impenetrable walls from jargon: perhaps renaming people 'objects' without saying why, or, equally, speaking in abstract, spiritualising vagaries. Ordinary people understand 'object' as 'a thing done to'. They get cross with 'object relations theory' if its users mistake a grammatical convention for pseudo-scientific 'rigorous' (stiff, unbending) objectification. Likewise, while it may seem comforting to reconstrue suffering as a spiritual gift, using archaisms, this can be felt as devastatingly patronising. Raising the nominative power of the analyst to 'spokesman for the baby' or 'spokesman for the divine in man' increases the semantic differential: as if a role for the analyst is to be surrogate mother or shamanic father.

If names increase the semantic distance between us and our patients, there is less room for affect. Analyst or patient, one becomes Humpty Dumpty, the other Alice, lost in a looking-glass world of 'part-objects', 'whole objects', and 'breast-penises' (Lewis Carroll's Victorian illustrator Tenniel might draw such a creature), or a fairy-land of 'prima materia', 'vasa hermetica', and alchemical retorts. We get mesmerised by magic words, forgetting, as Jung said, to take our theories *cum grano salis* – with a pinch of salt. The task of an analyst is to analyse, to 'do semantics': to reality test, humanise archetypes and allow completion of age-appropriate development. The aim is to permit individuation: finding one's own meaning. And, if we can't do these things, we could listen and remain ordinary in the presence of the extraordinary.

Languages let their speakers form concepts from percepts in specific, limited ways. Hours spent observing infants may teach us to talk 'infant observation'. This may teach us how to observe, or how to infantilise. Action follows thought. Taught to see certain phenomena between mother and infant, we'll see them. Told we'll see them in adults, then, there they are. So with archetypes or personality types – learn to see shadow, hero or anima, there they are too. If a fellow analyst meets me and opens with, 'Oh you're an ENTP' (guessing my Myers-Briggs personality inventory type, a Jungian's party-game), for them, I am. We invest our Self into our concepts: so, of course, they must exist. But if we invest in the concept of meaning, what are we investing in?

## Theories of person

We are investing in a theory of person. Such theories are intrinsically intersubjective; the correct pronoun is 'we', not 'he, she or it'. Theories of person are, after all, about us. We are in our meaning system and cannot create objectivity with pseudo-scientific objectifying language. In nominative relations theory, introduced in Chapter 1, to recognise objects, we must first name them consistently and reliably within a shared signifying system.

Maintaining a capacity to think in the face of another's overwhelming emotion and projective-identifications is easier (for me) if I keep to semantic tasks, tracking verbal and gestural narration for its meaning above 'the sound and fury, signifying nothing' (Shakespeare 1963b: *Macbeth* v. i: 15–16). In separating signal from noise, this resembles an anthropologist's participant-observation. I try to stay with physical sensations, be 'present' and 'not-present'. What our bodies say helps us recognise when complexes appear, as mismatches between spoken and gestural language occur when strings of meaning get 'tied in horrid knots inside' as in Hilaire Belloc's cautionary tale:

> At last he swallowed some which tied
> Itself in ugly Knots inside
> Physicians of the Utmost Fame
> Were called at once; but when they came
> They answered, as they took their Fees,
> There is no Cure for this Disease,
> Henry will very soon be dead.
>
> (1974: 17–20)

A meaning disorder (complex, or not) signifies a 'stuck' semantic differential. If nominative power moves only from 'them' to 'us', we have to swallow our feelings. Words stick in our throats. We may be so angry, astonished or amazed – we say 'Words fail me.' Analytical psychology treats complexes in archetypal metaphor as 'intrinsic structural contents', and in developmental metaphor as 'unfolding semantic patterns'.

Complexes form as archetypes 'install'. Archetypes, biological software for meaning, develop innate patterns: 'father archetype' develops fatherly behaviour. Developmentally, complexes are essential, non-pathological structures – unless an archetype installs prematurely. For example, ego is a complex with a vital reality testing function. Ego installs, according to Michael Fordham (1976: 18–32) through deintegrating and reintegrating of Self. This has age-appropriate phases, linking Self to other, distancing Self from other.

As genetic patterns for language-making exist within Self, then language ought to develop, if ego develops. If the patterns are imperfect at birth then the person has a congenital meaning disorder (in child psychiatry, called a semantic deficit disorder – early infantile autism, Asperger's syndrome, one of the multi-form dyslexias or an attention deficit disorder). If we can't attend, we can't make meaning. If, say, visuo-spatial awareness is impaired, then objects cannot be reliably named. Self cannot locate in space, it is 'autistic'. In these conditions there may be motor defects or stereotypic movements, there are always problems with language. If the patterns are present but inadequately humanised, the person has a primary meaning disorder.

Naming thoughts and feelings internally, communicating them both externally and internally (back to memory, forward into expectation) underpins theories of person. Problems arise if symbols become signs, if signs remain merely signs. Semantics, which neither infantilises nor spiritualises, can evaluate these theories and their place in a culture, as I'll show in the next chapter. Here, to illustrate how this applies in clinical practice, I'll tell a story about a man with alexithymia, a Greek word meaning 'with no names for feelings'. I'll apply semantics to the unconscious processes between us, to 'show the working' in treating a primary meaning disorder.

### *Clinical example – Jacques*

Jacques speaks five languages fluently, yet, starting analysis, he can't name his feelings in any. A dark, attractive man, whose family live in Brussels, a freelance journalist, he came initially because of difficulties with his girlfriend. He has a son by another woman, both of whom he hardly ever sees. On first entering my consulting room, I felt as if I was greeting a child frightened in the night. Reassurance came as he gradually learnt to make the soothing words and gestures of a parent to himself; turning on the light, discovering the 'nameless terror' was a fold in the curtains.

Alexithymia describes a state in which we have sensations but do not know what they mean as feelings. For Jacques, I could say there was failure of primary attachment. Achieving object-constancy was difficult or near-impossible, for, if there is no empathy, then there is no attachment. His mother lost her whole family in Auschwitz and herself hardly survived the Camp. His father, at sixteen, fled Warsaw and, after many harrowing adventures, ended up in Belgium. Jacques mother, unable to locate herself as a Camp kid, could hardly locate her infant – neither could his father: both were handling unbearable suffering and meaninglessness, common in holocaust survivors (see Dreifuss, in Samuels 1989b: 309–26).

### Symbol formation

Jacques was trapped, words for feelings were walled off. There were paradoxical operators: attachment signified separation, intimacy signified isolation. As parts of his languages re-installed, his complex lost its nominative power, its 'Oh, God, here I go again' quality. A symbol formed in a dream, the dream of *The Cat in the Bottle*. When Jacques told it to me we both, quite unconsciously, switched from English (my first language) to French, Jacques' childhood language. This helped us separate the language of use (dream content, French) from language of structure (dream form, analysed in English).

Jacques described to me his dream in which he is a boy again and sees a cat stuck in a bottle. He told me in monotone English (his adult language); phonemes slurred and became inaudible. Simultaneously he flushed, breathing shallowed and his jugular venous pressure and heart rate went up (it's easier to read body-language when using a couch). Mismatch between content and form, use and structure, words said with no feeling, clinical signs of strong emotion plus sensations of emptiness in my stomach told me *The Cat in the Bottle* was a potential symbol. It had a high semantic differential – 'high voltage' – it meant a lot for me, not much for him.

Remembering archetypes are genetic blueprints unfolding into meaning was useful here. As Jung said, archetypes have a biological and a spiritual pole. The biological pole is the DNA: giving tendencies to make meaning in certain ways. Highly social mammals, we reconfigure these tendencies into strategies at each *rite de passage* (*CW* 8: para. 420). Jacques felt he'd failed to make the passage to adulthood: he was a father who did not believe he was a man. He did not understand the semiotics of 'fathering', couldn't work on them with his son or his inner child. A possible reading of the dream could be, 'He's the cat, separated from his child.'

Imagining problems in his early life could give us a 'theory' which could 'explain' why he's like this. I could invent plausible tales about breasts and suckling. But such myths have a logical error – *post hoc, ergo propter hoc*. Whatever the dream meant, Jacques and I had to first of all find what the signs mean 'now', then, what they meant 'then'. We do so by examining the structure, the order in which signs appear.

We treat boy, cat and bottle as *signs* and *signifiers*. The words signifier (noun) and signified (adjective) bring together images (boy, cat and bottle) and concepts – all the meanings boy, cat and bottle might have – the signified. Signifier and signified are ways of speaking about equivalence, not equality. There are equivalencies between 'the boy in the dream', 'Jacques as a boy', 'Jacques' son', 'Dale as a boy' and 'all boys', but not equality. The signifier {boy} is a sign. The signified could be {infant experience} or {the child archetype}. The signifier {bottle} could signify {mother}, {container}, {analyst}. The signifier {cat} could signify {helplessness} or {Jacques as a child} or {X . . . an unknown}.

Myths have the semiotic form, *if* a *then* b, *if* b *then* c: so, *if* a *then* c, a syllogism. They make meaning by leaving something out (Barthes 1972: 117–74). If bottle then container, if container then mother: so, if bottle, then mother. Or, if boy then bottle, if bottle then cat: so, if boy, then cat – the cat is the boy, the boy is the cat. If {bottle signifies mother} and {mother equals alchemical vessel}: so, {analyst equals mother} then {bottle equals analytic container}. We can let anything signify anything else.

Analysts do this sort of mental juggling very quickly. Myth is a condensation of meaning: if bottle, then mother as container – if container then analyst – so, if bottle, then analytic container. Notice, 'mother' is left out. Or, if boy, then bottle; if bottle then cat; if boy, then cat – bottle is missed out. Analysts can mind-game with symbols forever, but we sometimes forget how the result, which may seem to us a casual observation, can seem like telepathy (paranoia, intrusion, hermetic wisdom or 'good mothering' . . .). The child-in-the-adult needs to find out *himself* that he feels like a cat in a bottle now. I made a semantic interpretation. It is not mutative (change producing), it is an attempt to start a meaningful translation, an intra-mural dialogue between Jacques' Self and his ego. I said, maybe . . .

D: 'When we switched unconsciously from English to French, Jacques, we spoke street-French, like boys . . .'
J: 'Yes, but we spoke Polish and . . . (hesitates) . . . Yiddish at home.'
D: 'So you still can't speak your parents' tongue . . . is your problem your own anti-Semitism?'

The family myth is 'Jews are not supposed to exist: we exist, therefore we are not Jewish.' Here is Jacques, a journalist, fluent in five languages – Yiddish, Polish, French, English and Japanese: a real person, existing for me in a confiding analytic space, and 'a myth', who now exists in public, in a fictionalised (mythical) account (Tuckett 1993). Our session may have continued:

Jacques feels 'flat'. I sense emptiness, and say,

D: 'The cat is a sign. I wonder what it symbolises?'
J: 'Moi, un petit garçon, pris dans le bouteille . . . le pauvre chat . . .'

He starts to cry.

His complex is a knot in his meaning-string. In English, his meaning-system is closed. 'Cat' *only* signifies trapped. English is, for him, the cold, experience-distant language of a cold, rainy country. The climate signifies the people (and his cold, distant analyst). He explains he loves jazz, he refers to himself and his teenage friends as *les cool cats*. His parents want him to like Mahler, a good Jewish composer. In French, in adolescence, *un chat* signified friend/jazz lover: his adolescent capacity for feeling and for change is bottled up.

I asked him to tell me the dream in each language he speaks, in turn.

In Japanese, he weeps at the cat's beauty.
In Polish, he senses the cat's rage.
In Yiddish, he howls with compassion for the cat.
In French . . . he can't speak.

He says the cat is himself, a boy trapped by his family's holocaust survivor mind-set. As Chris Hauke (1998) says, 'Childhood means nothing without a context,' and neither does a dream. I discuss with Jacques the difference between sign and symbol. Maybe I say,

> 'The sign "cat" is a symbol in the sentence, "The cat is in the bottle". Cat is a symbol for separated.'

Jacques in his present relationship, in the here-and-now relationship with me and with his parents felt like a trapped child. This is a classical transference triangle, between past-current analytic relationship (Malan 1982: 92–4). Maybe Jacques felt this way with his mother, he feels like this with his girlfriend and with me . . . but we need not argue backwards from effect to cause. Even if he felt that *then*, does the insight help *now*?

### Semiotics and analysis

Christopher Hauke (1998) describes how 'analysing "the child in the adult" has become the royal road to the unconscious'. He continues:

> this crude reductionism is only partly attributable to the attitudes and discoveries of Freud . . . in Kleinian thought especially, it is still infantile instinctual drives that are the motor of the object relating that is going on . . . Jung's theory of the archetypes already accounts for the instincts in a more satisfactory psychological way, not so dependent on chronology and diachrony, thus reducing the need for emphasis on the child as the locus of our instinctual nature and its struggles.
>
> (Hauke 1998: 18)

An 'inner child' has context, family and social setting. If we only use a theory of 'mother and baby', all we do is 'talk baby talk' when we re-mythologise. But, perhaps, it is the form itself that soothes? As a junior doctor in the East End of London I'm called to casualty. 'Gorra pain in me bleedin' wossname, doctor,' says a perky young cockney girl. 'Oh, which part of your wossname . . . ?', I ask. She grins cheekily at me, 'You tell me! You're the fucking doctor!'

My power to name is, itself, soothing. Or, an analytic fairy-story: Marie Louise von Franz supposedly once made a fifty minute interpretation. I imagine, that, when telling the story (in the bar?) afterwards the recipient of her largesse was asked:

*A:* ' . . . but did you understand what she meant?'
*B:* 'No . . .'
*A:* 'So, was it a waste of time, then? Her interpretation?'
*B:* 'Oh no!, I knew Dr. von Franz understood what she was talking about! Then I felt much better!'

My first analyst used this classical technique occasionally, calling it 'baroque interpretation': 'Take all the dreams, all the personal history, the transference and counter-transference, the object relations, Oedipus and his mother . . . add a few gilt plaster cherubs . . . stir well. Add a myth. Cook for fifty minutes.' She used the myth of Hephaestus, knowing I'd understand 'laming' literally (after polio as a boy, I was lame for months). She used all the information she had to allow that experience to become symbolic.

The Greek God, Hephaestus, brother to Apollo, like the Vedic god of fire, Agni, is a purifier. He allows metal to be worked by the blacksmith, or alchemist (Larousse 1989: 126–30). This myth helped transform a near-death experience frozen in my psyche into a symbol. She showed me there was a limit to meaning-making: some things are beyond meaning. As she said, 'There's no point trying to make sense of the senseless.'

Contemporary Jungians take meaning in language as pluralistic: a text with a multitude of meanings. Which meaning is selected depends on the purpose (and free will) of the persons choosing. Meaning is a matter of choice, an object for cultural negotiation. Jung, in *Psychotherapists or the Clergy* explored the problem by contrasting two overlapping meaning systems, psychology and religion:

> though the theories of Freud and Adler come much nearer to getting to the bottom of the neuroses than any earlier approach from the medical side, their exclusive concern with the instincts fails to satisfy the deeper spiritual needs of the patient. They are too much bound by the premises of nineteenth century science, too matter of fact, and they give too little value to fictional and imaginative processes. In a word, they do not give enough meaning to life, and it is only meaning that liberates. Ordinary reasonableness, sound human judgement, science as a compendium of common sense, they certainly help us over a good part of the road, but they never take us beyond the frontiers of life's most commonplace realities, beyond the merely average and normal. They afford no answer to the question of psychic suffering and its

profound significance. A psychoneurosis must be understood, ultimately, as the suffering of a soul which has not
discovered its meaning.

(*CW* 11: paras 496–7)

## Myth: a form of speech

If neurosis is suffering in a soul which has lost its meaning then
treating neurosis depends on its meaning, and not its origin; what it
means now, not what it meant then. Now subsumes then. Symptoms
have a purpose, a teleology (a knowing of place), demanding we find
new meaning. Change may occur in the meaning of a few words in a
vocabulary: 'is' may become 'as if'; concrete thinking may become
symbolic, if the attunement of the analyst leads to a reparative
change of names. Sometimes this is enough, sometimes not. The
analyst is Alice, not Humpty Dumpty high on a wall of theoretical
bricks.

Linguistic scholars study use (content) and structure (form). An
example of 'use' is literary criticism. Sociology, politics and
psychology study what is said, by whom, to whom and when. They
perform 'content analysis', look at a story, how it's told, analyse
narration. Analysing form looks at structures in a narration. 'Form
based' disciplines, looking at the parts in a narrative, include
semantics, linguistics, communications theory and depth psychology.

Special names are given to linguistic units: *phonemes* for sounds,
*morphemes* for words or gestures, grammar and syntax for forms in a
sentence. These parts move together according to sets of underlying
rules, 'transformational generative grammars' (Chomsky, in Lyons
1970: 47–55), which flex one meaning structure around another.
Roland Barthes, the French structuralist, in *Mythologies* (1972:
117–74) defines structuralism as a science dealing with value and its
attribution, that is, with feeling. Structuralism studies how sign and
symbol relate in signifying systems to make meaning, and comments
on the validity of meanings so derived.

Barthes argues that knowledge and epistemology are subjects for
linguistic analysis. Neither the form or content of knowledge exist
without words, grammar and syntax. The key to knowing (meaning)
lies in understanding the structures by which we know. Semiotics
is science applied to meaning. It works on deep structures – the
archetypes of, and in, language. One such structure is myth.

Structuralists define metaphor as 'a form of speech between a
symbol and sign'. Myths form when a metaphor is used in a

narrative. Chambers defines a metaphor as a 'figure of speech by which a thing is spoken of as being that which it only resembles, as when a ferocious person is called a tiger'. Similarly, a sad little boy might be called a cat in a bottle (or a boy terrified of staying lame is called 'Hephaestus'). Metaphor implies fluidity of meaning, ambivalence, *between-ness* (Siegelman 1990: 36–41, 101–07) which permits pluralism. Metaphors use logical operators, as in Hindi, *Usco-isco* (this thing and that thing), or, in Latin, *alii-alii* (some-others).

In the famous story of the blind men of Hindustan and the elephant, each of the six men touched only one part of the elephant. One, holding the trunk, says, 'The elephant is like a hose;' another, holding the tail, says 'No, it is like a rope;' a third, holding a leg, says, 'No, it's like a tree . . .' and so on. Each gives a true description of the part-object they perceive. Each is correct, and each wrong if they stick to one interpretation, naming only one part of the signifying system {elephant}.

Closed systems tend to mistake parts for wholes, open systems tend to mistake wholes for parts. Work on meaning as a whole object, I believe, underpins any analytic gesture. An elephant, we know, has a solid boundary: the boundary between conscious and unconscious is ever-changing, like the boundary between beach and ocean. It is a fractal pattern (there is one on the cover of this book), which shows self-similarity; whatever the magnification, the pattern stays the same. As the pattern is ever-shifting, we can only describe the rules which make it up – its generative grammar – rather than it as a thing in itself. When we interpret a symbol, we apply theories of signification. It has content and value (feeling) form, but its use and structure change from minute to minute.

## Sign and symbol

In a dream or narrative, what constitutes a sign? A sign describes a known. A sign is an icon *plus* a concept. An icon is only an image, picture or gesture. Usually there are direct, concrete relations between the icon used in a sign and the concept. A cross, signifier of a Roman State execution method, came to symbolise God's love for his creation. A lotus, a flower growing in mud, came to symbolise the Buddha nature, the link between samsara and nirvana.

Signs relate image to concept. {30 on a white background in a red circle} is an icon. It has no meaning till part of a language, a signifying system – road signs. Signs always have a lexicon, like the list of road signs at the back of a road atlas. A symbol is a sign plus {X}, when {X} is an unknowable – it is not an unknown which could become a known. There may be a relation between the content of the sign and the concept symbolised, but this is unquantifiable, as symbols 'express in a unique way psychological facts incapable of being grasped by consciousness in any other way.' They are 'two contradictory elements being held together . . .' (*CW* 6: paras 818–29). They cannot have a lexicon.

In Jacques' dream, separation is signified by the icon 'the cat in the bottle', yet he has no word for that feeling. The bottle, for me, was a symbol for separation, for Jacques, a sign. 'It is perfectly possible for a man to establish a fact which does not appear in the least symbolic to himself, but is profoundly so to another consciousness' (*CW* 6: para. 818). Myth is a form of speech: a structure in the form of a dialogue, for Barthes.

Analytic theory – indeed, any theory – is a narrative myth. Myth does *not* mean false; it means a narrative of a particular form. The French semiologist saw mythology as partly a science of form, and partly of ideology. Mythology is the study of ideas in form, their evolution over time, of archetypes and development. At least three features of myths can be recognised:

1  A myth isn't an object, a concept or an idea. It is a mode of signification within a semiological system
2  Any object can be mythologised – and thus opened to social appropriation
3  Myths do not, necessarily, arise 'from the things themselves'. The content is not intrinsic to the structure

Myth, says Barthes, form from two statements collapsing into one, leaving out a linking concept. By convention, the first statement is called 'the first system' {I am a boy} and the second statement 'the second system' {I see a cat in a bottle}. Myth forms when the signified in the first system becomes the signifier in the second: when {an associative image plus a concept} becomes {an image}. The myth is: the boy is the cat in the bottle.

Myth shapes language and perception. To myth, language is a subsystem. An example is in the ways the *Sun* and the *Times* newspapers reported the death of Lady Diana, Princess of Wales, turning her into a fairy-tale Princess. To see what mythologisation looks like you could read how 'developmental analysts' or 'archetypal analysts' made meaning from that same event (Haynes and Shearer 1998).

The language used determines what can be thought, argues

Barthes, and whether it can be said. Myth systems lead us to certain kinds of conclusion, to collect observations on that basis, and attribute meaning to certain signs, not others. The analytical psychologist's definition of myth is arguable: here is one from Joseph Campbell: 'A myth is . . . the function of nature and culture necessary to balanced maturation of the psyche – a carrier of archetypal content' (1991: 3). Can analysis release the archetypal elements in a myth from various local matrices and culturally conditioned references? It can, if myth is a linguistic enzyme, a culture-catalyst with a biological function. Culture creates a huge network to protect an infant against the experience of loss. Society is a social womb, symbols are the milk. Another definition of myth starts with dreams, psychic connections explicable in terms of myths:

> The pre-conditions for myth formation are pre-existent in the psyche – that is, the collective unconscious, which is a reservoir of archetypal experiences and themes, where myths are stories of archetypal encounter, metaphors for working out archetypes. The aim of all this is individuation . . . a dialogue with archetypal processes, mediated through myth.
>
> (Samuels *et al.* 1986)

Myths, therefore, humanise archetypes: inherited parts of the psyche, irrepresentable in themselves, evident only through their manifestation: all form and no content, numinous, unconscious and autonomous biopsychic seizures which need . . .

### . . . a symbolic attitude to assign meaning intersubjectively

In the myth 'analysis', analyst is both observer and participant. Fantasies about the (m)other's psychological processes are directed at us. Different analytic myths reflect different fantasies about a semiotic task, developing a symbolic attitude. This lets us and our patients learn to give meaning intersubjectively: to attain agency, coherence, continuity and form affective relationships. Jacques and I spontaneously changed languages when we noticed our lack of affective relating about his dream: an attempt by our 'collective unconscious' to talk to the cat in the bottle. Imagine this is what happened:

*D:* (singing) 'Ding dong bell, pussy's in the well, who put him in . . .?'

(I do not speak the language of his infancy (Yiddish). Instead, I associate to a childhood song).

J:    *'Moi!'*
      (In the dream, the first system is {the boy sees the cat in the bottle}. The second system is {being in a bottle means separated}).

D:    '. . . you dreamed of childhood separation.'
      (The cat signifies {separated}. If we take {separated}, and expand . . .).

D:    '. . . *vous avez l' impression qu' il y a un mur de verre entre vous et votre mere . . .'*
      (This is a myth).

J:    (crying) *'Et aussi, avec toi.'*

Being able to form and use symbols in a developmentally appropriate way marks successful linking between ego and Self along the ego–Self axis (Edinger 1962). Depth psychologists agree ego is a reality-testing area in the psyche, operating in chronological time. Self describes a sum of all potentials an individual could express. If communication is impaired between ego and Self, as in my patient, it's hard to link to parts of the psyche or to others. Failure of symbolisation creates a primary meaning disorder. In Jacques, internal splits interrupted communication between ego and Self. The growth of a capacity to symbolise followed the interpretation. We used active imagination: Jacques imagined the boy freeing the cat.

## Meaning and not-meaning

With patience, we wove a new myth using dream, synchronicity (he met my cat on the mat the day he brought the dream) and fragments of personal history (he was a 'jazz cat'). Curious juxtapositions of transference and counter-transference with personal history occur as we play our own mythology into and on to any one else. We'd both had experiences of childhood separation: mine through illness, his through the psychological 'absence' of his parents, still 'bottling up' their own traumas. In French, I'm a schoolboy; I can only speak to Jacques boy to boy, not mother to son. I amplify his words with my sense-response. Semantically, I notice when his language loses affect, and I acquire sensation.

When projective-identification occurs there is a resonance in two semantic structures, two value systems. When Jacques says *'Ma mère est de glace'* (My mother is ice), he's using a concrete metaphor. The hairs on my neck rise. My body adds gesture to words, changing and charging the signification of mother. I tell him. He laughs, *'Oui, j'ai peur d'elle,'* then, in English, 'she scares me.' Soft, with a still body, he tells me about being left outside on his tricycle when he was little, wanting his mother, but afraid what she might do if she heard him cry. I re-imagined a time when my go-cart broke. My father was there to help. So, I asked where his father was.

*'Au travail . . . ,'* he said.

Analytic work is like aesthetic criticism (studying the patient's myths) and semantics (studying their structure). Jacques' dream-text, as it changed through his five languages, showed he did have feelings, but they were 'bottled up'. In this renarration neither Jacques nor I believe we have recovered lost memory, relived infantile traumas at the breast, or connected his psyche to archetypal patterns. Nor have we 'unlocked the power of his higher self by liberating his wounded inner child'.

We are doing hermeneutics, playing with meaning, a game named after Hermes: trickster, god of crossroads, thresholds, liminal places; god of thieves, shepherds and magi, conductor of souls in the land of the dead (Kerenyi 1976). Jung had Hermes in mind in 1940 when he wrote *Transformation Symbols in the Mass* (*CW* 11: paras 296–448). Christ, with an early infant experience involving shepherds and magi, is a symbol for the suffering Self. But do we believe, 'The crucifixion was a direct consequence of the shepherds interfering with Jesus's first feed?' Hermetic tricks deconstruct meaning, allowing us to play in an intersubjective field. The term intersubjective was given by George Atwood:

> psychoanalysis seeks to illuminate phenomena that emerge within a specific psychological field constituted by the inter-section of two subjectivities – that of the patient and that of the analyst – (it is) a science of the intersubjective, focused on the interplay between the differently organised subjective worlds of the observer and the observed. The observational stance is always one within, rather than outside, the inter-subjective field . . . being observed, a fact that guarantees the centrality of introspection and empathy as the methods of observation . . . psychoanalysis is unique among the sciences in that the observer is also the observed . . .
>
> (Atwood 1984: 2–7)

It arises from an overlap of two perceptual sets: analyst's and patient's. The intersubjective field is the *between* area, the common ground, the language of word and gesture. My sense of 'I' in analysis – 'these thoughts are mine, these feelings are mine, this is really my consulting room and it's really three o'clock' – let me treat everything else (subliminal, pre-conscious and unconscious perceptions) as valid counter-transferential response. The intersubjective field has, as boundaries, two projective surfaces, the phenomena in the room as perceived by each person present. At this surface signification occurs.

So, when presented with a distressing dream image which gives me a gut reaction I ask, 'What's going on?' 'OK,' says my analysing mind, 'These "historical events" he's talking about? You know, they're re-imagination, not legal fact. His mother might be mourning the death of all her family in the gas ovens, does that make her a bad person?' I don't have to think so. But he feels it so. He felt she was separated from him by a glass wall – by a bottle . . . 'did she drink . . . or was she addicted to feeling sad? This is a feeling, his feeling. So, why am I feeling sad?' And so on . . .

I don't know whether I did think like that. It's a myth, using my 'inner voice' as a metaphor. Later, I did use a baroque interpretation, amplifying his story with Jung's story, *The Spirit Mercurius* (*CW* 13: paras 239–303). In it, a boy is out cutting wood with his father. He finds a glass bottle under a tree. When he opens it a Genie comes out. The Genie is furious at being imprisoned, and threatens to kill the boy at once. The boy says, 'All right! You can kill me. But I don't believe a Genie as big as you could possibly have come out of such a tiny bottle.' 'Oh no?' goes the Genie, 'Watch this!' And, of course, the stupid Genie gets back in the bottle.

Opening Jacques' complex was like releasing the Genie. It was essential to get the cat, the despairing, clawing furious cat of his feelings, back into the bottle. Jacques needed space to allow his mind to digest, to deintegrate without disintegration. I used the myth to help him, as a container (as my analyst had done with 'Hephaestus'). I told him how the genie, once back in the bottle, promised to be helpful. The boy let him out, and the genie showed him where three gold pieces were hidden. The boy used the money to learn medicine, to learn to heal.

## The language of meaning in analysis

Our capacity to form and use myth lets us make symbols out of anything that comes along. This speaks of a deep, inborn need to give meaning in our lives. We are meaning-making animals. We have to develop meaning, because survival of infancy and successful socialisation depend on it. Meaning is an archetypal experience, we can't help making it: in paranoid states we may wish we could, in depressive states we *know* we can't. In either position, meaning collapses.

Modes of concrete, abstract and symbolic thought evolve in a developmental sequence as archetypes install. We can take 'paranoid' or 'depressive' to refer to a style of internal narration. Arrest or delay in the first mode predisposes to 'paranoid ideation', a persecutory internal language which leaves us trapped in a concrete, objectifying world. We find the world full of 'hard autistic objects'; Jacques reconstructively imagined his mother as a woman who could not interpret his cries of distress. Overwhelming grief prevented her accurately naming his cries. Delay in the second mode prompts 'depressive ideation'. We *can* abstract from events, but place ourselves at the centre of all signifying – if something is wrong, then it's our fault.

Jacques then had a paranoid dream – 'The North Koreans are coming to get me'. In my counter-transference, I felt guilty, and guessed he might too. 'North Koreans' appeared as we interpreted the cat dream. They were 'border guards' and I'd gone too near 'de fences'. He felt paranoid, I felt depressed. A third mode, the symbolic, oscillates between the first two modes (positions). It brings a capacity for ambivalence which Melanie Klein said was the defining characteristic of an open system (1975: 1–25). Symbolic modes of speech and thought use both/and (and other pluralistic logical operators) rather than either/or, if/then. By definition, a symbol is {a sign plus X}, where {X} is an unknowable. Symbolising systems remain open. If {X} is known, the symbol has become a sign, and has closed.

Symbols live when full of meaning and decay as meaning precipitates out. The languages of depth psychology, developmental and archetypal, use metaphors of process, of journey. Both talk in experience-near words about individuation, defined as

> becoming a distinct self separate from others: ego is to integration what self is to individuation – consciousness may be

developed by analysis of ego defences and ego structure, but the self is always in a perambulation about the self.

(Samuels *et al.* 1986: 76–9)

## The place of meaning in analysis

Symbolic thought, with its cultural prevalence and power, is part of the collective unconscious. It provides, through the social matrix, mothering when 'mother' fails. 'Old wives' tales', fairy-stories and dreams mythologise us to ourselves; eulogise and satirise, re-member, carrying percepts and cultural history. People with this social function are called culture carriers. Herman Hesse, in *The Glass Bead Game* gave a novelistic treatment of semiotics (1946: 15–44). Glass beads are symbols. The game began as a toy for musicians and mathematicians, elaborated until each 'bead' represented an experience drawn from any field of human culture. The beads can be connected into sequences, which give life meaning. Ironically, in the end, Knecht (the hero, a Master of the Glass Bead Game) feels there is more to life than playing with symbols and leaves the sheltered scholar-world of Castalia. Hesse and Jung were friends with many interests in common: Chinese Philosophy, I Ching and Alchemy among them. Hesse had analysis in 1916, at the time of the death of his father, the serious illness of a child, and the breakdown of his wife. His analyst, Dr. Josef Lang, was supervised by Jung. Hesse wrote of the experience:

> There is . . . the lasting profit that might be called the possession of the 'inner relationship to the subconscious'. He experiences a warmer, more fruitful, and more ardent exchange between the conscious and the subconscious; his gain in this is clarity about many things that otherwise remain beneath the threshold and are enacted only in unnoticed dreams.
>
> (Zeller 1972: 84–5)

Semiotics helps give clarity about the 'many things that otherwise remain beneath the threshold'. Analysts look for semantic differentials in the narrative, to find where meanings have formed closed systems, for complexes and their resolution involves not only reinterpreting early experience but also a reconnection to the collective unconscious and the culture, through myths, which I will explore next.

# 9

# MYTH AND CULTURE

'Narnia?' she said. 'Narnia? I have often heard your Lord-
ship utter that name in your ravings. Dear Prince, you are
very sick. There is no land called Narnia.'
'Yes there is though, Ma'am,' said Puddleglum. 'You see, I
happen to have lived there all my life.'

(C. S. Lewis, *The Silver Chair*, 1953: 150)

## Belief and illusion?

The previous chapter looked at how language shapes what can be
said and what can be thought. Belief and illusion are constructions
of a meaning-making mind confronted with experiences beyond
words. Aged nine, Belfast-born boy Clive Lewis had such an experience when his mother died of breast cancer. With his elder brother
Warren, the orphans invented imaginary worlds based on Norse and
Greek mythology. They needed to create meaning in a world
suddenly made meaningless by mother's death and father's abandonment of them to his grief (Lancelyn Green and Hooper 1974:
19–49).

> The tragic tale was invented in ages that long preceded psy-
> chotherapy, and already at the time of its origins it sought to
> serve the very same purpose which its re-discovery was to
> posit for itself in the course of the last century: not pleasure,
> but meaning.
>
> (Zoja, in Casement 1998: 33–51)

Myths speak symbolic language, common to the collective
unconscious, and can transform painful realities. They are a cultural
aspect of the transcendent function. Strictly, myths differ from fairytales. The time-frame is not 'once upon a time' but 'when the world
began . . . dreamtime' (Kast 1996); 'when the world was new and all',
they're *Just So Stories* (Kipling 1987). Wilfred Bion called them

'basic assumptions' (Bion 1961: 158–65), all-subsuming meaning systems which add or subtract value, ethic and meaning.

As an adult, C. S. Lewis created the magical land of Narnia (1951). Frozen in the icy grip of the White Witch (a life-denying, terrible mother: villain of *The Lion, the Witch and the Wardrobe*), Narnia is liberated by the death and rebirth of its Lion-King, Aslan. While knowing an author's history isn't necessary to enjoy his story, it lets us deconstruct the purpose behind the narrative. We could imagine the White Witch represents his dead mother, and the story is a way of expressing inexpressible feelings of murderous rage at her for 'turning his world into a thousand years of winter'.

The form is a Christian allegory, written from Lewis's heart. The meaning of a symbol (Aslan), depends on *substance* (structural elements), *set* (who is narrating to whom), and *setting* (personal, familial and cultural). To Christians, the Lion, Aslan, signifies Christ. To a child raised on the African Savannah, 'lion' means a lion. The first is a symbol, the second a sign.

Analysis is a healing renarration of personal mythology which turns signs into symbols (Covington 1995). Myths are cultural tools which help us understand suffering, and use it creatively. As Mark Twain did by creating Tom Sawyer and Huck Finn, so Clive Lewis used his awful childhood experiences as source energy for *The Silver Chair*. Two bullied kids are called by Aslan to Narnia to rescue its rightful King, Prince Rilian, a young hero. A Green Witch, Queen of the Under Land, used drugs to keep him prisoner in her underworld kingdom. She tries to drug the children too, to get them to believe her myth: Narnia is an illusion. Puddleglum, their guide, bravely grinds out her magic fire with his bare foot saying:

> Suppose we have only dreamed or made up all those things – trees and grass and sun and moon and stars and Aslan himself. Suppose we have, then all I can say is that, in that case, the made up things seem a good deal more important than the real ones.
>
> (Lewis 1953: 156)

A classics scholar, Lewis reworks Plato's 'Cave' simile to show the difference between belief and illusion. In Plato's myth, percepts are a shadow of an image of the 'real thing' projected on to the cave wall. This, his translator Desmond Lee noted:

> is the moral and intellectual condition of the average man

from which Plato starts; and though clearly the ordinary man knows the difference between substance and shadow in the physical world, the simile suggests that his moral and intellectual opinions often bear as little relation to the truths as the average film or television programme does to real life.

(Plato, ed. and trans. Lee 1955: 316)

'Symbols are not allegories and are not signs, they are images of contents which, for the most part, transcend consciousness' (*CW* 5: para. 114). They have a {both/and/neither/nor} logical operator. Meaning, value and ethics link in culture-bound myths, symbolic communications {both/and/neither/nor} belief and illusion. In Chapter 2, I looked at *how* we individuate, now I'm looking at *where* we individuate, and what we individuate *with*. Do we use our myths, their myths, or both? Clearly, both. This is an argument about locus of control: who validates a myth?

Deconstructing the illusion 'inside and outside' is necessary. No individual (even a Hermit) can exist outside the collective. This reverses the immoral fib given in 1987 by British Premier Margaret Thatcher – 'There's no such thing as society.' Jung said there's no such thing as an individual:

Individualism means deliberately stressing and giving prominence to some supposed peculiarity rather than to collective considerations and obligations. But individuation means precisely the better and more complete fulfilment of collective qualities.

(*CW* 7: para. 269)

Neither Self nor ego are 'real' when viewed from the collective. They are cultural constructs, analytic heuristics. To imagine two opening and closing systems dynamically interacting, deintegrating and reintegrating, is also a construct. Self and ego are ideas, not facts. This constructivist argument developed in analytical psychology through the work (amongst others) of Louis Zinkin in London and Polly Young-Eisendrath in Vermont. Constructivists see development as a co-responsibility between mother and infant. They argue there is not (nor could there ever be) a state of undifferentiated separateness: no infant is an island. There is no primary, undifferentiated Self. We only exist as and in relationship, as described by Zen master and scholar of comparative religion Masao Abe in 'The Self in Jung and Zen' (1992: 128–140).

In Zen, there is no Self. The English analyst Warren Coleman (2000: 13), summarising the argument, points out that to assume a primary Self is to ask a Zen koan, 'What is the face you had before you were born . . . ?' Any answer has to be a myth (a 'Just-so story'). The content of a personal (developmental/archetypal) myth is unique, but its form (social involvement) is universal.

> In this sense there is a considerable difference between the archetype and the historical formula that it has evolved. Especially on the higher levels of esoteric teaching the archetypes appear in a form that reveals quite unmistakably the critical and evaluating influence of conscious elaboration. Their immediate manifestation, as we encounter it in dreams and visions, is much more individual, less understandable, and more naive than in myths, for example. The archetype is essentially an unconscious content that is altered by becoming conscious and by being perceived, and it takes its colour from the individual consciousness in which it happens to appear.
>
> (*CW* 9i: para. 6)

Myths describe delicate balances in naming rights between individuals and societies: do I call aggression what you call assault? What forms of intra- and inter-personal conduct do we see as necessary and sufficient for a free society? Analytical psychology gives us instruments to study naming rights in social systems. It makes semantic observations to measure competing political, scientific and religious myths about meaning for individuals in society: as, to an analytical psychologist, these fit together like Jung's 'infra-red' and 'ultraviolet' ends of the archetypal spectrum. Cultural myths are, themselves, 'made up things'–heuristics. As Puddleglum said, 'the made up things seem a good deal more important than the real ones . . .'

## Myth is a form of speech

Chambers dictionary defines a myth as 'an ancient traditional story of gods or heroes, especially one offering an explanation of some event; a story with a veiled meaning; a commonly held belief which is untrue.' The French semiotician Roland Barthes argued myths are constructed from two statements put together with subtraction of meaning (1972: 124), and anything can be mythologised. The

American analytical psychologist Joseph Campbell took an opposite view, arguing myths form when two statements are put together, adding meaning. Both may be right: Barthes takes myth as illusion; Campbell, myth as belief.

Myths are cultural equivalents of stimulus-meaning, social gestures designed to generate self-similar relational patterns and are intended to produce similar affect states in their audience. Barthes says myth is a type of speech, a mode of signification requiring two statements. A sign in the first statement becomes a signifier in the second. In the process, something is lost. Condensation occurs. In his essay 'Soap Powders and Detergents' he gives an example of how this trick is done:

> These products have been in the last few years the object of such massive advertising that they now belong to a region of French daily life which the various types of psycho-analysis would do well to pay some attention to if they wish to keep up to date. One could then usefully contrast the psycho-analysis of purifying fluids (chlorinated, for example) with those of soap powders (Lux, Persil) or that of detergents (Omo). The relations between the evil and cure, between dirt and a given product are very different in each case.
>
> (1972: 40–3)

Cleaning fluids are holy liquid fire, slaying dirt. Powders purify, detergent militant drives out demon dirt, liberating the garment. Religious metaphors sanctify soap. Appropriation of sacred imagery by soap salesmen, for Barthes, then, is about concealing meaning, closing it into a jingle – 'OMO . . . your washday Saviour!' A hallmark of the petit-bourgeois mind, he believed, is using myth to appropriate cultural products, to label and typify, bureaucratise and systematise, to prevent changes which threaten stability: myths are for conservation. And, by determining who has locus of control in a culture, myths dilute difference.

In analytic mythopoesis, jingles like 'good-enough mother', 'alchemical vessel' or 'negative counter-transference' have a similar function. They are beliefs and illusions – not facts. In contrast, in *The Flight of the Wild Gander* Joseph Campbell says:

> myths are a function of nature as well as of culture, and as necessary to the balanced maturation of the human psyche as is nourishment to the body . . . I have revived a formula,

first proposed by Kant, for the release of the archetypal
symbolic images of mythic thought from their various
matrices of culturally conditioned references and 'meaning'
so that, viewed apart from the uses to which they have been
applied in the social provinces of human life, they may be
recognised in themselves as natural phenomena . . .

(1991: 3)

Campbell suggests individuation releases archetypal elements
enclosed by local culturally-conditioned myths into open systems,
expressing what can be said only poetically, if at all. Analysts, like
Celtic Bards, create and interpret myth-symbols. The San Francisco
analyst Joseph Henderson said this is done by 'combining two or
more apparently incompatible things at the same moment without
any disturbance to the rational mind, a natural habit of an aesthetic
mode of thought' (1988: 53–4). Jacques, in the previous chapter
combined boy/cat/bottle to symbolise separation. In this version,
myths free aesthetic cultural products, remove labels, and create
changes which threaten stability: they are for liberation. By determining how locus of control moves in a culture, myths celebrate
difference.

## The 'truth' of myth

Is a myth 'true'? Self and ego are myth, projected images of collective analytic fantasies about the mind (constructions). What of the
myths separating religious from scientific explanations – freely trans-
lated as 'archetypal' and 'developmental' metaphors? In the mind–
body controversy, this dualism developed from beliefs of the early
Christian Church Fathers (and alchemists) that man below (microcosm, ego) reflected God above (macrocosm, Self) – 'as above, so
below'.
    These early theologians distinguished 'mythos' (beliefs about
God) from 'logos' (beliefs about humans) (Russell 1961: 325–51).
Interestingly, this split between 'head-knowledge' and 'heart-
knowledge' did not occur in Buddhism. Splits about which view was
'truth' developed, later, into open war between Cathars (Gnostics,
illusionists who wish to know, forerunners of empiricists) and
Catholics (believers, those who wish to love God, forerunners of
romantics). The threat arose from questioning whether one believed
what one was told, or, like Galileo (placed under house-arrest for
observing the Earth went round the Sun) what one experienced.

The Westerners' struggle to define boundaries between natural and super-natural, to decide whether myths are 'logos' or 'mythos', divided the Enlightenment from the Romantic movement, and still separates those who prefer open to closed systems. Social anthropology and comparative religion, in which Jung read deeply, take myths as naturally occurring cultural narratives. Jung studied them using empirical methods, to challenge romantic spiritual assumptions. In nineteenth-century scientific fashion, he discovered they can be classified into six groups each with a broad theme: creational; about the end of things; birth, rebirth and fertility; culture heroes; national foundation; and death and afterlife. The forms appear universal. Jung suggested they arise from the collective unconscious:

> Another well-known expression of the archetypes is myth and fairytale. But here we are dealing with forms that have received a specific stamp and have been handed down through long periods of time. The term 'archetype' thus applies only indirectly to the *'representations collective'* since it designates certainly those psychic contents which have not yet been submitted to conscious elaboration and are therefore an immediate datum of psychic experience.
>
> (*CW* 9i: para. 6)

Jung, like most young Europeans in the nineteenth century, approached myth by studying classical Greek and Latin, translating texts about slave-owning societies which, supposedly, exemplified 'right living'. This educational device could be read as a cultural projection, *embourgeoisement* of master–slave relations to justify dispossession of peasants, exploitation of the working class and colonial adventurism. Similar cultural imperialism appeared in linguistics, in attempts to trace the origin of language to a 'pure source' – Pali or Sanscrit – the vernacular and sacred languages of the 'Aryan Master Race'. From the German philologist Max Müller's work with Vedic texts, Jung learnt that myths structurally express natural phenomena in sensual and visual images, rather than by linguistic stereotypes. They are embedded, linguistic structures.

Jung's ideas link to subsequent developments in semiotics. The French anthropologist Claude Levi-Strauss took myth as a level of language describing clusters of social relationship (Leach 1974: 54–83). Structural linguists like Ferdinand Saussure searched out relations between the two levels in language itself – content and form (Cobley and Jansz 1997: 38–42). The semiotician Julien Greimas described the inter-relational patterns of ideas in myth as forming Semantic Squares. Myths use semantic squares as logical operators, linking cultural ideas to moral values, expressing the living experience of a community.

For example, the myth of the ballot box creates the illusion, 'I chose the leader,' with the reassurance 'I can always choose another.' It is an example of a messenger-myth: the voters' message, as in the original Greek, is a σψμ–βολον (Stein 1957) a thing split and then thrown together. In the culture-symbol 'voting', individual and social aspiration are thrown together. In a democracy, the meaning of the symbol is choice: in a dictatorship voting is a religious act, sanctifying the 'great leader'. This is hermeneutics. The word comes from Hermes, who, as Mercurius, is an alchemical symbol for links between conscious and unconscious, the transcendent function. Hero quests, Grail legends, messenger-myths (and analytic theories) are forms of this function, linking religious and scientific narratives in cultural structures.

The structure of a myth tells us about its meaning-making process. The Italian philosopher, semiotician and novelist Umberto Eco (1976) suggests myths develop through four stages: first, natural events are personified (sexual thunder becomes Zeus, intercourse takes place); second, the Gods are domesticated (like Hera, the scold); third, they embody civil institutions (Mt. Olympus) and fourth, they're humanised (baby Hermes naughtily caught stealing his big brother Apollo's sheep).

Freud used a myth to characterise unconscious sexual conflict, inventing an Oedipal variation on the archetypal incest theme. Jung understood incest as a purposive, creative, mythological urge. It is taboo because that protects its social value as a primary maker of meaning – the installer of sexuality. Sexuality does not define psychic energy (libido). Incest fantasy is 'projection, in which libido is seen to purposely regress to earlier levels of experience in order to find the appropriate symbol for further progression' (Hogenson 1983: 74–96). The conflict between Freud and Jung was one between belief and illusion: Freud was a believer, Jung, an illusionist. Mythologise their conflict as between monistic, closing interpretations (nothing but) and pluralistic, opening interpretations (both-and). Both are right and both wrong. Myths can open and/or close systems: the meaning-making problems of Self can be called spiritual emergencies, psychotic episodes, chemical imbalances in the brain, or meaning disorders. Which name we choose depends on the myths we prefer about Self, not on the 'true nature' of a made-up construct.

## Myths of Self and culture

Cultures need change (liberalism), and maintenance (conservatism) to survive. Social opening and closing are described in myths which help cultures accept transitions and mark them by traditions, socio-politico-religious rituals. For example, the voting myth is used to validate changes of governance: however, as the anarchists' say, 'It doesn't matter who you vote for, the government is always in power.'

Traditionally, the Chinese believed the Jade Emperor's Heavenly Court mirrored their Emperor's Earthly Court in the Forbidden City with Courtiers, Ranks – even a god of Salaries. The Emperor remained as a convenient political illusion till the mid-thirties (well after the Chinese Republic began in 1911) to legitimise a series of feuding, rapacious war-lords who seized power. With the victory of Chinese communo-fascism, and the deification of Emperor Mao Tse Tung, hereditary emperors were no longer needed to give the government the mandate of Heaven.

Descriptions of psychological structures (ego and Self) in analytical psychology are, similarly, projections, and, like the Emperor, persist after their usefulness has gone. The myth of Self has become a myth of legitimisation. To see Self as a higher organising centre causes problems. As Jung's junior colleague at the Burgholzli, Roberto Assagioli (the Italian founder of Psychosynthesis) pointed out, when in life there's too much meaninglessness, too much suffering, this gives Self a bad name (1973: 35–59). He suggested it is by the exercise of Will (volition) that we exorcise this daemon, the shadow of Self.

Analytical psychology is a constructed world-view, belief and illusion, a mirror glimpsing shadows of meaning in liminal experiences, not a religion or (as Richard Noll angrily claims) a successor to a 'Nietzschean cult' (1996: 247–9). It lacks myths of creation or hereafter. It is close to a political philosophy, as it is intimately concerned with power dynamics, governance in systems (their cybernetics) and the relations between Self and collective (ecology). Meaning formation in analysis, as in politics, is pragmatic, concerned with narrative, rather than 'truth'. We hear power dynamics in clinical settings, ask who is the namer, and for whom are they naming.

From the life-stories I've used in the clinical examples, here's how these people initially named themselves: Dekk – junkie rent-boy; Ben – mummy's baby (Chapter 2); Mike – coward and murderer (Chapter 3); Maisie – stupid epileptic, Billie – gutless victim and Jay – screaming queen (Chapter 4); Storm – dirty thief, Geoff –

wife-betrayer (Chapter 5); Yukio – ugly street-brat and Ann – failed mother (Chapter 6); Jacques – failed father (Chapter 8), – all shameful names. All these people had developmental delays, an after-effect of shame on emerging personae.

Believing internalised bad names, staying scapegoats in dysfunctional family systems let them stay with omnipotent feelings of guilt which, as Fairbairn pointed out (1952: 213, 215), allows maintenance of omnipotent responsibility: 'If it's my fault, then I can make it different . . .'. For Self, this has a corollary: 'If I believe their name, I'm bad, but if I don't believe it, I'm betraying them: heads they win, tails I lose,' – a double bind. If the myths we take as ours are in fact the myths of others, what's 'true'? Maybe nothing. This creates what French sociologist Emil Durkheim called anomie, loss of social meaning.

Controversies about which myths are 'true' in analytic narratives parallel those between: (1) pluralists (after Greek philosophers Plato and Aristotle) with 'small' explanatory ideas, who value experience, logic and reason over myth and take 'gods' as immanent in creation; and (2) monists (Jewish, Christian and Islamic) with grand narratives, who value both myth and history, and believe in a transcendent God outside space-time.

Pluralists see psychology and religion as myths: monists believe God shows Himself to creation through social acts (revealing Himself to His prophet, guiding His chosen people and so on . . .). Monistic cultural groups treat psychology and philosophy as branches of religion. Jung belongs to the first group, and Freud, 'Messiah of sex', to the second. It's hard for believers in a One God Universe (Chapter 5) who see 'Signs of God' (or 'Signs of Sex') in all creation, and Self as a unity, to accept as valid systems which define belief as illusion.

A contemporary social example comes from the 'autistically encapsulated' state of Albania, where, says journalist Priit Vesilind, (2000: 52–71) citizens honestly believed myths promulgated by the 'great leader', dictator Enver Hoxha: 'Ours is the richest country in Europe, the Americans are our enemy!' When Hoxha died, they discovered they and their ragged, starving children were the poorest in Europe and most Americans neither knew nor cared where Albania was, until the Kosovo war – caused by the closed Kosovan society imploding.

Closed myth-systems become dictatorships: whether in families, analytic tribes, societies or nations. Mark Twain said, 'Faith is believin' in what you know ain't so . . .'. Re-naming within a myth depends on faith in our ability to deconstruct a text, to treat myths as both belief and illusion, with one meaning (icons as signs) and many meanings (icons as symbols).

To have locus of control of our meaning-making is to acquire fluidity in our personal myths, and access to appropriate collective ones. I'll explore this further in Chapter 12, in the dialogue between Jung and Zen Master Shin' ichi Hisamatsu. Here it is mentioned as a problem of cultural relativism. Their argument turned on the meaning of 'Self' and fell apart as the 'Two Sages' couldn't agree whether they were discussing belief or illusion. On this question the East–West dialogue turns, as do arguments between analytic myths of meaning. As Wilfred Bion wrote:

> It is possible here to talk about psycho-analysis and alpha-elements and beta-elements . . . there is no evidence whatsoever to believe that beta-elements and alpha-elements exist, except by a kind of metaphor . . . It's a psycho-analytic game, like a children's game in which the arguments become so fierce and bitter as to who is father, who is mother, or who is baby . . . the ordinary adult can find it difficult to know why the children are so quarrelsome and why 'only a game' stirs up so much emotion. I suggest that it is equally difficult to know why an adult, mature psycho-analyst should feel angry about a psycho-analytic theory unless that theory is part of an adult game – the psycho-analytic game – which stimulates and engenders a good deal more heat than light.
>
> (Bion 1990: 15)

Analysts are seduced by myth-games into taking as signs, what are, in fact, symbols. To work against this, I believe, requires clarification of terms.

### The structure of myth: the semiotic square

In structuralist terms an icon is an image, (picture, sound or gesture; road sign, whistle . . . fist). Icons are arranged according to a generative grammar (Chomsky, in Lyons 1970: 83–95). A sign describes a concept. Link the icon (picture of scissors – a signifier) to the concept 'cutting' (signified) to form a sign: signifier (icon) + signified (concept) = sign. Symbols are a sign (concept) + X (unconscious, inexpressible, limitless concept). Link the concept (cross) with the inexpressible concept (God's infinite mercy) to form a symbol for

Christianity. Link the concept (lotus) with the limitless concept (Buddha links spiritual light and material mud) to make a symbol for Buddhism.

'Symbol-language' is poetic; 'meta-language' is common speech. Barthes' critique centres on the reduction of symbols to signs, replacing symbolic language (religious purity) with meta-language (salvation through using the right washing powder). Likewise, analytic theory may embourgeoise the psyche – reducing symbols to signs, especially the stigmatising signs of 'psychopathology' – 'narcissistic rage' for a response to a shaming hurt, 'anal retentive' for a person using closed system thinking.

Signs, according to Kant, are defined by categories. Symbols link categories, a transcendent function: 'transcendent' here means 'rising above', that is, giving equivalence in meaning-validity, not equality. Metaphor is between symbol and sign. Fowler's *Modern English Usage* (1965) categorises metaphors into new, old, overdone, spoilt, dead and mixed. They are a linguistic form which create new equivalences, a key building-block for creativity (Koestler 1969: 88–101; Siegelman 1990: 1–23). For example, we can metaphorise analytic work as creating a 'Sacred Space' or a 'Field of Healing'.

Barthes said the linguistic form 'myth' is a syllogism (if a, then b: if b then c: if a then c) which predisposes to certain conclusions, organises observations on that basis, and attributes meaning by substituting a sign in a first statement for a symbol in a second (unlinked) statement. They generate meaning as well as non-meaning. In mythologising, a thing is socially-appropriated while losing its social presence (1972: 117–19). As myth is a form of speech, Greimas says:

> the interest a linguist or semiotician – since the linguistic system is just one privileged system among so many other semiotic structures – can have in mythology is twofold. For them a mythology is a 'natural' meta-language that structures itself using an already existing human language as its object-language. Linguists or semioticians then try to identify and describe the functioning of the 'forms' of this new complex signifier that is being used to realise mythological significations.
>
> (Greimas 1987: 3)

He suggests feelings attach to signifiers in myths (syn-language) less strongly than to signifiers in everyday speech (meta-language); this is why their meanings are more fluid. He believed analysis of myths produced simple structural descriptions (archetypal patterns) and gives as example anthropologist Claude Levi-Strauss's reformulation of the Oedipal myth into what (at first) looks like a mathematical equation:

$$\frac{\text{overestimated family relationship}}{\text{underestimated family relationship}} \text{ is like}$$

$$\frac{\text{autochthonous human nature}}{\text{negation of autochthonous human nature}}$$

(Autochthonous means 'sprung from the soil' in Greek; hence aboriginal, native or natural.)

The Oedipal story describes an imbalance, a lack of humanisation of family relationship. The Theban chief Laius raped his 'guest son' (heir to the next-door kingdom). He violated a custom common from Greece to Ireland in those times that chiefs' sons were tutored by the neighbours (Chadwick 1970: 110–140; Delaney 1986: 61–82). The custom aimed to reduce risks of inter-tribal war by ensuring the lads were 'blood-brothers', enduring initiation together and likely to make love with the neighbours' daughters and 'marry out' (i.e., encouraging exogamy).

The entire cultural point of the Oedipus myth is lost in Freud's sexy rendition. Laius broke a kinship taboo, spurning his wife Jocasta for a pretty boy. Jocasta hopes having a child will win Laius back, but instead, the son is hung by his feet from a tree and found by shepherds, whom the boy takes as his 'real' parents. At adolescence, the boy goes to Delphi to learn his fate. Hearing he's going to kill 'mum and dad', he runs away . . . meets and kills an arrogant old man on the road (Laius) steals from the Sphinx what is rightfully his, marries the old Queen (Jocasta) . . .

When the Oedipal myth was acted in Greek theatres it said to the audience, 'Look! This is what happens when chiefs and fathers betray their duty to their people and their children.' That audience knew perfectly well Laius was a notorious paedophile. Oedipus lusting after his mother is a 'natural' consequence of a breakdown in the social order: 'With a father like that, what do you expect . . . ?', they might have said to each other after the play was over. Greimas says myths like this examine relationships between pairs of opposites (enantiodromia), representable by the following general semiotic equation: the semiotic square.

$$\frac{A}{\text{non A}} \text{ is like } \frac{B}{\text{non B}}$$

This is not about equality, but equivalence between concepts. Laius negated the natural order in both family and host–guest custom (A: a king and father's duty of hospitality / non-A: raping a guest-son). As counter-balance, fate sees that his own son is lamed, exiled, becomes a shepherd-boy instead of a prince, and eventually his murderer. Fate also sees that Oedipus, blind to who his mother is, blinds himself, escapes with his own daughter Antigone, to die when the Earth swallows him up at the crossroads at Colonnus (B: son's duty of fidelity to father / non-B: son murdering father).

Jung used the same concept – balance between opposites – and the same structure, the semiotic square, in his major work *The Psychology of the Transference* (*CW* 16: para. 422), thus:

$$\frac{\text{Adept}}{\text{Anima}} \text{ is like } \frac{\text{Soror}}{\text{Animus}}$$

Jung's approach to transference uses the alchemical myth of the mystic marriage to describe the semiotic square between analyst (system A) and patient (system B). He plays imaginal and symbolic meanings together through alchemical metaphors, alchemy being 'a pre-science based on the projection of the unconscious into matter . . .' (*CW* 16: para. 361). Events in the conscious (numerators, Adept and Soror) and unconscious (denominators, Anima and Animus) are mirrored in the transference and counter-transference, say, like this:

$$\frac{\text{Analyst}}{\text{Analyst's relationship to \textit{their} own analyst}} \text{ is like }$$

$$\frac{\text{Patient}}{\text{Patient's relationship to their own analyst}}$$

A semiotic square describes the form of personal and cultural myths. There can be any number of statements as denominator: parent figure, body-language, Self-image, social or political role. Patterns between two people in analysis mirror those between cultural groups in equivalence not equality: just as a chief's duty is equivalent but not equal to that of a father.

## Cultural meaning disorders

Evolving from primate gestures and sounds into linguistic representations, myths give a common ground for ethical development. When
we are kids in a world of heroes, princesses and dragons, our stories
have meaning, value and ethical significance. Ethical behaviour originates as we differentiate Self from other, through shame (Jacoby
1994: 49–50). Kids in all cultures understand 'you don't split on your
mates'. They have a natural sense of justice, and are ruthless
with each other in enforcing social mores with strong oral codes of
legislation (Opie and Opie 1982: 141–73).

Semiotics can be applied to polarising conflict. The 'tribal conflict'
in analysis has competing myths: which are 'true'? Answers require
deconstruction, not destruction. The term deconstruction, coined by
French philosopher Jacques Derrida in the 'sixties, described a way
to handle texts with multiple meanings (Derrida 1996). By looking at
different forces of signification in a text, exposing internal differences, inconsistencies and vulnerabilities we can locate the power
dynamics and hidden agendas of text and author to show how signification shapes symbol formation. I did this at the start of this chapter with a literary example (C. S. Lewis); now I'll do so again using
myths about 'Jung and the Jews'.

The myths arose from his taking on the Presidency of the General
Medical Society for Psychotherapy in Nazi Germany, just before the
Second World War, when Nazi persecution of Jewish analysts had
forced them out of the German society. Jung later claimed he took
the post so that the rights of Jews could be protected, and he did
alter the Society's constitution into an International society, with
the German Society becoming a national group (Samuels 1993: 287–
316).

Did something in Jung's psyche predispose him to anti-Semitism?
There was certainly carried-forward resentment (*Nachtraglicheit*) to
Freud, negative father-transference, failure of homoerotic playback
between them, and a background of anti-Semitic cultural feeling in
Middle Europe, well-described by Richard Noll as 'Volkish' culture:
a neo-Pagan idealisation of nature, nation and 'race purity' (1996:
75–108). There was a culturally opposite pole in Art Nouveau, a
powerful multi-national movement celebrating nature to redress the
gross social imbalance between man and nature created by the
Industrial Revolution (Greenhalgh 2000: 14–72).

The presence of powerful myths indicates social arguments about
locus of control. Who created the myth 'Jung and the Jews'? The

Jungian community, the Jews, the Nazis . . . all three? A 'hidden fourth' . . . ? Who needs to mythologise Jung and claim him as pro- or anti-semitic? Who gains power by asking, or refusing to ask such questions? Jung's acts cannot but be set against the National Socialist myth: a kitsch-and-death vision of a racially pure Aryan *volk*, radiating *gemutlich*; with a Pagan homoerotic warrior *broderbund* bringing peace and prosperity to the Master-Race of *Mittel Erde* for a thousand years. Their petit-bourgeois, utopian myth incorporates a simple lie, 'War is peace!' The aspiration had a dark shadow, the *Shoel* (Holocaust). Further, it is not possible to have a master-race without there being a slave-race, the Slavic people of Eastern Europe. Over twenty million were slaughtered.

Fascism, the military arm of fundamentalism, is the prototypical cultural meaning disorder, a closed and closing system. Jung failed to appreciate this. Nor did he realise that negotiation with a closed system under threat and closing ever tighter, is all but impossible. Such a system's closed beliefs (basic assumptions) have reached delusional, paranoid intensity: shadow is projected so strongly.

I think Jung was seduced by the hero archetype, seeing himself as *Ubermensch*, with a vision of himself 'rescuing the Jews'. He then fell into the 'victim-persecutor-rescuer' game. As described by Eric Berne, in its classic version 'Alcoholic' (1964) this game for three can be played indefinitely, provided the participants are willing to take turns playing the roles. Jung began playing as 'rescuer', quickly became construed as 'persecutor', and ended up as victim.

A question I personally find extremely hard is 'Why did more Jews not fight or flee?' Survivors, like Marianna Jacoby, co-founder of the analytic association, where I trained, answers 'Because we just could not believe the reality and horror of the shadow archetype . . .' When Jacques, whom we met in the previous chapter, was eventually able to visit Auschwitz to give respect to his ancestors, we were both struck by the words he found inscribed in the centre of the killing field: 'This is a monument to despair'. It would be so much easier if there was someone to *blame*. But Buchenwald, where the gas chambers were, is a pretty little village. Ordinary people live there, wash their cars, do the laundry, just as they did when the ovens burnt. Ordinary people drove the trains through its one way gate.

We could read Jung's story and suggest his attitude to Jews and Judaism put him in the same frame as the Nazis. To concentrate on this question but not ask questions about inter-group relatedness, or politics, is to miss the point. We can mythologise Jung as anti-Semitic, pro-Semitic, political idiot-savant, power-junkie or whatever. It's easy to deal with the shadow by projecting it, by refusing to see our ordinary, intrinsic ability to create meaninglessness. Despair is produced by destroying meaning, closed systems closing create despair. Locating analysis of Jung's political acts at an intergroup level lets us use it as a study in mythologisation (Samuels 1992a). We might read his behaviour as 'embodied countertransference', acting-out in response to a collective meaning disorder in his 'patient', German culture.

In *Wotan* (*CW* 10: paras 371–443) he described the culture-myth he felt dominated the *volkish* mind, derived from images of Norse Heaven, Asgard and Valhalla: an understandable hero-dream of the inglorious losers of the Great War. From that despair, a nationalistic myth arose, a wish to divide the world into *them* and *us* – splitting, denial and projective identification on a global scale. If we are trapped by what the rock singer Paul Simon calls 'The myth of fingerprints' (1986) then *only* black therapists could *really understand* blacks, Jewish therapists understand Jews, gay therapists understand gays . . . this is the fascist myth of difference disguised as liberal guilt.

Myths of exclusivity are universal responses to marginalisation. They increase closure in closed systems (whether the closure is voluntary or imposed). If we fall into Jung's naive cultural relativism (evinced in his ambiguous remarks about the difference between Aryan and Jewish psychology), if we follow him by talking about 'racial psychology', as he did on his North American and African journeys, then we are supporting a central, crucial self-contradiction to his theory of the collective unconscious operating at a level below language, the psychoid – that is, below our skins, whatever their colour.

Jung confused levels of meaning in his response to the Nazis (and to cultural difference) between what Piaget might call psychological racism (the racist myths we each have) and epistemophilic racism (the racist myths we all have in common). This depends upon recognising differences between 'my mother', 'mother-as-collective', 'motherland' and 'the Mother Goddess' – between psychological, political and religious narratives and between philosophy of knowledge, belief and morality.

Purpose-led approaches to myth (like that of Barthes and Campbell) assume their purpose is nominative power. What I (a Scot) call *careful* with money you could call *mean*. If I write 'nigger' instead of 'black', the feeling-tone depends on our skin-shade (the substance), our culture (the set) and the setting. If I'm with black friends, and one says to me 'You're one *baad* nigger . . .', it's a mark of deep respect. But if, like Mike (Chapter 3), my myth is 'I'm a white-trash loser boy-soldier,' I can't tell myself I'm a hero.

### Poetry and ritual

Analytical psychology deconstructs personal narratives allowing change (opening), *and* constructs them allowing maintenance (closure). In doing so, value is given to myths and cultures as educational tools. Jung's own journeys have been subject to social appropriation (Jung 1989: 238–88; Hannah 1991: 158–82); his 'anthropology' is equal proportions of travelogue, eulogy, and fantasy. It gives us more empirical data about his developing meaning-system than about any people he was 'observing'.

In oral traditions, poets eulogise, satirise, remember, hold and contain the culture. Similar figures exist in all cultures – 'culture carriers'. The symbol systems anthropologists examine are culture carriers, and, like Bards, anthropologists use poetic language. Jung's 'anthropology' is a poetic observation of ritual. Archetypes, as meaning-giving concepts, create *ritual*. Ritual is structure. Definitions of ritual might emphasise its function as holder and container of a culture, creator of social myths. For illustration, consider an advert featuring dining in an expensive restaurant:

> The diners assume the restaurant is going to give them respect.
> They choose a particular dress-code, form of social discourse,
> and may use special vocabulary – say, the language of wine
> (not just jargon here, or a technical vocabulary, but a true
> language in the public domain) to show they have appropriated
> to themselves certain status-giving cultural products. 'Fine
> Dining is back: eat at Joes': the icon, a dinner-jacketed Latin
> lover, with an ear ring, opening the passenger door of a smart
> open-topped white sports car driven by a slender woman in a
> strapless white evening gown and a seamless tan, as the sun sets
> behind a San Francisco waterfront . . .

The status-giving totemic cultural products signified might be the suit or dress, the car, or the kind of credit card being used to pay the bill. It might even be the restaurant. In advertising's private language, this is 'aspirational marketing': 'We want you to know what to want'. Advertising becomes art. Black art? Meanwhile, back in the restaurant . . . waiters and diners engage in ritual exchanges. Much play may be made of the serving and choosing of wine. However, the trick does not work if the staff know less about the ritual than the diners, or vice versa. Both should already know how to play the restaurant game, neither should require instruction or education.

The same is true in a religious (or analytic) system. The agreed pattern of ritual, once learnt, is repeatable almost without variation. 'Father forgive me for I have sinned . . .' or 'Tell me about your mother . . .'. Ritual has a special place set aside for observance (restaurant, Church, consulting room). There are conventions concerning dress, speech, and social exchange; ceremonies of greeting and leave taking; exchange of tokens (bill and tip, money in the collection plate, sessional fee). There is a system of initiation for the waiter-priest-analyst involving learning arcane and hidden language, ritual humiliation, and compliance to the 'Masters' of the trade. The content of the ritual is irrelevant as the function of ritual is 'sharing occult knowledge': *only* the waiter can turn our desire into a vintage; a priest, wine into the Holy Blood; an analyst, the complex into 'the gold of the Self'.

Jung's work on transformation symbols in the mass (*CW* 11: paras 376–448) shows the idea of ritual meals in which believers eat their Gods is neither new nor Christian, but common through history. A signifying game (restaurant game, the Mass or analysis) can be played 'open or closed'. Closed, the participant is allowed a sense of sharing the magic, numinous space – the corner table, the Altar, the couch are presented as 'Temenoi' ('Sacred spaces', 'stone circles') but actually the Gods at work are commercial ('fields of healing'). I'm playing fine dining against the Church and analysis, as the clients for one are often clientele for the other.

Mythology (the science of myth) is part semiology and part ideology (Barthes 1972: 117 *et seq.*). It concerns the evolution of narrative over time. A real mother feeding a real infant could be mythologised (say) into a 'breast–penis'. Information about the mother–infant relationship is lost. 'Breast-penis' is merely a sign. We can substitute 'vas Hermeticum' for 'breast–penis', and repeat. Analytic narratives are *myths*. They are not histories, being what we made of events rather than events themselves. In George Orwell's *1984* where 'Big Brother is watching you', the hero Winston Smith's job is the daily rewrite of history (1949). Similarly, 'Big Brother' analysts may attempt to substitute their culture-myth for the patient's (Balint 1968: 92–103, 105).

## Clinical application

Our personal narrative as *analysts* changes with our identity and our patient's identity, as we establish our sense of Self in each other's presence. We do this by working with parental and cultural counter-transference: the fantasies, dreams and strange effects at boundaries that occur with particular patients. As these enactments become first analytically, then socially present, so the patient becomes aware of their transference: they can recognise their body-language's emotional signifiers, pause before these become actions to let feelings become symbols.

Emerging symbols in the 'here and now' of the consulting room appear in the meta-language of the session – whether in analyst, patient or surroundings. Once my wife (also an analyst) dreamed: 'Your new patient has moved in: he's asleep on our bathroom floor. His head's bandaged from trying to force a man's skull on top. He looked just like a mummy . . .'. This was Ben, whom we met in Chapter 2: rich kid turned street-kid. He was living rough at that time. My wife (who met him 'by chance') was cross he sent a dream to her, instead of to me. I thought 'At least he's told mummy.' Ben did need 'immersion in the Bath' (an alchemical metaphor for the part of the transference where the intersubjective field is created – *CW* 16: 453–6) as well as a bath. He was 'wrapped up in his mummy'. I amplified the content: my wife, the form. She wondered why this boy's unconscious intruded into mother but not father? Who did he want to renarrate his story? I did not tell Ben the dream, but held it in mind as he told me about street-culture (a collective mother).

Other street-kids – down-and outs and lost souls recieving 'community care' with chronic mental illnesses – helped him learn to take care of himself in their world. And, as he learnt to give care back he discovered he had good in him. He developed a sense of being a character in his own story. People with little sense of personal history (narrative) use that as a defence: 'If I have no past, I can't mourn the bad things that happened . . .'. However, conditions for myth formation pre-exist in the collective unconscious, a reservoir of archetypal themes. With Ben, my wife's dream helped me see I was 'mother in the transference'. There certainly were vital issues about early rejection. Ben, a tramp, cared for by tramps, showed both of us how culture can act as a mother and retell our stories.

Michael Fordham, developmental analyst, saw story-making as a symbolic process and stories as transitional objects combining fact and imagination. He felt over-use of myth in amplification led away from dealing with early mother–infant issues. There is a long-running conflict over this issue with the 'classical' school – dependent on whether there are 'truths' about early experience, rather than beliefs and illusions.

The New York analyst Esther Harding (trained in Zurich) used Babylonian creation myths to metaphorise early relationships in her book *The Way of All Women*. She argued that personal parents are less important than archetypal ones (1971: 146–77), as did Erich Neumann (1973: 9–26). The previous generation of analytical psychology schools tend to treat myth as 'thing', rather than 'form of speech'. Fordham might concentrate on transference dynamics as *the* clinical sign, Harding on symbol formation. Certainly, both over-interpret from their own 'myth of theory'. A patient's ideas can be blocked by foregone conclusions, material distorted to fit analytic myth (Harding 1971: 243–4).

As Fordham (1995) says:

> This method, which can be so illuminated in other contexts where it amplifies the collective matrix in which the fantasies of individuals are embedded, becomes, unfortunately, a positive obstruction when studying the psychology infancy and childhood. . . . The use of myth easily leads to basic fallacies, for it is not the myth that makes understandable the overwhelming power of the parents for the child; it is the simple realities of the infant's dependence on his parents for his continued existence. . . . Such confusions arise because it is not understood that the developing psyche of the infant only gradually gets embedded in the collective forms exhibited in myths. These he may be expected to use, as part of maturation, to express his own inner psychic life and to relate to the adult world.
>
> (Fordham 1995: 244)

As 'myth is a form of speech', understanding the signification in a patient's narrative must 'amplify the collective matrix in which the fantasies of individuals are embedded' - including maybe myths of development? Maybe Fordham's view is as valid as its mirror image: 'The psyche of the child only gradually emerges from cultural myths about infants and small children?' I'm using Louis Zinkin's constructivist argument here (Zinkin 1999: 135–49), to ask again, 'Who is the namer, and for whom are they naming?' For example: Ben had to emerge from his myth of being 'mummy's baby'.

All the patients I've mentioned had to emerge from their family myths, and did so by linking creatively to the collective: Dekk – TV star; Ben – rock guitarist; Mike – artist; Maisie – veterinarian; Billie – designer; Jay – lawyer; Storm – eco-warrior; Geoff – conjurer; Yukio – musician; Ann – painter; Jacques – journalist. They treated their shame by providing themselves with cultural affirmation, as important as reliving infancy in the analytic setting.

Archetypal material unfolds in development: *that* it does is clear, the *order* in which it does so is far from clear. Maybe it's useful to start thinking about infants in a cultural matrix involving mother, mothering behaviour, her partner and the Tribe? Maybe patients need to look at their families' *myth of development* in a cultural context. For example, Yukio's experience of abandonment by his mother (Chapter 6) might be 'normal' amongst a certain social class, perhaps amongst the International business community: it is not normal amongst a traditional landowning Japanese family. His developmental dilemma took place between different cultural myths, its resolution involved leaving both of them behind.

Each of my patients, at first, could only attribute particular, closed meanings to signs. All of them went through 'it's my mother . . .', which, like proving milk causes crime, as all criminals drank milk as infants, is the post hoc, ergo propter hoc problem. The clinical value of myth is finding new meaning in a person's story, essential when faced with horror stories of abuse and neglect, which led to building a false self, a stiff persona, a compliant external identity used for survival in a family micro-culture that did not support the 'type' of a particular individual. Do we, like the lost (and drugged) Prince Rillian in *The Silver Chair*, have to believe the stories told us by the terrible witch Mother? Or are we able to free ourselves, to make our own stories about the origin of the world, belief and ethics . . . to make our own philosophy of meaning?

# 10

# PHILOSOPHICAL BACKGROUND

'It has been many years since anyone asked me to see Oz,' he said, shaking his head in perplexity. 'He is powerful and terrible and if you come on an idle or foolish errand to bother the wise reflections of the Great Wizard, he might be angry and destroy you all in an instant.' 'But it is not a foolish errand nor an idle one,' replied the Scarecrow, 'it is important. And we have been told that Oz is a good wizard.' 'So he is,' said the Green Man, 'and he rules the Emerald City wisely and well. But to those who are not honest, or who approach him from curiosity, he is most terrible, and few have ever asked to see his face. I am the Guardian of the Gates, and since you demand to see the great Oz, I must take you to his palace. But first you must put on the spectacles.'

(L. Frank Baum, *The Wizard of Oz*, 1993: 65)

## Green spectacles?

Dorothy and her dog Toto are carried by cyclone to the Land of Oz. To get back to Kansas, they seek the Great Oz, in his Emerald City. Through green spectacles, naturally, his city looks green. When Dorothy and her companions gain the presence of Oz they're terrified – till Dorothy notices 'The Wizard' is only a *projection*. Behind the big screen sits a little old man, who, like her, wants to 'get back to Kansas'. If theories are green spectacles, then philosophy is like optics: a reflective and refractive process, looking at three areas where we seek meaning – the origin and nature of the world (metaphysics, theories of existence), belief (epistemology, theories of knowledge) and conduct (ethics, theories of value). These measure reality testing, and provide means to validating meaningfulness.

Philosophy might be defined as 'thinking about thinking'. It uses reason and argument to seek the causes of things. Two views oppose – natural philosophy and idealism – in a system of Western thought in which objects of knowledge are held to be dependent on mental activity. That is, objects arise as a synthesis between experience and idea. Philosophy can't tell if what our theories let us perceive is 'true', but it can find blind-spots in an argument: as Nietzsche said, it can tell truths about truth.

This chapter examines how concepts about meaning (epistemology) evolved in Western philosophy and links this to arguments about meaning in analytical psychology – 'what colour spectacles do we wear?' (I'll look at analytical psychology and Eastern philosophy in the last chapter.) Western arguments about meaning turn on an age-old conflict: believers in 'absolute, objective truth' see 'truth' as a closed system existing in an 'out-there' object-world (pragmatic empiricism) whereas believers in 'relative truth' see 'truth' as an open system. Sense-perceptions may or may not relate to 'out-there' objects, and validation comes by 'in-here' experience (transcendent idealism). In this thumbnail sketch, I suggest Jung and the Post-Jungians are, mostly, transcendent idealists, like Kant and the neo-Kantians, following Plato and the neo-Platonists. To support this, I've to detach 'Jung the man' from Post-Jungians, separate Wizard from Oz, figure from the ground.

## Jung's philosophical development

Applying his theory of types to himself, Jung believed he was an introverted intuitive by nature, with a second, social persona of an extravert thinker (Jung 1989: 42–45; Hannah 1991: 19–38; Smith 1996: 159–60). Like the Wizard of Oz, Jung seems to have relished projections on to him as senex, the 'Wise Old Man', the 'The Wizard of Kusnacht'. Another projection is that he contributed significantly to philosophy: correctly, though disingenuously, discounted in the Terry Lectures at Yale, 1937 (*CW* 11: para. 2). As his critical biographer Robert Smith said,

> In theory, Jung did not hold the view that all truth is psychological and hence subjective. He was so impressed by unconscious determination, however, that he almost overlooked the fact that even though statements are conditioned, this will say nothing about their essential truth or falsity. From the time of the early Greek philosophers onwards, ascertaining truth has not been a matter of majority opinion. That is to say, a neurotic person may espouse a theory that is true. In short, psychological conditioning

factors need not, as he implied, limit philosophical truth to subjective appearances.

(1996: 113)

Like many who search for meaning, Jung struggled to separate psychological from philosophical issues. In his day, the two disciplines were mutually entangled with parapsychology; arguably, without his contribution, this entanglement would have continued. He began reading philosophy in adolescence. Like any boy in nineteenth-century Germanic culture, his first philosophical meeting was with Goethe. As Richard Noll correctly pointed out, Goethe was steeped in Graeco-Roman mythology (1996: 24–6), and father to the German Romantic Movement – Jung's philosophical home. At fifteen, Jung devoured *Faust*: its themes of sex, temptation and redemption would speak to any sexually awakening teenager.

In *Memories, Dreams, Reflections*, Jung, in his eighties, mythologised formative experiences in the light of what he'd made from them. He says he felt attracted and repelled by Pythagoras, Heraclitus and Plato – their 'reasoning was too abstract'. The early Christian Schoolmen 'left me cold', wanting to 'prove belief by tricks of logic', and he 'distrusted Hegel's linguistic arrogance' (1989: 68–70). He warmed to Schopenhauer, whom he later discovered was strongly influenced by Buddhist philosophy (*CW* 6: para. 223; *CW* 11: para. 769). Like many introverted, lonely adolescents he identified with and found comfort in Schopenhauer's 'pessimistic' view of the causes of suffering. But an appeal to the 'Will' and equating that with the Almighty seemed inadequate to a pastor's son in emotional turmoil. Jung turned to Kant, and became fascinated by *The Critique of Pure Reason* (1953). Kant's influence was to be profound.

The *Critique* examines classes of truth (existence, knowledge and value) asking whether or not synthetic truths are *a priori* possible. (Analytic truths are ones in which the predicated concept is contained in the concept of the subject: for example, snow is white. Synthetic truths are ones where this is not necessarily so: snow is for ski-ing.) Kant believed some synthetic truths are *a priori* (known from the beginning, with no outside evidence) rather than *a posteriori* (known after evidence, from sense experience). Such truths, he suggested, include mathematical truths. Jung agreed:

> Unperturbed by the philosophical pros and cons of the age, a scientific psychology must regard those transcendental intuitions that spring from the human mind in all ages as

projections, that is, as psychic contents that were extrapolated in physical space and hypostatized.

(*CW* 9i: para. 120)

Jung's next encounter was reading Friedrich Nietzsche (Professor of Philosophy at Basle University whilst Jung was a medical undergraduate). A profoundly positive, highly opinionated thinker, Nietzsche wished to find a way through and beyond the crisis of meaning at the end of the nineteenth century: how do we recognise truths about 'truth'? How do we move away from fundamentalism of all kinds, from political despotism to individual freedom?

The romantic tradition emphasised individual, unconscious motivation, understanding personal transformations of primordial phenomena as free, creative acts. Henri Ellenberger (1970: 205, 670–1) argues Jung was not only more committed to this tradition than Freud, but in Nietzsche's descent into madness saw the perils of his own 'night sea journey'. The iconoclastic theme (the death of God), emphasis on moral individualism and 'will to power' later led to Nietzsche's appropriation by the Nazis – a travesty, for he'd ruthlessly condemned moral absolutism.

In *Beyond Good and Evil* Nietzsche berates philosophy for 'selling out' – reducing itself to mere playing with words, abrogating its social responsibilities to 'science', which deals with theories of knowledge but not theories of existence or value. This confusion is a category error – theories of knowledge are, *de facto*, unable to provide moral guidance. Science's claim to 'disinterested knowledge' (spurious objectivity) is, according to Nietzsche, a simple lie: an insight one hundred years ahead of its time. Science depersonalises spirit and society, emasculating the will with its scepticism, and replacing the divine by 'Great leaders' who use superior knowledge to justify their power (Nietzsche 1973: 110–27).

To avoid premature closure of meaning systems, Nietzsche pioneered and advocated using multiple analytic vertices: circum-ambulating problems of meaning, illuminating them from as many disciplines as possible – a method Jung himself used (Freeman 1974: 13–14). Jung identified with his prophetic, 'great visionary' hero Zarathustra, another lonely outsider (Noll 1996: 257–9). The shared concern is not so much the 'death of God', as the death of metaphysics, the deep inability of 'science' to take God's place. In the 'authorised versions' Jung's thinking developed the tradition of Plato, who took mental imaging as the process which originates meaning – not 'objective science'. Plato's technique of 'Socratic dialogue' –

attention to the role of belief rather than affect – has parallels in contemporary cognitive therapies; his appeal to inherent knowledge and morality led to Jung's theory of archetypes (Mace 1999: 23).

The American analytical psychologist Paul Kugler traces the development of image-theory from Plato's cave simile (1997: 71–85), an historical starting point for epistemological arguments. People are imagined living in a cave, trapped in a world of images. Shadows of 'real objects' projected on to the wall are taken as real (Plato, ed. and trans. D. Lee 1955: 315). Plato assumed the images arose *a priori*, from ideals existing independently 'with the gods'. Aristotle, however, located image formation in the mind, it linked sensation and reason, outer and inner worlds. Neither saw imaging as originating (creating) objects; rather, it is a reproductive activity (like drawing).

Their ideas persisted. During the Middle Ages, mental images were believed to be reflections of ideas in the mind of God. From alchemists, such as Giordano Bruno (a Gnostic) came an (heretical) idea that images are products of the human mind rather than reflections of the divine. This cost Bruno his life. René Descartes located meaning-making in the mind – not a 'given', because he assumed the mind was a *tabula rasa*, a clean sheet. He held the thinking subject existed separately from the mind of God, from Platonic ideals or from the material world. David Hume, developing this theme, held meaning originated from association of image-ideas. There was no need to appeal to belief.

The problem their views created is this: if psychic images have no transcendent (trans-personal) foundation then giving any meaning validity outside of the subject only creates sets of overlapping fictions about the world – if you say red and I imagine red, how do we know we are imaging the same thing? And, if our subjectivism is unfounded, then how does meaning gain inter-subjective validation?

Kant, with his bold phrase 'percepts without concepts are blind', addressed this problem. He said imaging is both productive and reproductive, therefore transcendent to (above) reason. An act of imaging is trans-personal as it is culturally-mediated, creates consciousness, which, in turn, creates meaning. Jung synthesised Kant's ideas with his own in *Psychological Types* (*CW* 6). He traced the history of meaning-making from early conflicts between nominalists (naming is arbitrary) and realists (naming is derived from archetypal images) (*CW* 6: 41), through Schiller's notions of superior and inferior intellectual functions as derived from introversion and extroversion (*CW* 6: paras 101–214) to privilege symbol formation as the central epistemological act.

He learnt about the introversion–extroversion dichotomy when studying with the French psychologists Binet and Janet, from whom Jung also took the concepts of the subconscious, autonomous sub-personalities, complexes and, particularly, the idea of 'autism' as 'loss of sense of the real'. (Ellenberger 1970: 406, 702–3). An autistic defect is an inability to form symbols, mental images which hold together opposites and always contain unknowable terms – 'x' – that is, there is a metaphysical component to any symbol.

Symbols are by definition, objects with open signification. They create and survive by strong social consensus – agreement amongst Christians to accept the Cross as symbol for a sacred mystery (divine love) is an example. What 'divine love' means cannot be specified. It is an 'x' which can't be measured scientifically, yet each Christian in their own unique way will have an experienced-based understanding of 'x'. 'Divine love' is a member of a set of meanings referring to metaphysical concepts. Similarly, understanding the sign 'mother' requires theories of knowledge – understanding the symbol 'the Great Mother' requires metaphysical notions – beliefs. Theories of existence, conduct and belief are all required to categorise archetypes. Jung suggested archetypes are collective, *a priori* synthetic functions:

> we are not dealing with categories of reason but categories of the imagination . . . the original structural components of the psyche are of no less surprising a uniformity than those of the body. The archetypes are, so to speak, organs of the pre-rational psyche. They are eternally inherited forms and ideas which have no specific content. Their specific content only appears in the course of an individual's life.
>
> (*CW* 11: para. 518)

'Authorised versions' of Jung's philosophical journey emphasise his search for validation of meaning by direct inner experience. Philosopher and analyst Marilyn Nagy said Plato's notion of ideal types, Kant's theory of the categorical imperative and Jung's view of validation by 'inner experience' are forms of epistemological idealism – 'They give authority to the reasons in the mind in order to guarantee a moral world order and/or they grant authority to the things of the mind because of the moral order which is thought to exist' (1991: 45). This is crucial to the social project of analytical psychology, which I'll examine in the final chapter.

Jung's uses of philosophy reflected his unfolding psychological process. If his philosophical oscillations were teleological (purposive) then his breakdown-to-breakthrough created a shift from a closed pragmatic-empiricist 'rigorous, scientific' philosophical position to an open, transcendental-idealist 'mystical, artistic' view. This followed dis-illusionment with Freud, a painful circumnambulation of the Self, after which a new position arose between ego and Self. What did this mean for him? Nagy, analysing his philosophical antecedents, begins with his existential problem as the son of a clergyman who had lost faith.

In this new millennium, it is hard to imagine the hold Christian belief had on the Western mind but a century ago – unless we remember the war in Kosovo or the tribal 'troubles' in Northern Ireland, unless we recognise we too live in an all-pervasive belief system: 'scientific materialism'. Jung's repeated claim that his work had 'nothing to do with philosophy' was an attempt to separate psychology from the *massa confusa* in the crucible of, then contemporary, ideology. It may reflect his need to separate from father's failed 'arrangement of rules', from Freud as 'surrogate father', or from psychiatry as a fathering tradition. His appeal on behalf of the inner life arose

> not on the ethical value of recognising an alternative to the objective, scientific view, nor on the prophylactic value for the patient, but on an *epistemological assumption* that the *only* certainty we have is our knowledge of the Inner world. We are in fact imprisoned by the symbolic realm of the psyche.
>
> (Nagy 1991: 29)

He wished to bring scientific understanding to religion through hermeneutics, for example, by discovering meanings hidden in alchemical texts. His first attempt was a 'baroque' expansion round material gathered by his friend and mentor Theodore Flournoy: the fantasies of Mrs Frank Miller, first published as *The Psychology of the Unconscious*, (1915). When revised as *Symbols of Transformation* (*CW* 5, 1952) Jung had realised psychology could not make definitive statements about objective 'truth', as, like any natural science, it is subject to the 'observer effect'. Over forty years, he changed from being an experimental psychologist whose Word Association Experiments provided 'objective evidence' for the unconscious, to an intersubjectivist, constructivist, position: meaning is a construct, not an empirical fact. This development made explicit what was implicit in Jung's thinking as a lad searching for meaning.

And what of the 'unauthorised version'? The 'wannabe' analyst Richard Noll suggests Jung's philosophical roots dip into the well of '*volkish*' utopianism and sun-worship of the decadent Weimar Republic: 'bearded hippies' from the Art Nouveau, magical mummers from Rosicrucianism, theosophy, and 'the occult'; colourful philosophical roustabouts like 'private scholar' Bachoven, (whom Noll dubs 'the Von Daniken of the late nineteenth century', 1996: 162–9), are paraded before us. He makes but one reference to Jung's study of Kant (ibid.: 142); of twenty-eight to Nietzsche, half play up his (spurious) links to Nazi ideology. Noll's thesis 'Sun-worshippers were neo-Platonists, Jung was a neo-Platonist, therefore Jung was a Sun-worshipper', is a syllogism.

The positive value of Noll's critique is to help separate the ideologist from the ideas. Locating Jung within the philosophical traditions of his time, discovering which theories of meaning he used, lets us ask whether he was consistent in his usage. Did he add to epistemology, heuristics or hermeneutics? Conflicting versions exist, depending on the political mission of the author. I think he was not inconsistent, but developed the first, by theorising with the second and made a small, but important contribution to the third. What have his followers done with this?

### Post-Jungian's philosophies

Post-Jungians do not share a common philosophy. English analyst Warren Coleman argues post-Jungians approach the concept, 'Self as originator of meaning', in four ways (2000: 3–19). Drawing on Andrew Samuels' helpful three-part categorisation of analytical psychology (1985a: 1–22), he adds a 'hidden fourth' – the constructivist position. There is a spectrum between transcendent idealists and pragmatic empiricists in each of Samuels' groups – archetypal, developmental and classical positions.

The 'first way' (after Marie-Louise von Franz and James Hillman) theorises meaning as arising from archetypal patterns. They style themselves phenomenologists, like Husserl 'going back to the things themselves' (Vannoy Adams 1997: 101–18). As transcendent idealists, they hold meaning disorders arise when archetypal patterns can't unfold freely into an imaginal, validating, intersubjective field. Treatment approaches therefore include amplification of images (signifiers) by active imagination; 'dreaming the dream on'; using techniques such as sandplay, creative work with myths, music, drama, art and literature to re-engage an individual with their culture. For them, 'truth' is relative, open and fluent – unknowable, as it deals in symbols not signs. Analysis is, for this group, an aesthetics of meaning with a strong metaphysical component.

The 'second way' (after Fordham), the developmental perspective, theorises meaning disorder as arising in mismatches between mothers and infants; a primal meaning-validating environment. Pragmatic empiricists, they base arguments on the Butterfly effect – 'exquisite sensitivity to initial conditions'. This concept from Chaos theory says tiny changes when a system initiates rapidly become huge differences as a system develops (Chapter 7). For them, analysis is a 'science of meaning'.

However, working backwards from signified to signifier, '. . . if x is happening now in the transference and counter-transference then something like x happened before . . .', and empirically concentrating on 'here and now', may claim a higher degree of certainty than observations allow. Further, interpretation too easily falls into the post hoc ergo propter hoc fallacy, or, worse, infinite regress (. . . it was your, my mother, everybody's mother . . . all mothers, back to Mother Eve . . . back to an archetypal image). If we take 'truth' as a closed system, and construe analytic work as 'science', while this may work well with severe meaning disorders, in people who seem to need certainty and strong containment: it is, philosophically, unsound, with a weak metaphysical position.

The 'third way', 'classical' analysis, says meaning disorders appear in object relations and (which is saying the same thing) from failures of archetypal installation – lack of appropriate cultural meaning-validation. It has a semiotic approach (rather than a 'scientific' one), studying signifier and signified in meaning systems, to look for defects in symbol formation. The 'fourth way', constructivist, is less a 'school', more a deeper view of meaning disorders as problems in signification, arising between 'Self and not-Self'. As the semiotician Julien Greimas said 'signification can be concealed behind all sensible phenomena, it is present behind sounds, but also behind images, odours, and flavours, without being in sounds or in images (as perceptions)' (1987: 17).

He is echoing Kant's argument against 'objective truth' suggesting mental structures themselves structure 'objective' experience. This may look like a 'chicken and egg argument' – which comes first, archetype or development? I put it here to illustrate a consequence of using different logical operators, different philosophical frames of reference, different coloured spectacles: we are looking at an argument like that of the six blind men of Hindustan and the elephant – their descriptions differed depending on which part of the elephant they touched. Descriptions of meaning disorder differ depending on which logical operators we're using to 'touch' our data: and whether we're wishing to tell 'truths' about existence, belief or value (or any particular combination).

The dominant logical operators chosen by post-Jungian groups might be: archetypal, {both/and}; developmental, {if/then}; classical, {both/and//if/then}; constructivist, {both/and/neither/nor}. I'm drawing stronger contrasts between the first two groups (the archetypal/developmental pole) and the second two (the classical/constructivist pole) than may exist in 'reality' to suggest the latter argue against the existence of objective truth, while the former have a habit of belief, and of claiming 'the truth'. The latter are open meaning systems, tending to open – the former are closed meaning systems, tending to close.

Practising analytical psychologists are more pragmatic than the theories suggest. We use a broad spectrum of meaning-making strategies from wide-open to tightly-closed, depending on who we are working with: '. . . from each according to his abilities, to each according to his needs' (Marx 1875). A shared meaning-making (epistemological) hazard is to assume altering the degree of openness or closedness of a system resolves its meaning disorder. Maybe 'the rate of change of flow of information' is more important? 'How does meaning accelerate?', is a better question than 'How fast is it moving?'. 'Classical' and 'constructivist' analysts are concerned with 'level errors' and 'category errors' as originators of meaning disorder. Assume there are different quantum levels of meaning: energy is required to accelerate from one to the other. These errors slow change of meaning.

When looking for agreement over naming in a meaning dysfunction, we notice potentially meaningful signifiers may belong to one level (or one category) when in fact, they belong to another (Sandner and Beebe 1982: 294–335). For example: 'What you call aggression, I call assault,' is a level error in the philosophy of conduct (ethics). If you say, 'God made the universe,' and I say, 'No, it made itself,' we're discussing level errors in the philosophy of existence (metaphysics). If you say, 'God made the world,' but I say 'There is no such being . . .' *then* you shoot me: we've a category error and a level error. A debate about belief (epistemology – theory of knowledge) collides with a bullet about conduct (ethics – theory of value) ... I get killed for my beliefs.

A level error is a mismatch in value within a category – belief, in this example. We have here a category error; a confusion between metaphysics (your belief does not equate with my belief), epistemology (my knowledge is better than yours) and ethics (your values matter more than mine). Most so-called analytical 'theoretical disputes' result from category errors, are maintained by projection of self-similar patterns of mutual envy, typological difference and wish to stay at the top of a semantic gradient (that is, to keep the power and the money). Such differences caused a split in the Society of Analytical Psychology in the 'seventies (Casement 1995).

First, theories are used to create unequal power gradients in the analytic community. Second, as 'extravert' and 'introvert' mean 'open' and 'closed'; what 'feels right' to an introverted feeling type probably is 'vague and woolly' to a thinking type. If the 'real world' is related to by projecting psychic contents into it, and/or introjecting the psychic content of others, then whatever 'reality as such' (Kant's *ding an sich*) may be, it can't be apprehended. Third, belief (a *form* of mental process) is *a priori* to what we 'believe' (a *content* of mental process). To confuse an epistemological meaning (mother means something about scientific observation of mothers and infants) with a metaphysical meaning (mothering means something about a belief in what makes a mother), is a category error.

Elias Canetti (1984: 29–31) shows, given any crowd of human beings, 'belief' of some sort or other inevitably arises. Because a prime function of a collective gathering together is survival, sharing meaning – any meaning at all – provides a crowd with direction and purpose. Analytic meaning-making structures are no different, the 'crowd of analysts' uses the same instinctual religio-political structures as any tribe: sometimes people (or things) have too much, too little, the wrong sort of meaning – their theories of meaning are liminal, 'out-group' rather than 'in-group'.

For example: in 'Symbols of transformation' Jung ran into an epistemological problem: how do we know what a symbol is? Flooding the reader with images and arguing by analogy, he attempted to give Mrs Miller's psychic images transcendent foundations by drawing endless cultural parallels. He says we analyse symbols in two ways:

1   From an initial personal idea which works itself out in words, 'thinking with directed attention' – 'The material with which we

think is a language and verbal concepts – something which from time immemorial has been directed outwards and used as a bridge, and which has but a single purpose, namely that of communication . . . the most abstract system of philosophy is, in its method and purpose, nothing more than an extremely ingenious combination of natural sounds. Hence the craving of a Schopenhauer or a Nietzsche for a recognition and understanding, and the despair and bitterness of their loneliness' (*CW* 5: para. 12). Whether this is true or not, Jung is projecting his feelings at suddenly finding himself in a meaning-making 'outgroup' on to his two great philosophical heroes.

2    From social validation of the initial idea. He suggests the transition from pre-judgmental to judgmental meaning requires social confirmation, established by trial and error. The transcendent function links these two modes of thinking.

In logic and science, argument by analogy is weak argument. There is no hypothesis being tested. However, if these statements are taken as hypotheses about communication theory, and the nature of symbols, then they could be tested. These ideas are derived from Kant and the German idealists, particularly Hegel, Schopenhauer and Nietzsche: they concern the form and function of mental images.

## Imaging and idealism

In the *Critique of Pure Reason* (1781 [1953]), Kant claimed acts of imaging produce reason and sensation: are productive and reproductive. Synthetic categories underpin imaging, and, though transcended, the transcendence is not between God and man, but man and man – agreement to use the same terms to refer to objects. Ability to form mental images between people creates consciousness, and consciousness then creates the external world (in autism, this is lacking). We do not perceive what *is* at all. Perception, as cognitive psychologists say, is 'internally driven'; or, as Fairbairn put it, we actively seek objects to relate with. Contemporary neurophysiology strongly supports this hypothesis – Gerald Edelman argues in favour of a biologically based epistemology, underpinned by realism and Darwinism, which does not 'sell out' to what he terms 'silly reductionism' – the causalistic, deterministic thinking of fundamentalist believers in 'scientific materialism' (1993: 157–72).

We need to watch for category errors: within philosophy, arguments around meaning question how language reflects reality, within biology arguments around meaning reflect 'fitness to function'. These may or may not overlap. The meanings of words, like archetypes, look both 'out' and 'in', stand as signs for things in the world, that is their function. Semantic theories have to explain how signs can reflect reality through signification and form symbols, that is, deal with an ecology of meaning. The German idealist Gottlob Frege suggested each part of a language had its 'reference': objects it stands for in the out-there world. References contribute to the truth or falsehood of a statement. However, as we can replace one 'reference' (sign) by another (using synonyms), there is no 'one on one' match between a sign and a thing signified.

Frege tried to get round this by introducing the idea of 'sense', the sense of an expression is not what is referred to but the *way* it is referred to. The reference of an expression is the object it stands for, the 'sense' is the mode of presentation, its context (Frege 1980). For instance, 'the wise old man of Kusnacht', 'the boy who saw God's turd shattering Basle cathedral', 'the author of Aion' or 'the founder of the Jung cult' are one person. Jung (the reference) is presented (sensed) differently, to show different aspects of his life. Frege does not explain how different signs relate to different words.

Logical positivists, like A. J. Ayer (1956) held that meaning is given by accounts of what it would take to prove a statement true or false. Karl Popper applied this argument to the philosophy of science, with his concept of empirical falsification. Both concentrate on processes of signification – which is not symbol formation, but an essential precursor. The Harvard philosopher Willard Quine suggests falsification relates to theories of meaning rather than to individual statements of meaningfulness. He did not believe in Frege's idea of 'sense', and claimed translation (like hypothesis generation) is indeterminate, as, strictly speaking, there can never be any facts about what words (or hypotheses) mean: if we can't agree what 'black' and 'white' mean (name) we can happily argue 'black is white'. He's describing the difference between a sign and a symbol – a sign plus an unknowable, 'x'.

Philosopher Donald Davidson (1984) expanded this idea, suggesting that belief and meaning are interdependent. Beliefs acquire their existence if they are public language: an idea first put forward by Wittgenstein in *Tractatus Logico-Philosophicus*. 'The book deals with the problems of philosophy, and shows . . . that the reason why these problems are posed is that the logic of our language is misunderstood' (1961: 3). He attempted to answer a Kantian question, 'How is language possible?', concluding it is only possible if it is not private (that is, closed). Empirical and phenomenological perspectives on meaning are semiotic playing with words, unless there is a social contract. For the Greeks, semiotics was an intrinsic part of philosophy, examination of the 'well-formedness' of propositions. Semiotics can permit agreement, including the hardest agreement of all – to differ.

## Dialectical spirituality?

The differing perspectives on meaning-making in analytical psychology arise from category errors, using {either/or} as logical operator: meaning is either an epistemological or metaphysical construct. The problem is resolvable: as London analyst Hester Solomon (1994) suggests, the bridge is Jung's notion of the transcendent function. She carefully traced commonalities between Jung's idea of this function and Hegel's dialectic: the movement from thesis, antithesis to synthesis parallels Jung's concept of enantiodromia – movement between opposites to a synthesis, holding both. She makes a case for Jung's theory of meaning to be what I'd like to term 'dialectical spirituality' – a contrast to Marx's dialectical materialism. However, she does not address the adding of Nietzsche's opinions to the melting pot. As Lucy Huskinson (2000) points out, this is an essential component of Jung's concept of the telos (purpose) of the psyche.

In his chapter on 'the Apollonian and the Dionysian' in *Psychological Types* (*CW* 6: para. 225, quoting Nietzsche 1871 [1966], 21) Jung takes Nietzsche's stand; the first represents ordering, structuring (Apollo being god of music) and the second represents anarchy, the 'free-spirit' at play with music. The first is dreamy, the second intoxicating: the first is conscious, the second, unconscious, as when the player is 'possessed' by their muse. I develop this theme of tension between order and anarchy again when I look at the religio-political impact of Jung's theories of meaning, in Chapter 11.

He named the opposites he sought to reconcile 'nature and spirit', instead of 'experience and idea', attempting to apply Hegel's insights to his own religious dilemma – what to do when 'faith' in an omnipotent creator is not sustained by experience. The transcendent function replaces {either/or} by {both/and}: meaning can be both epistemological and metaphysical, agreement as to which at any given moment is an ethical decision, reflecting an individual's individuation – that is, a measure of their personal and social integration (Solomon and Christopher 2000: 191–216).

The 'classical' analyst Ann Casement sketches parallels between

Jung and Kierkegaard (1998: 67–80) to relate Jung's concept of individuation to Kierkegaard's idea of dread – anxiety about the future (negative temporal perspective). Both men had difficult relationships with fathers who had lost their faith, both believed validation for belief arose internally and both distrusted Hegel's dialectic method (deriding it, then renaming the terms, as Solomon suggests).

Kierkegaard saw dread as a precursor to sin, not its sequel. It has a function; to prepare us for change by challenging accepted social boundaries and morality – challenging ethical meanings. Such a challenge could be defined as 'Sin – a concept common in the monotheisms'. Buddha talked about this as desire – the origin of suffering. 'Desire' concerns future perspective, including positive hope for the new (welcoming change); greed, (hope to have more) envy (hope to have a thing another has, and to spoil it if we don't get it), and jealousy (hope to have a relationship we imagine another has).

The resolution Kierkegaard reached was to propose a 'leap of faith' – Jung's vision of God's turd shattering Basle cathedral caused him to dread. When he accepted his thought, his anxiety faded, having separated from an identification with his father. 'This qualitative leap brought home to Jung that from then on he had to accept responsibility for himself through listening to his inner experience and to think his own thoughts based only on what he understood' (Casement ibid.: 71). This is an example of 'acceleration' in meaning being used to bring about a level shift in meaning. From understanding 'God' as a sign, there is a rapid movement to understanding 'God' as a symbol. These writers show the value of using philosophical concepts to clarify meaning-making strategies.

The German analyst Wolfgang Giegerich (1997) further defends the place of philosophical thought in analysis. He argues against taking 'thought' as 'mere thought', which needs something added (feeling) for it to have validity. He sees pleas to the contrary (as, for example, in the writing of analyst Cecile Tougas, 1996) as dissociative splitting – the opposite of synthesis. If thought is taken always as an antinomy to feeling, it can't have its own passion, its own Eros.

Pointing to the work of Heidegger and Jung he restates the importance of 'social context' as the field in which the Eros of thought operates – that is, ideas have a social, erotic presence as well as a social meaning. He gives a good example of a category error in social meaning making ('how not to do it'). An attempt to introduce 'ebonics' (black street-kid language) as 'official school language' in California, to 'empower' disadvantaged kids merely replaces one unequal power gradient by another, increasing rather than decreasing the kids' marginalisation. Like the fashionable notion of 'politically correct language' this reinforces a 'ghetto' mentality. Turning a private language into a public one does not solve meaning disorder.

The kids' problem is not epistemological but ethical, the gross devaluation of black people and black culture for economic ends. Effect has been mistaken for cause. He suggests thought works against such closures against and within individuals because it depends on a capacity to relate to 'non-I', non-egoic transcultural commonalities – like thoughts about human rights – in common speech and with a common philosophical tongue. Philosophy is 'ego-abandoning' – it depends on the collective for validation.

He goes on to imply we don't want (or need?) to know about a philosopher's private life to evaluate his ideas . . . as ideas. Or do we? I suggest we need the {both/and/neither/nor} logical operator again here. As mentioned in the previous chapter, knowing an author's story lets us deconstruct the purposes behind their narrative. In a postmodern world, we are obliged to include uncertainty, and, with it, the dread of 'not-knowing', of 'thinking sinful thoughts', or recognising the inevitability of desires. Postmodernists no longer believe in 'universal' grand narratives, as there are no absolute theories of existence, knowledge or value. As Jung said,

> If it be true that there can be no metaphysics transcending human reason, it is no less true that there can be no empirical knowledge that is not already caught and limited by the *a priori* structure of cognition.
>
> (*CW* 9i: para. 150)

This does not mean there are no standards by which to evaluate theories of meaning. It implies meaning requires evaluation in terms of the structures of cognition and its social consequences – assessment of the degree of openness and closedness in the meaning-making systems any theory generates, consequences in terms of development of Self's meaning-making cognitive ability and the purposes 'free Selves in free society' produce. I discuss these next.

# 11

# RELIGION, POLITICS AND THE COLLECTIVE UNCONSCIOUS

> Now she had got a start, and she went on and told me all
> about the good place. She said all a body would have to do
> there was to go around all day long with a harp and sing for
> ever and ever. So I didn't think much of it. But I never said
> so. I axed her if she reckoned Tom Sawyer would go there
> and she said, not by a considerable sight. I was glad about
> that because I wanted him and me to be together.
>
> (Huck Finn, in *The Adventures of Huckleberry Finn*, Mark
> Twain 1991: 186)

## Involvement

If religion or politics look like this, they're mere 'arrangements of rules'. Unable to give depth and meaning to life, their social, boundary-marking (hermetic) activity fails. Culture-myths, religion and politics define and determine power gradients: who is master, who is slave, who says playing a harp all day is 'paradise'. Huck, a 'real' kid, values friends over ideas, 'here and now' over 'pie in the sky'. For him, as a young hero, the archetype, 'religion and politics' meant action. He bravely helped Jim, a runaway slave, to escape: an intensely political act in the pre-Civil War slave-owning Deep South where his story is set. To do so, he uses his own ethical boundaries and meanings about human rights: choices about exercising his own rights were stolen by his violent alcoholic father. As a street-kid, Huck lived on the threshold of society, liminal. Analysts are involved in individuation, for which a prerequisite is civil rights. But,

> It is an easy thing to talk of patience to the afflicted,
> To speak the laws of prudence to the homeless wanderer . . .
>
> (William Blake, 'The Price of Experience', in Blake 1977)

If that's all the meaning-enhancing work of analysis amounts to, it's worse than useless. We have nothing to say to people like Huck Finn.

I first 'met' him when I was a child, living in a commune in the Western Isles of Scotland in Iona Abbey, a former Benedictine Monastery on the enchanted, beautiful island where St. Columba brought Christianity to Scotland from 'Holy Ireland' in the sixth century. It was home to The Iona Community, to which my parents belong. The Community don't see politics as separable from religion. George MacLeod, the founder, told me how he'd walked past his church in the tough inner-city district of Govan, Glasgow during the Great Depression in the 'thirties, despairing at the plight of his starving parishioners. 'By chance', he looked up and noticed a pane missing from a stained glass window. It read, 'Glory to God in the High st.'

> State it how you will, the true Christian life, at every point, is compacted of the concrete and the ethereal. Ever since God elected to become Man; since the mystic Word wrote itself down on human parchment; 'took flesh and dwelt amongst us'; the Spiritual and the material must alternate and interfuse, disparate but conjoined.
>
> (MacLeod 1962: 50)

The Community consisted of craftsmen and clerics: helped during the summer by hundreds of volunteers of all ages and nationalities. Their collective concern was not just to 'rebuild the Abbey' (which they did) but to rebuild people and society by placing *involvement* at the centre of the Church's agenda. This led, amongst other things, to the formation of Shelter (the UK campaign for the homeless), and the Campaign for Nuclear Disarmament (CND). Analysis, involvement in meaning, for me, belongs in the High Street as much as in a consulting room.

If spiritual and material interfuse, then their social manifestations, religion and politics, go together. Both were once a prerogative of Lords (temporal and spiritual) but are now our co-responsibility; we share one planet, have the same archetypal meaning-making strategies – and a common human spirit. Analytical psychology comes from a philosophical position of epistemological idealism – we 'give authority to the reasons in the mind in order to guarantee a moral world order and/or (we) grant authority to the things of the mind because of the moral order which is thought to exist' (Nagy 1991: 45).

The problem with the word spirit is, like property, its value depends on location, location and location. Does it name something 'out there', 'in here', both of these, neither, all at once? Regardless of whether 'spirits' are 'real', let's ask what logical operators are used to respond to spirit – a closed {either/or} of fundamentalism, or an open {both/and/neither/nor} of pluralism? Religion and politics are two sides of one coin, one meaning-system. Like Janus, Roman god of thresholds (*limen*) symbolised by the key and the night watchman's staff, this meaning-system protects boundaries.

Any religio-political system can be a door to greater involvement in the collective, or an agency for social control – a door out to the margins? Herbert Read, co-editor of Jung's collected works, art critic, author and anarchist, is a guide; his seminal work, *Anarchy and Order* (1974: 13–31) opens with an essay on revolution and reason. His theme is the absurdity, the paradoxical nature, of the anarchist position. He states, 'The growth of authoritarian politics is due to a realisation of this absurdity: it is an attempt to replace the rule of an ignorant majority by the rule of an intelligent elite: but unfortunately the only judge of an elite's intelligence is the elite itself.' Theory making is an elitist activity, and analysis is an elitist game, unless we remember continually that the meaning-making task of individuation is impossible without active involvement of an individual in the real, social world.

Read, like MacLeod, saw no boundary between personal and public political acts: for him, the compelling human problem is realising in all its aspects our freedom of being, the essential nature of man – individuation is a political engagement. To take this approach to religio-political meaning-making requires giving up views of Jung as 'the Wise Old Man' and Post-Jungians as a quasi-mystical 'new age' guru-cult. Jung's engagement with meaning in religion and politics are the heart and soul of analytical psychology. In his seminar on psychological aspects of the mother archetype first given at Ascona, Switzerland, he wrote:

> we have even come to believe that Kant's personality was a decisive conditioning factor of his *Critique of Pure Reason*. Not only our philosophers, but our own predilections in philosophy, and even what we are fond of calling our 'best' truths, are affected, if not dangerously undermined, by this recognition of a personal premise. All creative freedom, we cry out, is taken away from us! What! Can it be possible that a man only thinks or says or does what he himself *is*?
>
> (*CW* 9i: 150)

Theories are our 'best truths', but we cannot have freedom to theorise without responsibility, or responsibility without freedom to choose to be responsible for our actions. Religion and politics form an archetype – 'Governance', a social form of the transcendent function. As explored in the previous chapter, this idea derives from Hegel's idea of dialectic: the dialectical materialism of Marx, and the 'dialectical spiritualism' of Jung. Religion and politics (often seen as thesis and antithesis) can be synthesised into a whole – governance.

Analysts treat counter-transferential responses to governance as co-equal to unresolved developmental issues when renarrating personal history (Samuels 1993: 111–34). The goal is what Andrew Samuels calls 'resacralisation' – revisioning the sacred (the numinous) in ordinary life – 'Glory to God in the High Street'. We do not create compliant, socially adjusted 'happy workers' or Neitzschean Supermen, but enhance personal and social integration, the finding of personal and social purpose, by increasing an individual's skills at making meaning.

As Self is of equivalent value in every person, with equal rights to a say in governance, social meaning disorders could be defined as the presence and maintenance of unequal power gradients in social systems. A common symptom is liminality, a common theme for many of my patients. Jung believed analysis does not 'convert' anyone from one religious or political belief to another, but allows reconnection with the belief system from which they came. Ben and Jacques found new meanings in Judaism; Storm, in the Pagan religion; Yukio in Zen; Jay and Ann in Christianity. Maisie, Billie and Mike renewed connections on the political left, Geoff deepened his commitment to the Conservative party. Rediscovery of personal meaning, redefining of personal morality, arose from reconnection to the Self – and had social consequences.

## Governance and social meaning disorders

Governance arises as culture myths interact with personal myths to form socially coherent meaning patterns, validating certain percepts (and precepts) over others. It creates these patterns using totems (numinous signifiers, like the Star of David) and taboos (like kosher food). Individuals and groups obtain meaning validation by acts of closure and opening. For example, for Christians, baptism closes into membership and opens up the benefits of membership. By giving freedoms and responsibilities, it changes meaning and status

(MacLeod 1962: 57–62). At births, marriages and deaths there are 'religious' and 'civil' records of this change.

Social rites reflect negotiations about governance between human and 'spirit' (however understood). 'Spirits' are often imagined living in mirror societies, beyond mortal reach: Tir Na Nog, The Western Land, Mt. Olympus, the Court of the Jade Emperor, the Happy Hunting Ground, Asgard, The Kingdom of Heaven. Contact with 'divine society' validates changes in status. If 'spirit' says nothing to 'here and now', it's just grand narrative: explaining everything, worth nothing. Such narratives tend to collapse into closed systems, or cults. When social systems cannot adapt to change, conflict results.

Western civilisation repeatedly tore itself asunder over the separation and/or identity of Church and State: the English Civil War between Charles I (God's Representative on Earth) and the People; the American Revolution, between 'One Nation, Sovereign under God', and the 'Evil Empire' of mad King George III; and the American Civil War – open, liberationist North versus closed, slave-owning South, are historical examples of conflicts between open and closed systems. The concept 'open and closed social systems' is both historical (developmental) and anthropological (archetypal).

When describing societies, anthropologists say closed societies 'marry in' (endogamy), and open ones 'marry out' (exogamy). Early Quakers, like some present-day Puritan groups in New England, practised endogamy: slaves raped by plantation bosses were (compulsorily) exogamous. Exogamy and endogamy are ritualised patterns giving social meaning for young adults. Religious and political signification is actively sought in adolescence, validated in *rites de passage*, whether they involve fasting and a vision quest, adult baptism or a Bar Mitzvah. For instance, Yukio and Storm both 'acted-out' with tattooing and piercing, expressing their personal vision; Maisie, Billie, Ann, Mike and Geoff, older, 'acted-out' by sublimation into art forms, which brought increased social validation. For them, a *social coniunctio*, getting and giving affection and recognition from others for their cultural products, became a purpose in itself.

If a culture does not supply adequate rituals, adolescents make them up (Zoja 1989). They seek governance. Learning to share in governance is a developmental task, taught as 'civics'. If the archetype is not well-installed, say as a result of marginalisation, it can form a complex – involvement in a cult or other 'closed' group. I suggest governance complexes result from interweaving between the archetypes of Trickster, Shadow and Rebirth as young adults attempt (and often fail) to negotiate for meaning with the collective. Governance (a meaning-making act) is, itself, liminal – a between activity – as are its practitioners (whether priest, analyst, shaman, senator or Native American Chief). Political and religious acts are themselves liminal, {both/and/neither/nor} anarchy and order: for example, voting for a new government takes place between parliaments; 'the Sabbath' is a day between weeks.

At adolescence, two meaning states co-exist (child and adult). In governance there is also a 'holding of twoness' – childlike wishes for society to be an ideal parent and childlike rage when governance fails to 'meet every need' oppose adult recognition that any form of governance relies on compromise, on politics as 'the art of the possible' and religion as a 'toleration of difference'. Individual and social needs balance envy, which, as Melanie Klein saw, is a product of twoness (Hannah 1991: 39–53). As sociologist Michael Rustin pointed out, examining inter-relations between psychoanalysis and social justice, Klein's views (with her focus on early object relations) have a social implication: we cannot, for example, be value-neutral about the care of mothers and infants – a social process (1991: 41–56).

Envy functions to maintain vigilance at boundaries, governance works with envy: for instance, ensuring the envy of a vulnerable mother–infant dyad is not exploited by other social groups. A grievous example of this *not* working is the social exclusion of unmarried teenage mothers in Western society. An ethical function of the governance archetype is to work against social exclusion, a form of collective unconsciousness.

We could, like the ancient Chinese, see successful governance as ensuring social equilibrium (Menicus, in Schurmann and Schell 1968: 12–21). The archetype concerns justice and human rights, 'the green movement', 'new age spirituality' as well as theories of political revolution. Its archetypal imagos are both order bringers, 'God-Kings' and 'God-Queens' (world creators), and 'anarchist' deities – Hermes, Monkey, Coyote, Loki, dancing Shiva and his consort Kali (world destroyers). Balances between creation and destruction depend on communication: whether through an open judicial system and a free press or the closed world of spies, secret police and torturers: liminal figures, symptoms of social meaning disorder.

## Trickster

A shaman's social function is sanctification and social validation (Vitebsky 1995: 10–22). Shamen have temporal and spiritual authority, represent both 'Church' and 'State' and negotiate between human and Spirit world. They mediate inter-tribal and inter-personal conflict; sanctify change in social status; initiate; treat illness; and bid farewell to departing souls (Eliade 1964: 300–02). Mana personalities, with extraordinary charisma, (*CW* 7: paras 374–406), they use empathic abilities to identify the needs of the tribe and to sacrifice for them. They are culture-carriers, structuring chaos into order, by means of group projective identifications of power. They are 'God-Kings' and tricksters (like politicians).

As Shamen use 'tricks', does this mean politics, like religion, is trickster-based? Take my opening clinical example again. Huck Finn was a youthful trickster, his survival depended on it. Trickster is used by adolescents, 'when all else fails', and was used by Ben, Storm and Billie. Trickster ensures societies (tribes) survive, and the younger generation acquire new adaptive skills – it is 'a comprehensive drive towards integration and relatedness' (Whitmont 1969: 176). Governance concerns communication (Samuels 1989a: 135–40). Hermes, a young Trickster god, was evoked at medieval New Year, when the power of the Church-State could be publicly mocked (*CW* 9i: paras 458–65). Playing tricks with sacred symbols dissociated the normal balance between ruler and ruled, between haves and have-nots. Trickster is

> a 'psychologem', an archetypal psychic structure of extreme antiquity. In his clearest manifestations he is a faithful reflection of an absolutely undifferentiated human con-sciousness, corresponding to a psyche that has hardly left the animal level.
>
> (*CW* 9i: para. 465)

His function is to open communication. Jung, in his foreword to the Native American Winnebago Trickster myth-cycle went on to say:

> It is a personification of traits of character which are some-times worse and sometimes better than those the ego-personality possesses. A collective personification like the trickster is the product of an aggregate of individuals and is welcomed by each individual as something known to him,

which would not be the case if it were just an individual
outgrowth.

*(CW* 9i: para. 468)

In the myth, Trickster, a handsome young Brave, reaches the edge of
a Lake. The Chief's beautiful daughter is swimming naked with
other girls by the opposite bank. He gets aroused, takes his firm
penis from a box on his back, and puts it in the water. The girls see it
coming, and flee, shrieking. He uses stones to weight it, till it's able to
swim over and enter the Princess (Radin 1972: 57). Here, the penis is
both a part object and a bridge (Gordon 1993: 69–84). This is Trickster's role in governance: thrusting and penetrating, using a part
object (an individual 'member') to relate to a whole object (woman/
society). He creates a *social coniunctio*: the subtle interplay between
penetrating and nurturing, hunting and gathering, hearthing and
housing, holding and containing by which we live.

Men and women have different sacred symbols mirroring differing socio-biological functions. Each layer of sexuality and gender
identity reflects and depends on individual and cultural boundaries, reflecting archetypal images: say, sun for man and moon for
woman (Harding 1955: 3–20). Images of governance (belief systems and ethical codes) are herms – boundary markers around
which meaning is negotiated. Louis Zinkin summarised Jungian
insights into the nature of Self as (and *in*) group negotiation
(1989). The problem is maintaining meaning boundaries between
Self and collective.

Though numinous symbols (father sun and mother moon) may
bridge gaps between Self and Other, concentrating on symbolisation
alone can lose sight of developmental issues involved in object relating. Damage to patterns of early attachment and damage to meaning acquisition, creating social meaning disorder. Talking about
symbol formation while losing sight of the social background
in which it occurs, risks it becoming 'reifying abstraction' – an
intellectual defence. Dazzled by theory, we mistake models for facts.

In this light, Zinkin hesitantly used Zurich analyst Jolande
Jacobi's topographical map of Psyche: ego at the top; Self next; and
collective at the bottom – noting its intrinsic elitism. He contrasts
Jung (and his tendency to abstraction) with Jewish theologian
Martin Buber, whose model, the 'I-thou' relationship, reintroduced
the personal to the spiritual. Drawing on the work of the semiotician
Korzybski, Zinkin says the problem for analysts seeking to under-
stand the meaning of 'Self *as* and *in* the group' arises from a

confusion of meaning levels: what is a sign in an individual may be symbolic for the group (and vice versa).

For example, the pentagram Storm cut over his heart with his flick knife was for him (and other Pagans) a symbol of man's bridging place between father sun and mother moon. For his parents, it was a sign of mental disorder: for us, analyst and patient, it was essential to move the meaning from sign to symbol – by means of a 'trick' (positive connotation): '. . . it's really good you did this, it tells us both about your commitment to Paganism.' Self deals in absurdity, paradox, ambiguity and symbols, but ego 'wants facts' – signs.

When a demagogue confuses their ego with society, any 'I-thou' dialogue against the wishes of 'dictator Ego' is taken as a personal threat – symbols cannot be permitted to remain ambiguous – as Salman Rushdie, author of *The Satanic Verses* (1988) found. As his example shows, when ideas are abstracted from feeling individuals, we create 'people like us' and 'people like them' – in-groups and out-groups – opposition between which serves to keep the crowd of Self (group or nation) together, and to marginalise the out-group. Wilfred Bion describes three common patterns in such 'basic assumption groups' which coalescence around unquestionable ideas (or theories), stops growth of meaning. A society sticks in the depressive or paranoid-schizoid position. I've just described 'the Army', defending the Great Leader's ego-image: an imagined threat maintains cohesion. 'The Church' hopes for a Messianic solution, a Holy Couple have to produce a 'divine heir' and 'the Aristocracy' maintain unequal power gradients by doing as little as possible and keeping the peasants ignorant (Bion 1961): as true of analytic communities as elsewhere. For example, our tribal disputes, like that between the different heirs of the Prophet, mistake a natural need for ancestors with 'theoretical purity' – splitting heirs.

Jung, helped by the robust de-mythologising of Richard Noll (1997) is now separable from his ideas. Jung's dream of God dropping a turd on the beautiful green, gold and red diamond-patterned tiles of Basle Cathedral's roof (1989: 36–41), is a Trickster projection, as well as a social statement: adolescent hostility toward his priest-father (and mother Church), and inner confirmation that God can dump on any human structure, religious, political or architectural. As a boy, maybe he felt '. . . father pays all that attention to the Almighty, but he doesn't pay any to me.' This might be bearable if Carl believes father believes. But if he doesn't, belief is a Trick.

As tensions between the 'Holy Spirit' of his father and 'the spirits' of his mother led him to appreciate, the archetype 'religioning', an ability to make space sacred around us, develops through life (Mathers 2000: 217–32). Governance negotiates at such developmental change points, giving guidance in situations of choice and a basis for socialisation, law and morality. It expresses archetypes of ethical behaviour (Solomon and Christopher 2000: 191–216).

However, Trickster is a-ethical (neither ethical nor unethical), an image for acts of governance arising from Self (or society) *in extremis*. For example, if a starving kid like Huck steals bread, is he mad, bad or sad? Do we put Huck, or any juvenile Trickster in an asylum or a reform school? Do we blame the young offender or do we 'blame the system' for politico-religious failure? If Oedipus (a dispossessed lad who stole Thebes, which, by birthright, was his) is a thief and crime is envious attack, then crime represents a failure of reality testing – individual *and* collective. It is a sign a need is not being met. The need is for validation, for social justice as much as for bread.

For example: 'affirmative action programs' in certain American states attempt to reintroduce socially excluded kids (truants, under-achievers, those with serious behavioural problems) to social justice. They are offered a choice of community work in which they learn to give and receive care and affirmation (*Guardian*, 7 December 1999); an open system approach. Other states have 'Boot Camps'. 'Bad boys' are 'broken' like Marine recruits by fierce discipline and (negative) affirmation. This, for some boys, 'grows 'em up' by forcing them to develop close bonds with fellow sufferers, by identification with the persecutor's values; a closed system approach. Both work – sometimes. But in both, the kids' agreement is crucial. There has to be recognition of a problem and consent to solve it, agreement about naming between individual and collective, agreement about what 'justice' means.

In Holland, both approaches are used. Delinquents are punished first; then rehabilitated, taught skills and given extensive after-care. Holland has the lowest recidivism rate for juvenile crime in the world. The principle was the same amongst Plains Native Americans. If youths broke the tribe's ethical code – charging a buffalo herd on their own instead of waiting for the others, for example – punishment was immediate and followed by explanation and restitution of the lads' rights (Hoebel 1964: 53–5). The aim of justice was re-involvement of the offender in society, essential for a hunting people's survival.

Social systems in which crime thrives, whether theft of goods or labour, of products or the means of production, lack 'ego function' (reality testing). The hermeneutic function of analysis (Greek: ηερμενευτος, interpreter, from Hermes) – interpretation for social beings – can assess a governance system's ability to reality-test, using qualities of Self (agency, coherence, continuity and emotional arousal) to measure its adaptive capacity and predict its likely responsiveness to change. Does a society's youth have qualities of Self . . . how many sleep rough? Trickster, like Hermes, asks such questions.

## Rebirth and the Shadow: the alchemy of governance

Born in a closed system, (a fundamentalist Swiss Reform Church household), Jung knew his approach to governance wore 'Christ-tinted spectacles': the Cross is simultaneously a symbol for opening and closing, for life and death, for rebirth and the shadow. Jung saw similarities between Khidr, 'the green man' of Islam (an Hermetic figure), the transformation of moon and sun in Mithraic ritual and Navaho healing ceremonies (*CW* 9i: para. 240). These illustrate the archetype of rebirth – which Jung felt was absent from political and religious experience in the war-torn twentieth century.

He used this insight during his last twenty five years to 'treat' Christianity. His 'treatment' (interpretation) reasserted religion's function as a bridge between individual and collective; a remedy for anomie, alienation and social disintegration (Stein and Moore 1987). Despite attempts to suggest otherwise (Noll 1996: 286–91, countered by Shamdasani 1998), analytical psychology is not a religion, a political creed or system of governance. It is an art and a science. Herbert Read quotes the Russian anarchist Bukanin on the difference between art and science, reminding us that:

> Science cannot go outside the realm of abstractions. In this respect it is vastly inferior to art, which, properly speaking, has to do with general types and general situations, but which, by the use of its own peculiar methods, embodies them in forms which, though not living forms in the sense of real life, nonetheless arouse in our imagination the feeling and recollection of life. In a certain sense it individualizes types and situations which it has conceived; and by means of those individualities without flesh and blood – and consequently permanent and immortal – which it has the power to create, it recalls to our minds living, real individuals who appear and disappear before our eyes. Science, on the

contrary, is the perpetual immolation of fugitive and pass-
ing, but real, life on the altar of eternal abstractions.

(Bukanin, in Read 1974: 236)

Governance is not an 'eternal abstraction', but a lived-out and lived-
in social network. In *Introduction to the Religious and Psychological
Problems of Alchemy* (1944), Jung places pluralism and paradox at
the centre of analysis:

> Oddly enough the paradox is one of our most valuable spir-
> itual possessions, while uniformity of meaning is a sign of
> weakness. Hence, a religion becomes inwardly impoverished
> when it loses or waters down its paradoxes, but their
> multiplication enriches because only the paradox comes
> anywhere near to comprehending the fullness of life. Non-
> ambiguity and non-contradiction are one sided and thus
> unsuited to express the incomprehensible.
>
> (*CW* 12: para. 18)

This pre-echoes Anthony Giddens (1997, quoted in Chapter 1): 'the
greatest threat at present to individual freedom and liberty is the rise
of fundamentalism of all kinds.' Paradox is an anti-fundamentalist
linguistic structure, used in alchemical metaphors. Appearing as
paradoxical injunction, it's a key ingredient of family therapy – 'pre-
scribing the symptom' (Madanes 1981: 65–94) as I did with Storm
and his cannabis use (see Chapter 5). Alchemy, a signifying system so
baffling it's never been decoded, allowed an esoteric tradition to
survive political and religious persecution. There is a polyphony of
meaning in its terms, in the duality and non-duality of alchemical
gold – both spirit and matter, neither spirit nor matter.

Jung believed alchemy viewed religion as a collective expression of
the numinous, particularly the archetype of rebirth. Value (gold and
ethics) is reborn through its suffering in the retort. The logical
operator is {both/and/neither/nor} – distillations, coagulations, con-
densations and sublimations, repeated over and over again. Jung
believed the central feature of the signifying system from which
alchemy derived (Gnosticism) was projective identification of Self
on to and into matter. 'Gold', 'the philosopher's stone', 'aqua
permanens' (and so forth) are metaphors for Self.

Heirs of the gnostic tradition (Freemasons: my father's family
have been members for generations) inseparably link religious to
social obligations. 'The Craft' has little to do with rolling up your

right trouser leg, wearing robes and muttering quasi-mystic non-sense. The apron, a masonic symbol, was daily work-wear for free (non-serf) stone-cutters, cathedral-builders. The trade union pro-vided education, health care, widows' pensions – all the benefits of a welfare state. No wonder they were persecuted – socially envied – in the past. The 'mystic' side of the Craft concerns rebirth: the symbol of the skull and crossed bones commemorates the murder of Hiram, Royal Architect to King Solomon and his burial in a grave too small for his body. His heirs represent the rebirth of his spirit in their rituals (Knight and Lomas 1997: 47–56).

In the Gnostic tradition, there was no separation between politics and religion. The God-King of Egypt made a political response (crop storage) to Joseph's interpretation of his dream of seven fat cows and seven thin cows (Genesis 40: 1–46). A religious leader is a political father to his people. The reverse is true in 'cults of the Great Leader', closed in a closing system, talking out of their fundament (Latin for bottom) and dumping on their subjects. We may be tricked by such figures, who, like Mighty Oz, fulfil projections of our own need, but, are themselves, ultimately empty.

Belief in political/religious values in family and culture involve paradox: are my meanings defined by my Self, the Selves of others or what the Shaman says? Having found Self, how do I relate to the collective? How does the social stance of my tribe relate me to the wider world? What are my values? Is the gold Spiritual or material? If 'Non-ambiguity and non-contradiction are one sided and thus unsuited to express the incomprehensible . . .' (CW 12: para. 18) – yet any system describing meaning has to be describable in terms of itself or it is meaningless, solipsistic, private language – what limits descriptions of Self made by Self?

Governance systems meet primary survival needs, help us 'feel good'. As border-defining activity, it provides a channel for tribal energies. The dangers of secondary narcissism – omnipotence fan-tasies, grandiosity, lack of reality testing, ego-inflation (Edinger 1962) – are apparent in many governance figures' careers. Moving from idealism to pragmatism is one possible interpretation, moving from idealism to ego-inflation is another. Jung used alchemy's para-doxical symbols to describe individuation: Solis and Luna in coni-unctio, giving birth to the gold, a vision of 'the image of the parents in bed' (Samuels 1985b: 111–34).

In developing Self, psychic contents are projected into the material world. Governance is a collective enactment, a social intercourse through which we negotiate space/time. Analysis of Self, establishing, or reestablishing links between Self-in-analysis and a person's cultural context requires renewing myths and metaphors: the archetype of Rebirth.

Strong psychological charges, and strong shadows, attach to symbols of governance. Analytical theory here has much in common with Tarot cards, the I Ching or astrology. Governance is a mantic system; we mythologise acts in, at or around the boundaries. For example, a supervisee of mine struggled to contain his rage after one of his patients urinated in his front porch. The patient, like God 'dumping' on Basle Cathedral, enacted what he could neither say nor symbolise, 'I'm pissed off . . .'

Religious and political acts are tribal responses to dangerous negotiations with the unknown. Alchemy was a smelly, sweaty process toiling beside hot retorts, on the edge of the unknown. But every apprentice alchemist knew, 'You only get gold out, if you put gold in . . .'. Here's how: the Master turns up at Court, saying 'I'll turn lead into gold'; the King gives us a bag of gold, for expenses; we put some into the retort, live well for six months; then, miraculously we 'find the gold!' (which we had prepared earlier . . .). This is a creative use of the shadow.

'Self', to an alchemist meant, as to a shaman, a divine pattern repeated in nature and man, space and time (Vitebsky 1995: 15). If the divine is both inside and outside, then there is no separation between spirit and matter, no Cartesian dualism, for 'If I am in God, and God is in me, then this has to be so in all people. Indeed, it has to be so for all creation.' This Gnostic myth is hidden in the signifying system of alchemy: creating and reflecting a sense of collective and individual wholeness. All are equal and all are equally divine. Christianity originates in sensual mystery traditions – the (feminine) Cult of Isis, the Moon Goddess, a Blessed Virgin with her miraculously conceived child, Horus (Jesus); and the (masculine) Mithraic Cult, in which a solar god is redeemed through the blood of an ox, shed over the initiate.

Gnostic views underpinned medieval science. Natural philosophy derived from alchemy, adding, 'If God created, then there is meaning and purpose in creation, which I, being part of creation, may share.' I juxtapose alchemy, religion and politics with gnosticism, to bring together issues of freedom and responsibility: today, not only can we can combine tin and copper together in a particle accelerator and *really* make gold (Roob 1997: 32–3), we can also make a 'star appear on Earth' (for a few seconds) followed by 'world peace' – the peace of nuclear winter. Controlling such forces requires constructive argument about the meaning of signs and symbols. It means confronting our sense of narcissistic importance, or impotence, in governance.

We cannot tell if our world was made specially for us (if the 'anthropic principle' is true, Davies 1995: 41–4), or results from 'chance'. Modern physics suggests a 'yes and no' answer. The continual exchanges between energy and matter are like the continual interchange between religion and politics. Light, a metaphor for Self, includes dark, the shadow of Self. Physics introduced uncertainty in knowing as a certainty: we now *know we cannot know*. The physical world is an open system.

Movement between open and closed, on a feeling level, is a movement between subjectivity and objectivity. If 'x' feels good, I'll be open to 'x' again; if not, not. Although subjectivity and objectivity exist separately as concepts, they do not exist separately in the experiential world. For some (like Dekk and Ben, Chapter 2) who met maternal omnipotence, only confrontation with their own mortality, discovering 'life has an end' brought awareness of intersubjectivity. Others have near-death experiences at or near birth: the end presents itself at their beginning (Yukio, Chapter 6). This produces too much opening, a 'blurred boundary' between Spirit and matter – such people may be psychic . . . or autistic.

Most of us flip between opening and closing, between sensing gods inside which can provide everything if propitiated, or gods without, unaware of our dependency needs. If our 'closed box' is dependency, we cannot validate our perceptions using other frames of reference, we have a meaning disorder. In 'pre-individuated' states the need to resolve this uncertainty is a primal epistemophilic need. Politico-religious systems address such needs in the collective.

## The Self, the crowd, and social presence

Analytical psychology sees exchange of value between people as a collective operation of a transcendent function, bringing spiritual and material 'gold' together. 'Gold in equals gold out . . .', the gold is Self – in at the start, out at the end. Self is a group, an interplay of sub-personalities and archetypal imagos. To understand social presence, and the Self as socially present, we need to know about crowds. A crowd is a collective, linked through the transcendent function. Elias Canetti (Nobel prize winning author of *Auto Da Fe*) in his treatise on social systems, *Crowds and Power*, describes large scale relationships and their mass psychology:

The crowd: suddenly there when there was nothing before, is a mysterious and universal phenomenon. A few people may have been standing together – five, ten or twelve, not more; nothing has been announced, nothing is expected. Suddenly, everywhere is black with people and more come streaming from all sides as though streets had only one direction. Most of them do not know what has happened, and, if questioned, have no answer; but they hurry to be there where most other people are. There is a determination in their movement which is quite different from the expression of ordinary curiosity. It seems as though the movement of some of them transmits itself to the others. But that is not all; they have a goal which is there before they can find words for it. This goal is the blackest spot where most people are gathered.

(1984: 16–21)

Canetti says this extreme form, a spontaneous crowd, once it exists, wants to grow. A natural crowd is an open crowd. But 'the openness which enables it to grow is, at the same time, its danger . . . the closed crowd renounces its growth and puts the stress on permanence. The first thing to be noticed about it is that it has a boundary.'

Crowds tend to closure, moving from initial charismatic togetherness to ritual, repetition and compulsion. A crowd's economy is controlled by leaders (functioning as its ego) to prevent it becoming an open crowd. Open crowds grow, discharge and disperse. Closed crowds institutionalise, invent 'arrangements of rules' and social rituals. Canetti gives the crowd's main attributes as a wish to grow, a sense of equality, a love of density which increases up to the moment of discharge: its most important event is a cathartic moment when the crowd simultaneously lose their sense of difference and feel equal.

Prohibitions against approach gestures are suspended (we hug total strangers). Crowds have a need for purpose and respond with hostility to threats from without, or collapse due to panic from within. Fear of disintegration means a crowd can accept any goal. The hazard is the crowd becomes a mob: nothing holds back the individual or collective shadow. In a large crowd, who can tell if it's me or the person next to me who set the city ablaze?

Politico-religious movements begin in open crowds – the Sermon on the Mount, Buddha preaching in the Deer Park, the French or American Revolutions. Crowds erupt from closed to open in war, when the crowd turns on real or imagined enemies. Attacks from outside strengthen the crowd. As each person making it up wishes for individuality, the enemy is within and has to be projectively identified outwards.

Crowds can be rhythmic or stagnating (rock festival vs. classical concert) slow moving or quick (pilgrims to Mecca vs. a football crowd), invisible (the dead) or visible (a parade). They can be classed by feeling tone: a baiting crowd (the Foxhunting troupe, the lynch mob) seeks discharge in death; a flight crowd (refugees) seeks sanctuary; a prohibition crowd (pickets) seeks reward; a reversal crowd (storming the Bastille) seeks justice; and a feast crowd seeks pleasure.

Natural symbols for crowds are fluent forms, like symbols of Self. They include forests, rain, wind, sand, fire and ocean. Self, like a parliament, is fluent. In a crowd, as in Self, boundaries between opening and closing depend on meaning-making. Maybe 'borderline' crowds are 'too open' – invasive, liable to flood, insecure . . . 'narcissistic' crowds are 'too closed', locked in repetitive patterns to secure fragile boundaries? A spectrum for crowds and Self-as-a-crowd might be: charismatic; liberal; conservative; fundamentalist. 'Open' and 'closed' are not moral judgements, simply tendencies for information to move in positive or negative feedback loops.

Any governance system is designed to give feedback on meaning to a society, to enable it to adapt purposively to change. Groups do this by defining membership, creating 'in groups' and 'out groups'. Theories of religion, politics and depth psychology are not co-foundational. Depth psychology analyses structures – social, religious and political – yet

> With all our efforts we cannot imitate the nest of the very smallest bird, its structure, its duty, or the suitability of its form, not even the web of the live spider. 'All things', said Plato, 'are produced either by nature, or by chance, or by Art; the greatest and most beautiful by one or other of the first two, the least and most imperfect by the last.'
>
> (Montaigne 1958: 109)

Exploring the politics of 'one to one' in an analytic micro-society of two, needs to result in analysis becoming socially present. 'For, we cannot imitate . . .'; no analyst can make anyone *believe* in Self. We can't interpret psyche if we don't speak its individual and social language. Only as the analyst forms as an internal image in the patient, sharing projections from Self and collective, like a religious or political talismanic figure (a shaman) are we, *de facto*, engaged. If politico-religious needs are met only by liturgical ritual at specific times (whether in an analytic session, synagogue on Friday, mosque on Saturday, church on Sunday), then the individual and their beliefs lack social presence, which George MacLeod called involvement. Andrew Samuels, in his essay 'Person and Psyche', says:

> The psyche creates a social presence for itself, for example, its presence in the binding role played by language. Hence, as it creates, the psyche cannot stop itself from moving more and more in the direction of culture. The psyche did not create the culture but, when the psyche functions as a source, it is engaged in a re-creation and re-formation of itself in cultural, and ultimately, in political terms. The psyche creates something from nothing, but such creation is on the move and in the general direction of cultural and political change.
>
> (1992b: 85–94)

Self creates social presence with the transcendent function through politico-religious structures. Anthropologist Brian Morris (1994: 192–9) examined these structures in major cultural systems, finding commonalities about the concept of Self. Its function is determining social boundaries. In anthropology such descriptions tend towards opposites: Western, 'I-based' egocentric models and Eastern, group-oriented, socio-centric. Morris argues against this dichotomy, showing negotiation of social presence of Self occurs at four main boundaries: individual, material, social and spiritual.

None of these have a universal form in which they occur. Many archetypes interact to create social presence. Morris does not argue against the existence of archetypes (by their nature, unseeable) but for the plurality of archetypal images – as 'doing words' verbs, forming verbal nouns, gerunds, '. . . ing' words: like 'mothering', from mother archetype. We usually think of religion and politics as nouns. Governance is a many-sided archetype. Trickster, balancing the creative drive for Rebirth with the, often destructive, drive of the Shadow.

## The transcendent function in the social world

In Chapter 3 I introduced the metaphor of luminous and non-luminous presence and absence. Stephen Joseph (1997), the

Californian analyst who wrote about these mirroring abilities in the psyche, gave us two concepts which can describe how 'Spirit in matter' might appear. Luminous presence – an Angel, Moses and the burning bush, illumination like St. Paul on the road to Damascus: luminous absence – the pain of doubt, the dark night of the Soul: non-luminous presence – the receptive silence of meditation: non-luminous absence – a Zen Koan – 'what is the sound of one hand clapping?' Or, to use the concepts on political acts: luminous presence? NATO bombs on Kosovo: non-luminous absence? The depression of the thirties: non-luminous presence? The disappeared in Argentina: luminous absence? The holocaust, Hiroshima, Nagasaki.

There is nothing man-made as luminous as an atom bomb (full of Plutonium – named after Hades, King of the Dead). Perhaps it's been necessary for us to recognise our inter-dependence by facing our collective shadow, weapons of mass destruction? Perhaps only by seeing religion (and its social corollary, ethics) as equal partner with politics can this shadow be contained (Redfearn 1992b: 18–34).

Jung's approach to governance, arising from his fascination with Gnosticism, was pluralist. Central to his argument with the Jesuit scholar, Father Victor White (*CW* 11: paras 449–67) was Jung's take on the tragic conflict between Man and God spelt out in the Book of Job (*CW* 11: paras 553–758). In *Answer to Job*, Jung suggests the conflict between God and the Tempter mirrors the conflict between Self and ego: God is to Self as Self is to ego (McKenna 2000: 173–90).

Western and Eastern value systems differ on Spirit's location: Westerners struggle for ego differentiation from God in order to return thanks to God, Easterners struggle to surrender ego into Self. Jung didn't doubt that negotiation between them was essential for our survival, but was doubtful if it was possible to 'switch' from one to the other (*CW* 11: para. 768). During his life, his preoccupation with religion became political. He first addressed this from within, creating images of Self in mandalas, seeing Self as a repeating form, a 'group within a group'. For individuation to occur in relation to a matrix of politico-religious myths requires discrimination of meaning. This allows involvement, the act of an individual Self 'religioning and politicking', in a collective.

The archetype of governance, holds, contains and cannot answer open questions. It may offer certainty in the face of doubt, or doubt in place of certainty. It is a paradox. Religious (or political) arousal, a collective expression of the numinous, provides cultures with 'myth based' signifying systems. In such systems the two economic laws of supply and demand and diminishing returns describe value attribution and the movement of ideas in a society. In the next chapter, I look at how we hold these paradoxes of meaning together.

# 12

# THE ART OF MEANING

Ged sighed sometimes, but he did not complain. He saw that in this dusty and fathomless matter of learning the true name of each place, thing and being, the power he wanted lay like a jewel at the bottom of a dry well. For magic consists in this, the true naming of a thing. So Kurremkarmerruk had said to them, once, their first night in the Tower. He never repeated it, but Ged did not forget his words.

'Many a Mage of great power', he had said, 'has spent his whole life to find out the name of one single thing – one single lost or hidden name. And still the lists are not finished. Nor will they be, till the world's end.'
(Ursula Le Guin, *A Wizard of Earthsea*, 1968: 59)

## Names and magic

In Le Guin's fairy-tale, Sparrowhawk, a young apprentice magician, accidentally releases a nameless Shadow from the Land of the Dead during a fierce magical competition. In it, he defeats Jasper, a fair-haired Court-reared snob, whom the copper-skinned goatherd Sparrowhawk imagines envies his skill. The Shadow almost kills him. He's badly scarred, but recovers. His hero-quest is to find the Shadow and name it. A dragon promises to tell him the Shadow's name in exchange for its life, but Sparrowhawk refuses this easy way out. After many adventures, on a Night Sea Journey, he confronts the Shadow over the Ocean and names it with his own, true name – Ged.

His story is an allegory of analysis. It also involves a magical duel with the snobbish, proud and envious parts of psyche ... till we meet our Shadow on a Night Sea Journey and name it with our true name – our Self. Jung said Shadow is everything we believe we are not, our unrealised potential for good or for ill. If we imagine ourselves as 'good' the shadow hides in our murderous sub-personalities, if we were 'shadow children' (conceiving badly of

237

ourselves because we failed as narcissistic objects for our parents) 'shadow' is the good in us. Ego experiences Self as Shadow: unrealised potential. Self can experience ego as Shadow too, blocking potential, preventing Self-actualisation. Shadow is a moral problem, highly resistant to change as it is usually only experienced in unconscious projection:

> While some traits peculiar to the shadow can be recognised without too much difficulty as one's own personal qualities, in this case both insight and goodwill are unavailing because the cause of the emotion appears to lie, beyond any possibility of doubt, in the other person. No matter how obvious it may be to the neutral observer that it is a matter of projections, there is little hope that the subject will perceive this himself. He must be convinced that he throws a very long Shadow before he is willing to withdraw his emotionally-toned projections from the objects.
>
> (*CW* 9ii: para. 16)

Shadow is a closed or closing psychic system, a set of emotions which *have* us, rather than a set of feelings which we have. When we're possessed by it, its meaning remains opaque, and purposes become circular, closed systems. Yet Shadow is an essential part of Self. From a Buddhist perspective, Self is a *function* giving a transcendent coherence to existence, yet, on a human level, there is a perilous tendency to make Self into something more – more permanent, more essential – a *thing* rather than a process, a form rather than a function. The more ego reifies Self, the more it turns into Shadow.

Self, like a child, learns through play, as conscious negotiates for meaning with the unconscious. This is a group process amongst a group of sub-personalities, and requires involvement in a group – as we are social organisms whose purposes include making meaning. Like magic, knowing the name of an object gives us power to negotiate with it, not to control it with our ego.

> The attribution of comprehension to consciousness leads to contradictions which are avoided by accepting, for purposes of the theory I wish to propound, Freud's later conceptualisation, 'but what part is there left to be played in our scheme of consciousness, which was once so omnipotent

and hid all else from view? Only that of a sense organ for the perception of psychic qualities.'

(Bion 1962: 2)

Ego comprehends meaning by sensing, feeling, valuing and naming objects. Self's qualities of coherence, continuity, agency and affective relationship permit object use. Each Self expresses its purpose, its karma, uniquely in the collective, naming Shadow, by shipwrecking on the Ocean of the unconscious, by, eventually, drowning in fate. Our capacity to do this, to let go into meaning, accepting meaning comes from Self, rather than as an ego-drive, reflects our psychological type. To experience the magic of being our Selves is to be free to name and use our own objects, our expressions of archetypal qualities: to enjoy our type, be who we are, rather than who we are *supposed* to be – to create ourselves. But how can we create ourselves, how do we 'catch our shadow'?

## The ten Ox Herding Pictures

I'm going to use a Zen teaching story, the ten pictures by Master K'uo Shih'yuan drawn in the twelfth century, to illustrate an Eastern approach to this dialogue between Shadow and Self (Hisamatsu 1994: 509–20). Then I'll place this in the context of Jung's dialogue with Master Hisamatsu, to demonstrate a cultural meaning disorder – a failure of naming between East and West. The problem centres round the meaning of the word Self. When this word is misunderstood, the whole meaning-making process aborts, with disastrous consequences. The ten pictures describe awakening to Self.

First is 'seeking the ox'. The original commentary says, 'turning away from awakening, becoming estranged': paths become entangled, 'the two forks of gain and loss, right and wrong pop up like sword points'. The ego loses sight of the reality of its shadow, which, at the beginning of life, is Self, as unrealised potential. Second, 'seeing traces'; footprints of our ox appear as we gradually awaken to the unconscious. Third, 'seeing the ox'; at first we catch only a glimpse of its tail, its fundament. We see Self as shadow till we realise shadow is Self. We need it, as we are *dependent* on it. Fourth, 'getting hold of the ox', requires all our might. Unless we pull with it, grab Self by the tail and hold tight, we lose all our ego-strength. Fifth, comes 'herding the ox'; we manage to get a rope round its neck. We form an ego-Self axis. But

239

still the question remains, who is herding whom? Can trust be established?

Sixth, 'astride the ox returning home'; the rope is removed, trust established, the man relaxes and plays his flute. He becomes creative. Of the seventh picture, 'forgetting the ox, remaining the man', the commentary says 'A *dharma* is not two *dharmas*': man and ox are not two, but one. There was no duality between ego and Self in the beginning, but if the authentic Self is lost, part of it yet seeks the whole. Ego is a 'temporary expedient'. Eighth, 'man and ox both forgotten'. The picture is a completely empty circle – a swift brush-stroke which is a symbol of the Zen mind. There is no man, there is no Buddha. The distinction between man and ox, ego and Self is irrelevant. There is not-Self. At this point, ideas of transcendence, transcendent functions and 'ego-Self axes' are seen for what they are – fictions. There's nothing to transcend anymore, there never was anything to transcend anyway.

There is no duality, no Hegelian thesis, antithesis, synthesis. No opposites. Not fusion, but reunion. The commentary says 'feelings of ordinariness fall away, all ideas of holiness empty'. This is 'the jewel in the lotus' – no matter what happens, this experience is indestructible, as it is no-thing. Hence follows, non-action. This is not idling, for, as Hisamatsu said, 'Calmly abiding in non-action means, wherever we are, without losing our Self, everywhere and anywhere we arrive will be our mountains of home. Here we have what we call freedom.' The ninth picture, 'returning to the phenomena', is reinvolvement in the world, back where we started, with the ox. This is individuation, not-Self and Self at the same time, a paradox. In the tenth picture, 'entering the market place open handed', we go into our village, our community; '. . . we re-enter society, create the historical world and let man awaken to their authentic self. In short, this is compassion and love in a very profound sense.'

Which speaks to us? Western imagery of Night Sea Journey or Eastern imagery of herding the ox? Unfortunately, Jung did not know this series of pictures, nor did he understand the Eastern concept of Self. In my view, unfortunately for the East–West dialogue, he thought he did. His dialogue with Shin'ichi Hisamatsu, Professor at Kyoto University took place in Kusnacht and centred on the 'mind vs. no-mind' (self vs. not-Self) question. As the translator Daniel Meckel makes clear, different versions were recorded by Hisamatsu's translator and Jung's secretary Aniela Jaffe (Meckel and Moore 1992: 101–27), reflecting their views of the meaning-exchange, or lack of it.

The conversation is like the ox-herding pictures – seeking the ox, the two men immediately got down to 'fundament' – Jung wanted to know what Hisamatsu understood by 'psychology'. Jung made a distinction between philosophy and psychology (logical operator {either/or}), Hisamatsu countered with 'Zen is a religion and a philosophy' (logical operator, {both/and/either/or}). Reading the exchange is like following a chess game: a classic Western opening, 'try splitting to get closure on meaning', and a classic Eastern defence, 'pluralism', to prevent closure. They reached picture three – 'seeing its tail'. They did not spend enough time with pictures one and two.

From the transcript, the fault lay with Jung. I think the idea that suffering can 'just stop' was one his physician sub-personality couldn't bear: '. . . if there is no suffering then I have no role'. Hisamatsu told him that when we awaken to our Original Self, there can be no such thing as suffering. Things are as they are. To a Swiss Reform protestant, the idea that justification by works, the fundament of the Calvinist heresy, is not so much nonsense as completely meaningless, is a slap in the face. Jung had been striving to get away from his father's belief system his whole life – he was dedicated to *the struggle*, rather like, as a communist's kid, I might have become 'dedicated to the class war'. Now he's told there is no struggle: like telling a rebellious communist child there is no 'class war'. Here is another example:

Last year, two young Traveller friends of mine met a 'Jesus Soldier' at Glastonbury Festival. The boys' 'tribe' are eco-warriors; festivals are where they rest up, meet up, share skills and information, and plan campaigns. So, the Jesus soldier met two young eco-warriors, and he challenged them, 'Are you kids Saved?'
'From what?' said Yurt (nick-named after his home).
'From sin!' the Jesus Soldier thundered.
'What's that?', ten-year-old Yurt innocently asked, having never heard the word.
The Evangelist turned to Sky, named after the sky he was born under. 'Jesus loves you!' he announced.
'Cool,' said Sky. 'Love is free! I am a Pagan and the Earth is my mother!' And to prove it, he sang a Pagan hymn from Sabbat school.

Jung and the Jesus Soldier, like the road builders against whom the boys' tribe protest, have a cultural meaning disorder: premature closure of a threatened meaning-system. We are not supposed to challenge their orthodoxy. Unlike the man and the ox, Hisamatsu, or

Yurt and Sky, they can only play with meaning if they get to make the rules: 'It's my ball and I want to play football!' Hisamatsu had the last word, 'The true Self has no form and no substance. Therefore the true Self can never be bound by a myriad of things. Liberation, the essence of religious freedom, rests on this point . . . my earlier statement, that Zen is a philosophy and a religion at the same time, derives from this.'

If this is hard to see, then try this. Reread the section, but delete the word Self and substitute the words 'meaning-making function'. Place this in the context of Jung's dialogue with Master Hisamatsu, to demonstrate a cultural meaning disorder – a failure of naming between East and West. The problem centres round the meaning of the words 'meaning-making function'. When these word are misunderstood, the whole meaning-making process aborts, with disastrous consequences. The ten pictures describe awakening to 'meaning-making function'. We are replacing a thing with a concept.

## Creativity and freedom

Jung's typology gave structural models for different aspects of the meaning-making function (the artist formerly known as Self). After enlightenment (analysis), perceptual functions are more acute (sense), we understand better what percepts mean as values (feel), we learn how to reflect on value changing over time (think), and, a hidden fourth, learn to respond to the gestalt {percept–value–reflection} all at once (intuit). Psychological types are like mountain tracks merging into each other (sensation becomes feeling becomes thought becomes intuition becomes . . .). Naturally, we prefer certain paths over others. However, no path is better than another, they are simply different. Earlier, I discussed the consequences of being a child of one type in a family when the parents' types are different, and, crucially, tending to close. Analytical psychology can never say to anyone, 'This is your type so this is your meaning and purpose', any more than a music teacher could say, 'Only play this instrument, and this tune, and play it like this', to a pupil. We have to interpret typology in our own unique, creative way.

To create means to bring into being out of nothing, by force of imagination. It involves an interplay between archetypes: parental archetypes provide a safe space; child archetypes play; trickstery archetypes operate when 'free play' is difficult; rebirth archetypes bring about renewal (*CW* 9i: para. 205) – and Shadow holds unlived potential. Creativity changes the quality of meaning in body, mind and spirit. In creative process there are subjective transformations: in creative acts our ego-persona feels diminished – we get lost in the process, which Jung (after Janet) called *abaissment du niveau mental*, a diminution of consciousness.

Following which, personality enlarges as we discover we can create meaning in new ways. This is not ego-inflation, nor grandiosity: rather, the opposite; because with creativity comes an increased awareness of shadow. We can destroy what we make, and we have an ethical responsibility for our creations. I'm thinking of nuclear scientist Richard Oppenheimer's shock on seeing the detonation of his splendid creation, the first atom bomb: quoting the Bhagavad Gita he said, 'Behold, I am become death, the destroyer of worlds.'

Creativity changes internal structures. It may release an over-identification with persona, or cause over-identification with the shadow, an inflation which 'blows ego away' like an atom bomb as opposites collide (Redfearn 1992b: 82–3). This changes our relation to the collective: we may identify with a particular group who have had similar transforming experiences through *participation mystique*, unconsciously sharing identity, or we may identify with a creative culture hero (a 'Star'). In terms of the development of meaning-making capacity, it is not what is created that matters, rather it is the act of creating meaning, as this requires an engagement with the collective unconscious.

Analytical psychology makes a vital contribution to freedom, by validating pluralistic approaches to meaning and purpose. In Chapter 1, I suggest three sciences help us understand meaning and purpose in changing systems. Cybernetics and ecology describe processes of negotiation for meaning *between* ego and Self and between Self and Society. Semiotics, the science of meaning, shows us how meaning is made. And there is a 'hidden fourth', governance: grounding meaning and purpose in social religio-political structures through involvement.

However, ego can't help from looking outside for a guarantee. The opening and closing meaning systems of analytical psychology (developmental and archetypal approaches) both permit holding fragmented parts of a psyche, which lets us accept the continuing process of change and becoming. Analytical concepts are used by feminists, holistic therapists, liberation theologians, the Green movement: giving the 'new age' tools to test meaning and purpose, creating a political impact that is just beginning to have effect.

To see how naming, giving meaning, is a key to individuation, we needed to understand consciousness (a prerequisite), explore 'autistic' as a word for parts of the psyche which can't engage in meaning-making, and deconstruct the reification of the concepts 'ego and Self'. Individuation is an unfolding of 'Self-as-purpose' (will, or volition): my clinical examples showed how dependency is a volitional disorder. In meaning disorders, whether bodily, primary or social, we can't *will* our own purpose. Michael Fordham (1976) suggested the opening of Self begins at, or before, birth. It is about awareness, free choice:

> personality is not controllable by the conscious mind, which is only part and not even the centre of an inner psychic reality. At first this fact is only vaguely appreciated by the ego, which yet, slowly, gives up its illusions of dominance. As that happens, the archetypal images, laden with effect, come more and more into the field of consciousness: if ego relates to these adequately, a development begins and progresses in a fairly regular way, which can be described in terms of a sequence culminating in the emergence of symbols . . .
>
> (1985: 35)

Freedom (liberty, unbound, not arbitrarily governed) is an act of will, creating symbols, which, as they are indefinables, raise unanswerable, open questions about purpose. Freedom comes through being able to form, name and use internal self-objects, to attribute meaning and have meaning culturally validated. Contemporary analytical psychologists don't see individuation as elitist, for the concept 'individual' has no meaning outside of 'collective'. A baby can't exist without mother, nor mothering without a 'tribe'. Large systems shape, hold and contain the small (see Erikson 1977: 102–49, on child rearing amongst Plains Native Americans). Individuation occurs in a social context (*CW* 6: paras 757–62), develops personality, pre-supposing and requiring collective relations.

Attribution of meaning negotiates for identity between infant and mother, individual and society, by determining locus of control. The naming process is central to object relations theory. To misquote the 'fifties hit song, *It's not what you name, it's the way that you name it.* Self and ego are loci of control between which meanings emerge – concepts, without neuro-physiological correlates. The concepts name two sides of a fluent boundary between time-bound and time-free experience (Chapter 7). The heuristic, 'borderline/narcissistic' personality names 'strange effects' at this boundary. Individual or collective psychopathology is evidence of primary or secondary meaning disorder, occurring when consciousness and reality-testing are impaired.

## The Night Sea Journey again

The metaphor, 'Ocean as collective unconscious, boat as ego and individuation as the Night Sea Journey', can be used to show the centrality of the teleological, purposive perspective in analytical psychology. Jung described it as an *opus contra naturam*, a work against nature. There are psychological dangers during the journey: inflation, depression, psychotic illness, premature death. Night sea journeys (like dreams) shift consciousness, freeing movement of information between psyche and society as we name shadow as Self. The present move in the world from domination by paternalistic, colony-rich Western society, the product of a generation of 'absent fathers' (the First and Second World Wars) is not a move back to matriarchy, but a move forward to 'person-archy' – 'democracy'.

> But, insofar as political aims and the State are to claim precedence, psychotherapy would inevitably become the instrument of a particular political system, and it is to its aims that people would have to be educated, and at the same time seduced from their own highest destiny.
>
> (*CW* 16: para. 223)

Insight into meaning and purpose provides a helpful critique of this change, as negotiation at boundaries is easier when the boundaries are seen clearly. Problems arise if therapies (of individual or society) rely on suggestion – or a power cult of 'the great leader': propaganda is also a form of 'guided imagery'.

A problem with the 'New age' is that too much of it is old, too much recapitulates the fin-de-siècle fascination with the occult. A second problem is naïveté: any unquestioning assumption that if it is alternative, then it must be 'better' than orthodoxy. This, once again, creates a closed, authoritarian system. Deconstructing masculinity to produce 'wishy-washy new age men' is no advance, it's a regression, an abdication of the hero-quest (Samuels 1995: 103–5, 177–9).

Richard Noll did useful work here on links between a 'volkish' (nineteenth-century trippy-hippie) attitude, and the Jungian gatherings at Ascona. Problems arose from using this logical operator: {belief without science} means 'any thing can signify anything else'.

This is a lazy way of construing experience, in part arising from a perambulation around the Self – all foreplay and no intercourse, no release into orgasm or creativity. We could coin the word 'mandalized' to describe this attitude – getting so lost in symbol-formation and meaning-making that we forget the activity is supposed to have a social purpose. Lacking involvement, it is a form of primary meaning disorder – narcissism.

Imagine young Narcissus, forever in love with his beautiful body but yet never in it. He'd forever imagine the result of his analysis but never *be* in analysis. This is a religious and political, as well as a personal, problem. If our religion and politics, or analytic theories, are not embodied, not lived, not involved, what use are they? They contribute nothing to freedom. Western religion has, likewise, tended to become disembodied. A 'New Age man' attempting soft-edged masculinity, denies the murderous, aggressive testosterone-fuelled rage and anger which makes men male. Feminism does not mean women have to behave like men, and masculinism does not mean men should behave like women, 'in touch with their sensitive inner feminine'.

The medieval habit of mortification of the body, seeing 'the flesh' as the enemy, and sex as a source of guilt, rather than a healthy part of life as natural as breathing, laid a narcissistic emphasis on 'works' and made shame a definer of meaning in Christianity: 'Jesus saves', said the Jesus soldier, 'From what?' asked Yurt. There is a borderline emphasis on 'faith' – a habit of projectively identifying 'evil' into those who do not believe. A long-term result for Western society has been to create social patterns of dependency. Luigi Zoja (1989) made clear that for many young people a lack of validation, a lack of meaning through acceptance into 'the tribe' by a *rite de passage* reversed Marx's famous dictum, 'Religion is the opium of the people.' Now, 'Opium is the religion of the people.'

Narcissus bulbs are a natural narcotic, getting 'stoned' has a narcissistic time-stopping quality. Psychedelics, which time-slow, may bring us to the border of liminal, perhaps numinous, meaning-making – but they also bring paranoia, literally, 'being beside one's Self' (Jaffe 1970: 68–75). A healthy 'New age attitude' has, for the ego, the advantage of bringing 'body' in all its variations back into play as part of a search for meaning – with practical implications directly relevant to lifestyle. Popular culture is full of 'fights against . . .', whether it is cancer, heart disease or a 'war on drugs'. This is to treat a problem primarily related to an individual's own lack of individuation by using helicopters to bomb poppy fields. As William

Burroughs (1968) said in *The Naked Lunch*, 'You treat the junk pyramid by removing the junkie . . .'

So, do I mean we treat meaning disorders by 'removing the meaning . . .?' Yes, I do. Removing a compulsion to search after meaning and purpose, to 'convert' others to our meaning and purpose, allows the appreciation of meaning for its own sake, developing an aesthetics of meaning as well as a science. The archetypal analytical psychologist James Hillman sees analysis as a dependency culture in which unmet dependency needs rapidly become unmeetable dependency needs (Hillman and Ventura 1992). He does not think re-experiencing unmet, infantile dependency needs and renaming them of itself allows a change of purpose – something extra is required: the free act of creative imagination, the capacity of the Self to form and use symbols instead of making symbolic equations.

## Wisdom

My aim has been to show the central place the concepts of meaning and purpose have in analytical psychology. I examined the development of the skills necessary to perform meaning-making task. They are:

1   the formation of a 'stable enough' ego, a temporal reality-testing neural network, which depends on
2   adequate perceptual systems (sensations)
3   repeatably and reliably validated in terms of survival (feeling) allowing
4   reconstructive comparison (thought) and
5   predictive feedback (intuition)

This cybernetic system of feedback between four levels of mind, four perceptual modes, is designed to give maximum ecological adaptability. If I were a xeno-anthropologist, that is, an 'Alien' studying our species, I might ask, 'What is this species for?', as a human ecologist addresses other bio-systems. If we look at what man does, then one clearly defining characteristic which marks us out is our capacity to communicate, to make meaning.

I began this chapter with a fairy-tale, using magic as a mythologem for meaning. Meaning-making is a sleight of hand between primary and secondary process, occurring when we are not quite aware whether it is 'I' reading this text (engaging in here and now) or 'Self'. Through the creative reworking of myths, whether perceptual, personal, religious, political or the competing myths of analytic theory, Self navigates through life.

Semiotics is a mythological language of signs and symbols, an attempt at a mathematics of the transcendent function, which I used to name aspects of the meaning process. In his essay on the Tibetan book of liberation, Jung identified 'the mind' as 'the means of attaining the other shore'. He points to a connection between the transcendent function and the idea of the mind as Self. The symbol-forming function is a 'means of attaining the other shore', a means of transformation, an act of magic. And, as Kurremkarmerruk said, 'And still the lists are not finished. Nor will they be, till the world's end.' There is no end to meaning, no end to naming.

> Myths and fairy stories both answer the eternal questions: 'What is the world really like? How might I live my life in it? How can I truly be myself?' The answers given by myths are indefinite, for the fairy-tale is suggestive; their messages may imply solutions, but they never spell them out.
>
> (Bettelheim 1975: 45)

There can be no definitive conclusion to a book on 'meaning and purpose', as the two terms describe fluent, ever-changing forms. Although I used an epistemological and semiotic approach, I'd like to suggest that, rather than being forms of knowledge, these are forms of wisdom. The motto of the Royal College of Psychiatrists, is 'Let wisdom guide'. I found this of practical value at three o'clock in the morning when assessing acutely mentally disturbed people brought into hospital by the Police. It didn't matter what I 'knew': and, in fact, as a junior psychiatrist, that was precious little. What did matter was reaching a wise, compassionate decision. I believe knowledge of meaning and purpose is of no value whatever without the wisdom to use it well.

Wisdom might be defined as 'the ability to make right use of knowledge', or, in the words of the wise English author, John Cowper Powys:

> Wisdom, this miraculous talisman, of which all of us are privileged to steal a modicum before we die, is no logical *quod erat demonstrandum*. On the contrary it is made up of paradoxes and contradictions, of shifts, compromises, transformations, adaptations, adjustments, balancings, calculated blindness, artful avoidances, premeditated

foolishnesses, cultivated simplicities! It is made up of the suppressions of curiosity, of the suppressions of cleverness, of narrowings down, diggings in, bankings up, not to speak of a cautious, guarded, tentative, gingerly use of reason.

(1967: 158)

# BIBLIOGRAPHY AND
# REFERENCES

Abe, Masao (1992) 'The Self in Jung and Zen', in Meckel, Daniel and Moore, Robert L. *Self and Liberation*, Manwah NJ: Paulist Press.

Adams, Douglas (1979) *The Hitch-Hiker's Guide to the Galaxy*, London: Penguin.

Alexander, F. (1952) *Psychosomatic Medicine*, Norton: New York.

Alister, Ian and Hauke, Christopher (eds) (1998) *Contemporary Jungian Analysis: Post-Jungian Perspectives from the Society of Analytical Psychology*, London: Routledge.

Andersen, Hans Christian (ed. Amy Ehrlich) (1986) 'The Snow Queen', *The Walker Book of Fairytales*, London: Walker Books.

Assagioli, Roberto (1973) *Psychosynthesis*, London: Turnstone.

Astor, James (1998) *Michael Fordham: Innovations in Analytical Psychology*, London: Routledge.

Atwood, G. (1984) *Structures of Subjectivity: Explorations in Psychoanalytic Phenomenology*, Hillsdale, NJ: Analytic Press.

—— (1994) *The Intersubjective Perspective*, London: Jason Aronson.

—— and Stolorow, R. (1979) *Faces in a Cloud: Subjectivity in Personality Theory*, New York: Jason Aronson.

Attwood, Tony (1998) *Asperger's Syndrome*, London: Jessica Kingsley.

Axline, Virginia (1969) *Dibs: in Search of Self*, London: Pelican.

Ayer, A. J. (1956) *The Problem of Knowledge*, London: Pelican.

Aziz, Robert (1990) *C. G. Jung's Psychology of Religion and Synchronicity*, Albany NY: State University of New York Press.

Balint, Michael (1968) *The Basic Fault*, London: Routledge.

Barker, Eileen (1987) *Religious Cults*, London: HMSO.

Barthes, Roland (1972) *Mythologies*, London: Paladin.

Bateson, Gregory (1973) *Steps to an Ecology of Mind*, London: Paladin.

Bauby, Jean-Dominique (1997) *The Diving Bell and the Butterfly*, London: Fourth Estate.

Baum, L. Frank (1993) *The Wizard of Oz*, London: Wordsworth Editions.

Belloc, Hilaire (1974) *Cautionary Tales*, London: Duckworth.

Benedek, Lazlo (1953) *The Wild Ones*, Los Angeles: Columbia Pictures Ltd.

Bennett, Angela (1997) 'A view of the violence contained in chronic fatigue syndrome', *Journal of Analytical Psychology* 42,2: 237–52.

Berne, Eric (1964) *Games People Play*, London: Penguin.

Bertalaffy, L. von (1968) *General Systems Theory*, London: Academic Press.

Bettelheim, Bruno (1975) *The Uses of Enchantment*, London: Penguin.

Bion, Wilfred (1961) *Experiences in Groups*, London: Tavistock.

—— (1962) *Learning from Experience*, London: Tavistock.

—— (1990) *Brazilian Lectures*, London: Karnac.

—— (1993) *Second Thoughts*, London: Karnak, Maresfield Library.

Bird, Jonathan and Harrison, Glyn (1982) *Examination Notes in Psychiatry*, Bristol: Wright.

Blake, William (1977) *The Complete Poems*, London: Penguin.

Blakeslee, Thomas (1980) *The Right Brain*, London: Papermac.

Bly, Robert (1990) *Iron John*, Shaftesbury, Dorset: Element Books.

Bolton, Derek and Hill, Johnathan (1996) *Mind, Meaning and Mental Disorder*, Oxford: Oxford University Press.

Bovensiepen, Gustav (1988) 'Individuation in Childhood', in Sidoli, Mara and Davis, Miranda, *Jungian Child Psychotherapy*, London: Library of Analytical Psychology, Karnac.

Bowlby, John (1951) *Separation, Attachment and Loss*, (3 vols) London: Pelican.

Boyle, D. G. (1969) *A Student's Guide to Piaget*, Oxford: Pergamon Press.

Brandon, S., Boakes, J., Glaser, D. and Green, R. (1998) 'Recovered memories of childhood sexual abuse: implications for clinical practice', *British Journal of Psychiatry* 172: 296–308.

Breuer, Joseph and Freud, Sigmund (1895) (trans. A. A. Brill, 1937) *Studies in Hysteria*, Boston MA: Beacon Press.

Brown, George W. and Harris, Tirril (1978) *The Social Origins of Depression*, London: Tavistock.

Bullock, Alan and Trombley, Stephen (eds) (1999) *The New Fontana Dictionary of Modern Thought*, London: HarperCollins.

Burroughs, William (1968) *The Naked Lunch*, London: Corgi.

—— (1987) *The Western Lands*, London: Picador.

Campbell, Joseph (1974) *The Mythic Image*, Princeton, NJ: Princeton University Press, Bollingen Series C.

—— (1991) *The Flight of the Wild Gander*, London: Harper Perennial.

Camus, Albert (1970) *The Plague*, London: Penguin.

Canetti, Elias (1984) *Crowds and Power*, New York: Farrar, Strauss and Giroux.

Capra, Fritjof (1975) *The Tao of Physics*, London: Fontana.

Carroll, Jim (1997) *The Basketball Diaries*, London: Penguin.

Carroll, Lewis (1965) *The Annotated Alice: Alice in Wonderland and Alice Through the Looking Glass*, (ed. Martin Gardner) London: Penguin.

Carter, Rita (1999) *Mapping the Mind*, London: Seven Dials.

Casement, Ann (1995) 'A brief history of Jungian splits in the United Kingdom', *Journal of Analytical Psychology* 40,3: 327–42.

—— (ed.) (1998) *Post-Jungians Today*, London: Routledge.

Castaneda, Carlos (1968) *The Teachings of Don Juan: a Yaqi Way of Knowledge*, London: Penguin.

Chadwick, Nora (1970) *The Celts*, London: Pelican.

Chambers Dictionary (1993) London: Chambers.

Charlton, Randy (1997) 'Fictions of the internal object', *Journal of Analytical Psychology* 42,1: 81–99.

Chomsky, Noam (1972) *Language and Mind*, San Diego: Harcourt Brace.

Christopher, Elphis and Solomon, Hester (2000) *Jungian Thought in the Modern World*, London: Free Association Books.

Clay, John (1996) *R. D. Laing: a Divided Self*, London: Hodder and Stoughton.

Cobley, Paul, (ed.) *The Communication Theory Reader*, London: Routledge.

—— and Jansz, Litza (1997) *Semiotics for Beginners*, London: Icon.

Cohen, Jonathan (1962) *The Diversity of Meaning*, London: Methuen.

Coleman, Warren (2000) 'Models of the Self', in Solomon, Hester and Christopher, Elphis (eds) *Jungian Thought in the Modern World*, London: Free Association Books.

Condon, W. S. and Ogston, W. D. (1967) 'A segmentation of behaviour', *Journal of Psychiatric Research* 5: 221–35.

Corcoran, D. W. J. (1971) *Pattern Recognition*, London: Penguin.

Covington, Coline (1995) 'No story, no analysis? The role of narrative in interpretation', *Journal of Analytical Psychology* 40,3: 405–19.

Cowan, Lyn (1982) *Masochism: a Jungian View*, Dallas, TX: Spring.

Cowper Powys, John (1967) *Autobiography*, London: Picador.

Crowley, Aleisteir (1979) *The Magical Diaries of Aleisteir Crowley*, London: Neville Spearman.

Cummings, E. E. (1962) *Complete Poems 1904–1962*, (ed. George J. Firmage), London: W. W. Norton & Company.

Dahl, Roald (1990) *Charlie and the Chocolate Factory*, London: Puffin.

Darwin, Charles (1998) *The Voyage of the Beagle*, New York: The Modern Library.

Davidson, Donald (1984) *Inquiries into Truth and Interpretation*, Oxford: Oxford University Press.

Davies, Peter (1995) *Are We Alone? Implications for the Discovery of Extraterrestrial Life*, London: Penguin.

Davison, Gerald and Neale, John (1978) *Abnormal Psychology*, New York: John Wiley and Sons.

Dawes, G. S., Fox, H. E., Leduc B. M., Liggins G. C. and Richards, R. T. (1972) 'Respiratory movements and rapid eye movement sleep in the foetal lamb', *Journal of Physiology* 220: 119–43.

de Beauvoir, Simone (1989) 'Must we Burn Sade?', in de Sade, Marquis *The One Hundred and Twenty Days of Sodom*, London: Arena.

Dee, Nerys (1989) *The Dreamers Workbook*, Wellingborough: Aquarian Press.

Delaney, Frank (1986) *The Celts*, London: BBC Publications.

Derrida, Jaques (1996) 'Semiology and Grammatology; Interview with Julia Kristeva', in Cobley, Paul (ed.) *The Communication Theory Reader*, London: Routledge.

de Sade, Marquis (1989) *The One Hundred and Twenty Days of Sodom*, London: Arena.

Dick, Philip K. (1968) *Do Androids Dream of Electric Sheep?*, London: Grafton Books.

Dreifuss, Gustav (1989) 'The Analyst and Damaged Victims of Nazi Persecution', in Andrew Samuels (ed.) (1989b) *Psychopathology: Contemporary Jungian Perspectives*, London: Karnac.

Eco, Umberto (1976) *A Theory of Semiotics*, Bloomington and London: Indiana University Press.

Edelman, Gerald (1987) *Neural Darwinism*, New York: Basic Books.

—— (1989) *The Remembered Present: a Biological Theory of Consciousness*, New York: Basic Books.

—— (1993) *Bright Air, Brilliant Fire: on the Matter of the Mind*, London: Penguin.

Edinger, Edward (1962) 'The ego–Self axis', *Journal of Analytical Psychology* 5,1: 3–18.

Eliade, Mircea (1964) *Shamanism*, Princeton NJ: Bollingen Foundation.

Ellenberger, Henri (1970) *The Discovery of the Unconscious*, New York: Basic Books.

Ellison, Arthur (1988) *The Reality of the Paranormal*, London: Harrap.

Erikson, Eric (1968) *Identity, Youth and Crisis*, London: Faber and Faber.

—— (1977) *Childhood and Society*, London: Paladin.

Estes, Clarissa Pincola (1996) *Women Who Run with the Wolves*, London: Rider.

Fairbairn, Ronald (1952) *Psychoanalytic Studies of the Personality*, London: Routledge.

Fenwick, Peter and Fenwick, Elisabeth (1999) *The Hidden Door: Understanding and Controlling Your Dreams*, London: Headline.

Field, Nathan (1992) 'The therapeutic function of altered states', *Journal of Analytical Psychology* 37,2: 211–34.

Fiske, John (1990) *Introduction to Communication Studies*, London: Routledge.

Fordham, Michael (1976) *The Self and Autism*, Library of Analytical Psychology, vol. 3, London: Heinemann.

—— (1978) *Jungian Psychotherapy*, London: John Wiley and Sons.

—— (1981) 'Neumann and childhood', *Journal of Analytical Psychology* 26,2: 99–122.

—— (1985) *Explorations into the Self*, Library of Analytical Psychology, vol. 7, London: Academic Press.

Fordham, Michael (1995) (ed. Roger Hobdell) *Freud, Jung, Klein: the Fenceless Field*, London: Routledge.

Foucault, Michel (1965) *Madness and Civilisation*, Cambridge: Cambridge University Press.

Fowler, H. W. (1965) *A Dictionary of Modern English Usage* (second edition, revised by Sir Ernest Gowers), Oxford: Clarendon Press.

Frazer, Colin (1987) 'Social Psychology', in Gregory, Richard L. *The Oxford Companion to the Mind*, Oxford: Oxford University Press.

Frazer, J. T. (ed.) (1972) *The Study of Time*, Berlin: Springer Verlag.

—— (1981) *The Voices of Time*, Amherst MA: The University of Massachusetts Press.

Frege, Gottlob (1980) *Sense and Meaning*, (ed. P. T. Geach and M. Black) Oxford: Oxford University Press.

Freeman, John (1974) 'Introduction', in Jung, C. G., *Man and His Symbols*, London: Aldus Books.

Freud, Anna (1986) *The Ego and Mechanisms of Defence*, London: Hogarth Press.

Freud, S. (1898) *Sexuality in the Aetiology of the Neuroses*, *SE*, vol. 3.

—— (1917) *Mourning and Melancholia*, *SE*, vol. 2.

—— (1953–73) *Standard Edition of the Complete Psychological Works of Sigmund Freud*, *SE*, 24 vols (ed. and trans. James Strachey *et al.*). Except where indicated, references are by volume and paragraph number. London: Hogarth Press and the Institute of Psychoanalysis.

Fuller, Buckminster (1983) *Intuition*, San Louis Obispo, CA: Impact.

Gallant, Christine (1996) *Tabooed Jung*, London: Macmillan.

Garner, Alan (1997) *The Voice that Thunders*, London: Harvill.

Giddens, Anthony (1997) Quoted in 'Influences', Brasher, Steven, *The New Statesman* 126, 4319: 32.

Gilbert, W. S. and Sullivan, A. (1997) *The Complete Plays of William Gilbert and Arthur Sullivan*, London: W. W. Norton.

Giegerich, Wolfgang (1997) 'The dignity of thought: in defence of the phenomenon of philosophical thought', *Harvest* 43,1: 45–59.

Glasser, Mervyn (1986) 'Identification and its vissicitudes as observed in the perversions', *International Journal of Psycho-Analysis* 67: 9–17.

Gleick, James (1987) *Chaos*, London: Abacus.

Gordon, Rosemary (1978) *Dying and Creating*, Library of Analytical Psychology, vol. 4, London: Karnak.

—— (1993) *Bridges: Metaphor for Psychic Processes*, London: Karnak.

—— (1998) 'Individuation in the Age of Uncertainty', in Alister, Ian and Hauke, Christopher (eds) *Contemporary Jungian Analysis: Post-Jungian Perspectives from the Society of Analytical Psychology*, London: Routledge.

Greenhalgh, Paul (2000) *Art Nouveau, 1890–1914*, London: Victoria and Albert Museum.

Gregory, C. C. L. and Kohsen, Anita (1954) *Physical and Psychical Research: an Analysis of Belief*, Reigate, Surrey: The Omega Press.

Gregory, Richard L. (1987) *The Oxford Companion to the Mind*, Oxford: Oxford University Press.

Greenberg, Jay R. and Mitchell, Stephen A. (1983) *Object Relations in Psychoanalytic Theory*, Cambridge, MA: Harvard University Press.

Greimas, A. Julien (1987) *On Meaning: Selected Writings in Semiotic Theory*, London: Frances Pinter.

Groocock, Veronica (1998) 'The Swiss Dionysus: A review of "The Aryan Christ"', by Richard Noll, *Times Literary Supplement*, London: News International, 16 January.

Grotstein, James (1979) 'Who is the dreamer who dreams the dream and who is the dreamer who understands it?', *Contemporary Psychoanalysis* 15: 110–69.

Gunderson, John G. and Singer, Margaret T. (1975) 'Defining borderline patients: an overview', *American Journal of Psychiatry* 137,2: 1–9.

Guntrip, Harry (1971) *Psychoanalytic Theory, Therapy and the Self*, London: Maresfield Library.

Hall, James and Young-Eisendrath, Polly (1991) *Jung's Self Psychology*, New York: Guildford Press.

Halligan, Peter W., Bass, Christopher and Wade, Derick T. (2000) 'New approaches to conversion hysteria', *British Medical Journal* 320: 1488–9.

Hannah, Barbara (1991) *Jung: His Life and Work*, Boston MA: Shambhala.

Harding, Esther (1955) *Woman's Mysteries: Ancient and Modern*, London: Rider.

—— (1971) *The Way of All Women*, London: Rider.

Hauke, Christopher (1998) 'The Child: development, archetype and analytic practice', *San Francisco Jung Institute Library Journal* 15,1: 17–38.

Haynes, Jane and Shearer, Ann (eds) (1998) *Death of a Princess: Reflections from Jungian Analysts*, London: Harvest Books.

Hegel, G. W. F. (1807a) (ed. L. S. Stepelevitch) *Phenomenology of Mind*, London: Collier Macmillan 1990.

Hegel, G. W. F. (1807b) (trans. A. V. Miller) *Phenomenology of Spirit*, Oxford: Oxford University Press.

Henderson, Joseph (1984) *Cultural Attitudes in Psychological Perspective*, Toronto: Inner City Books.

Herman, Judith Lewis (1992) *Trauma and Recovery*, London: Basic Books and HarperCollins.

Hesse, Herman (1946) *The Glass Bead Game*, London: Penguin.

—— (1951) *Steppenwolf*, London: Penguin.

—— (1974) 'Inside and Outside', in *Stories of Five Decades*, London: Jonathan Cape.

Hillman, James (1979) *Puer Papers*, Dallas TX: Spring Publications.

—— (1983) *Archetypal Psychology*, Dallas TX: Spring Publications.

—— and Ventura, Michael (1992) *We've Had One Hundred Years of Psychotherapy and the World's Getting Worse*, New York: Harper San Francisco.

Hisamatsu, Shin'ichi (1994) (trans. Claudia Grimm, 2000) 'On the Ten

Ox Herding Pictures', in Hisamatsu, Shin'ichi chosakushu, vol. 6, Kyorokoshu Kyoto: Hozokan.

Hoebel, E. Adamson (1964) *The Cheyenne: Indians of the Great Plains*, London: Holt, Reinhardt and Winston.

Hoeg, Peter (1996) *Miss Smilla's Feeling for Snow*, London: Harvill.

Hoeller, Stephan (1982) *The Gnostic Jung and the Seven Sermons to the Dead*, Wheaton IL: Quest Books, The Theosophical Publishing House.

Hogenson, George B. (1983) *Jung's Struggle with Freud*, Wilmette IL: Chiron Publications.

Holland, P (1997) 'Coniunctio – in bodily and psychic modes: dissociation, devitalisation and integration in a case of chronic fatigue syndrome', *Journal of Analytical Psychology* 42,2: 217–36.

Honderitch, Ted (ed.) (1995) *The Oxford Companion to Philosophy*, Oxford: Oxford University Press.

Hopke, Robert (ed.) (1991) 'Synchronicity', in Schwartz-Salant, Nathan and Stein Murray (eds) *Liminality and Transitional Phenomena*, Wilmette IL: Chiron.

Horney, Karen (1946) *Our Inner Conflicts: a Constructive Theory of Neurosis*, London: Routledge.

Howe, Ellic (1972) *The Magicians of the Golden Dawn*, London: Routledge.

Hultberg, Peer (1989) 'Success, Retreat, Panic: Over-stimulation and Depressive Defence', in Samuels, Andrew (ed.) *Psychopathology: Contemporary Jungian Perspectives*, London: Karnac.

Huskinson, Lucy (2000) 'The relation of non-relation: the interaction of opposites, compensation and teleology in C. G. Jung's model of the psyche', *Harvest* 46,1: 7–25 (London: Analytical Psychology Club).

Huxley, Aldous (1968) *The Doors of Perception: Heaven and Hell*, London: Chatto and Windus.

Jackson, Murray (1979) Psychosomatic Medicine – the Mysterious Leap from the Psychic to the Somatic, London: Institute of Psychiatry.

Jacoby, Mario (1989) *Individuation and Narcissism*, London: Routledge.

—— (1994) *Shame and the Origins of Self Esteem*, London: Routledge.

Jaffe, Aniela (1970) (trans. R. F. C. Hull) *The Myth of Meaning in the Work of C. G. Jung*, London: Hodder and Stoughton.

Jaspers, K. (1959) (7th edn, trans. J. Hoenig and M. Hamilton) *General Psychopathology*, Manchester: Manchester University Press.

Jones, David (1994) *Innovative Therapies*, Milton Keynes: Open University Press.

Jones, R. M. (1978) *The New Psychology of Dreaming*, London: Pelican Books.

Joseph, Steven M. (1997) 'Presence and absence through the mirror of transference: a model of the transcendent function', *Journal of Analytical Psychology* 42,1: 139–56.

Jung, C. G. (1915) (trans. Beatrice Hinkle) *Psychology of the Unconscious*, London: Routledge and Kegan Paul.

—— (1936) 'Dream symbols of the individuation process': mimeographed transcript of the seminar held at Bailey Island, Maine, 20–25 September.

—— (1953–77) *Collected Works of C. G. Jung*, 20 vols (ed. Herbert Read, Michael Fordham and Gerhard Adler; trans. R. F. C. Hull). Except where indicated, references are by volume and paragraph number. London: Routledge; Princeton NJ: Princeton University Press.

—— (1989) (with Aniela Jaffe) *Memories, Dreams, Reflections*, London: Vintage Books.

Jung, Emma (1978) *Animus and Anima*, Dallas TX: Spring Publications.

Kalsched, Donald (1998) 'Archetypal Affect, Anxiety and Defence in Patients who have Suffered Early Trauma', in Casement, Ann (ed.) *Post Jungians Today*, London: Routledge.

Kant, Immanuel (1953) *Critique of Pure Reason*, London: Macmillan.

Kast, Verena (1996) 'The clinical use of fairy tales by a "classical" Jungian analyst', *The Psychoanalytic Review* 83,4: 509–25.

Kawai, Hayao (1995) *Dreams, Myths and Fairy Tales in Japan*, Einsiedeln, Switzerland: Daimon Verlag.

Kenny, Anthony (1963) *Action, Emotion and Will*, London: Routledge.

Kerenyi, Karl (1951) *The Gods of the Greeks*, London: Thames and Hudson.

—— (1976) *Hermes*, Dallas TX: Spring Publications.

Khong, Belinda and Thompson, Norman (1997) 'Jung and Taoism', *Harvest* 43,2: 86–105.

Kipling, Rudyard (1987) *The Just So Stories*, London: Puffin.

Kitamura, T. and Kumar, R. (1982) 'Time passes slowly for patients with depressive states', *Acta Psychiatrica Scandinavica* 65: 415–20.

Klein, Melanie (1975) *Envy and Gratitude*, London: The Hogarth Press.

—— (1985) *Love, Guilt and Reparation*, London: The Hogarth Press.

Knight, Christopher and Lomas, Robert (1997) *The Hiram Key: Pharaohs, Freemasons and the Discovery of the Secret Scrolls of Jesus*, London: Arrow.

Koestler, Arthur (1969) *The Act of Creation*, London: Pan.

Kohut, Heinz (1971) *The Analysis of the Self*, New York: International Universities Press.

Kopp, Sheldon (1978) *If You Meet Buddha on the Road, Kill Him!*, London: Sheldon Press.

Kubler-Ross, Elizabeth (1969) *On Death and Dying*, London: Tavistock.

Kugler, Paul (1997) 'Psychic Imaging: Building a Bridge between Subject and Object', in *The Cambridge Companion to Jung* (ed. Polly Young-Eisendrath and Terence Dawson) Cambridge: Cambridge University Press.

Kutek, Ann (2000) 'Jung and his Family, a Contemporary Paradigm', in Christopher, Elphis and Solomon, Hester (2000) *Jungian Thought in the Modern World*, London: Free Association Books.

Lambert, Kenneth (1981) *Analysis, Repair and Individuation*, London: Academic Press.

Lancelyn Green, Roger and Hooper, Walter (1974) *C. S. Lewis, a Biography*, London: Fount.

Langs, R. (1979) *The Therapeutic Environment*, New York: Jason Aronson.

Larousse (1989) *New Encyclopaedia of Mythology*, London: Hamlyn.

Lawrence, Gordon (1991) 'One from the void, formless infinite', London: *Free Associations* 22: 259–94.

Leach, Edmund (1974) *Levi-Strauss*, Glasgow: Fontana Modern Masters.

Ledermann, Rushi (1981) 'The robot personality in narcissistic disorder', *Journal of Analytical Psychology* 26,4: 329–44.

Le Doux, Joseph (1998) *The Emotional Brain*, London: Phoenix.

Le Guin, Ursula (1968) *A Wizard of Earthsea*, London: Penguin.

Le Shan, Lawrence (1974) *The Medium, the Mystic and the Physicist*, London: Turnstone.

Lewis, C. S. (1951) *The Lion, the Witch and the Wardrobe*, London: Puffin.

—— (1953) *The Silver Chair*, London: Puffin.

Lyons, John (1970) *Chomsky*, Glasgow: Fontana Modern Masters.

MacDougall, Joyce (1989) *Theatres of the Body*, London: Free Association Books.

Mace, Chris (ed.) (1999) *Heart and a Soul: the Therapeutic Face of Philosophy*, London: Routledge.

McKenna, Christopher (2000) 'Jung and Christianity – Wrestling with God', in Solomon, Hester and Christopher, Elphis (eds) *Jungian Thought in the Modern World*, London: Free Association Books.

MacLeod, George F. (1962) *We Shall Rebuild*, Glasgow: The Iona Community.

McNaughton, William (1971) *The Taoist Vision*, Ann Arbor MI: University of Michigan Press.

Madanes, Cloe (1981) *Strategic Family Therapy*, San Francisco: Jossey Bass.

Mailer, Norman (1968) *Miami and the Siege of Chicago*, London: Penguin.

Main, Roderick (1997) *Jung and Synchronicity*, London: Routledge.

Main, Thomas (1957) 'The ailment', *British Journal of Medical Psychology* 30,3: 129–45.

Malan, David (1982) *Individual Psychotherapy and the Science of Psychodynamics*, London: Butterworths.

Mansfield, Victor (1995) *Synchronicity, Science and Soul Making*, Chicago: Open Court.

Marx, Karl (1875) (ed. C. P. Dutt, 1938) *Criticism of the Gotha Program*, London: Lawrence and Wishart.

—— (1961a) *On Economics and Sociology*, London: Pelican.

—— (1961b) 'Kapital VA I pp. 82–84', in Bottomore, Tom and Rubel, Maximilien (eds) *Karl Marx*, London: Pelican.

Mathers, Dale and Ghodse, Hamid (1992) 'Cannabis and psychotic illness', *British Journal of Psychiatry* 161: 648–53.

—— (1994) 'Psychosynthesis', in Jones, David (ed.) *Innovative Therapies*, Buckingham: Open University Press.

—— (2000), 'Jung and Religion', in Solomon, Hester and Christopher, Elphis (eds) *Jungian Thought in the Modern World*, London: Free Association Books.

Mathew, Marilyn (1992) 'Stranded starfish', *Journal of the British Association of Psychotherapists* 23: 109–25.

Meckel, Daniel J. and Moore, Robert L. (eds) (1992) *Self and Liberation: the Jung/Buddhism Dialogue*, New York: The Paulist Press.

Meier, C. (1962) 'Psychosomatic medicine from a Jungian point of view', *Journal of Analytical Psychology* 8,2: 103–22.

Meredith, Patrick (1972) 'The Psychophysical Structure of Temporal Information', in, Frazer, J. T. (ed.) *The Study of Time*, Berlin: Springer Verlag.

Miller, Alice (1987) *The Drama of Being a Child*, London: Virago.

Miyuki, Mokusen, (1992) 'Self-realisation in the Ten Oxherding Pictures', in Meckel, Daniel J. and Moore, Robert L. (eds) *Self and Liberation: the Jung/Buddhism Dialogue*, New York: The Paulist Press.

Modell, Arnold (1990) *Other Times, Other Realities*, Cambridge MA: Harvard University Press.

—— (1993) *The Private Self*, Cambridge MA: Harvard University Press.

Molière, (1959) (trans. John Wood) *La Malade Imaginaire*, London: Penguin.

Money-Kyrle, Roger (1971) 'The aim of psychoanalysis', *International Journal of Psycho-Analysis* 52: 103–6.

Montaigne, Michel de (1958) (trans. J. C. Cohen) *Essays*, London: Penguin.

Moody, Raymond (1975) *Life after Life*, London: Bantam Books.

Moore, Norah (1975) 'The transcendent function and the forming ego', *Journal of Analytical Psychology* 20,2: 164–82.

Morgan, Helen (2000) 'The New Physics through a Jungian Perspective', in Christopher, Elphis and Solomon, Hester *Jungian Thought in the Modern World*, London: Free Association Books.

Morris, Brian (1994) *Anthropology of the Self*, London: Pluto Press.

Morrish, Ivor (1980) *The Dark Twin: a Study of Evil and Good*, Romford, Essex: L. N. Fowler and Co.

Morrison, Toni (1987) *Beloved*, London: Picador.

Murray Parkes, Colin, (1972) *Bereavement*, London: Pelican Books.

Nagy, Marilyn (1991) *Philosophical Issues in the Psychology of C. G. Jung*, Albany NY: State University of New York Press.

Neumann, Erich (1973) *The Child*, London: Karnac Books.

—— (1989) *The Origins and History of Consciousness*, London: Karnak.

Nietzsche, Friederich (1973) (trans. W. Kaufmann) *Beyond Good and Evil: Prelude to a Philosophy of the Future*, London: Penguin.

Noll, Richard (1996) *The Jung Cult*, London: Fontana.

—— (1997) *The Aryan Christ*, London: Fontana.

Ogden, C. K. and Richards, I. A. (1938) *The Meaning of Meaning*, London: Kegan Paul, Trench, Trubner.

Ogden, Thomas (1990) *The Matrix of the Mind*, Northvale NJ: Jason Aronson.

Opie, Iona and Opie, Peter (1982) *The Lore and Language of Schoolchildren*, London: Paladin.

Orbach, Israel (1988) *Children Who Don't Want to Live*, San Francisco: Jossey Bass.

Ornstein, Robert E. (1968) *On the Experience of Time*, London: Penguin.

Orwell, George (1949) *Nineteen Eighty Four*, London: Penguin.

Owen, David (1999) *Nietzsche, Politics and Modernity*, London: Sage.

Patrick, Mathew, Hobson, R. Peter, Castle, David, Howard, Robert and Maughan, Barbara (1994) 'Personality disorder and the mental representation of early social experience', *Development and Psychopathology* 6: 375–88.

Paykel, E. S., Myers J. K., Dienelt, M. N., Klerman, G. L., Lindenthal, J. J. and Pepper, M. P. (1969) 'Life events and depression: a controlled study', *Archives of General Psychiatry*, 21: 753–60.

Pereira, Sylvia (1986) *The Scapegoat Complex*, Toronto: Inner City Books.

Perls, Fritz (1951) *Gestalt Therapy: Excitement and Growth in the Human Personality*, London: Pelican.

Perry, John (1953) *The Self in Psychotic Process*, Dallas TX: Spring Publications.

Pincola-Estes, Clarissa (1992) *Women Who Run with the Wolves*, London: Rider.

Piontelli, Alessandro (1992) *From Fetus to Child*, London: Routledge.

Plato (1955) (trans. Desmond Lee) *The Republic*, London: Penguin.

Prince, Morton (1900) 'The development and genealogy of the Misses Beauchamp', London: *Proceedings of the Society for Psychical Research* 15: 466–83.

Pullman, Philip (1998) *Northern Lights*, London: Scholastic.

Quakers, The (1995) *Quaker Faith and Practice: the Book of Christian Discipline of the Yearly Meeting of the Religious Society of Friends in Britain*, London: The Yearly Meeting of the Religious Society of Friends.

Quenck, Alex T. and Quenck Naomi L. (1982) 'The Use of Psychological Typology in Analysis', in Stein, Murray (ed.) *Jungian Analysis*, London: Open Court.

Radin, Dean (1997) *The Conscious Universe*, London: HarperCollins.

—— (1997) Letter, *The Network Newsletter*, Gibliston, Fife: The Scientific and Medical Network.

Radin, Paul (1972) *The Trickster*, New York: Schocken Books.

Read, Herbert (1974) *Anarchy and Order*, London: Condor.

Redfearn, Joseph (1985) *My Self, My Many Selves*, London: Academic Press, Library of Analytical Psychology, vol. 6.

—— (1992a) 'Getting into the body', *Journal of the British Association of Psychotherapists* 23: 24–43.

—— (1992b) *The Exploding Self*, Wilmette IL: Chiron Publications.

—— (1994) 'Movements of the I in relation to the body image', *Journal of Analytical Psychology* 39,3: 311–30.

Roffwarg, Howard P., Muzio, Joseph N. and Dement, William C. (1966) 'Ontogenic development of the human sleep dream cycle', *Science* 152: 604–19.

Roob, Alexander (1997) *Alchemy and Mysticism*, Köln: Benedict Taschen Verlag.

Rushdie, Salman (1988) *The Satanic Verses*, London: Viking.

Russell, Bertrand (1961) *History of Western Philosophy*, London: Unwin.

Rustin, Michael (1991) *The Good Society and the Inner World*, London: Verso.

Rycroft, Charles (1981) *The Innocence of Dreams*, Oxford: Oxford University Press.

Samuels, Andrew (1985a) *Jung and the Post Jungians*, London: Routledge.

—— (1985b) *The Father: Contemporary Jungian Perspectives*, London: Free Association Press.

—— (1989a) *The Plural Psyche*, London: Routledge.

—— (1989b) *Psychopathology: Contemporary Jungian Perspectives*, London: Karnac.

—— (1992a) 'National psychology, national socialism, and analytical psychology: reflections on Jung and anti-semitism', *Journal of Analytical Psychology* 37,1: 3–28.

—— (1992b) 'Person and psyche', *Harvest* 38: 85–94.

—— (1993) *The Political Psyche*, London: Routledge.

—— (1996) 'Jung's return from banishment', *The Psychoanalytic Review* 83,4: 469–90.

—— , Shorter, Bani and Plaut, Fred (1986) *A Critical Dictionary of Jungian Analysis*, London: Routledge.

Sandner, Donald F. (1986) 'The Subjective Body in Clinical Practice', in Schwartz–Salant, Nathan, and Stein, Murray (eds) *The Body in Analysis*, Wilmette IL: Chiron Clinical Series.

—— and Beebe, John, (1982) 'Psychopathology and Analysis', in Stein, Murray (ed.) *Jungian Analysis*, London: Open Court.

Sayadaw, Ven. Mahasi (1971) *Practical Insight Meditation*, Kandy, Sri Lanka: Buddhist Publication Society.

Schopenhauer, Arthur (1970) *Essays and Aphorisms*, London: Penguin.

Schurmann, Franz, and Schell, Oliver (1968) *Imperial China*, London: Pelican.

Schwartz–Salant, Nathan (1982) *Narcissism and Character Transformation*, Toronto: Inner City Books.

—— (1989) *The Borderline Personality: Vision and Healing*, Wilmette IL: Chiron Publications.

—— and Stein, Murray (1986) (eds) *The Body in Analysis*, Wilmette IL: Chiron Clinical Series.

Scott, Ridley (1992) *Blade Runner: the Directors Cut*, Los Angeles: Time Warner Entertainment Ltd.

Segal, Hanna (1975) *Introduction to the Work of Melanie Klein*, London: The Hogarth Press.

Shakespeare, William (1963a) *The Tempest*, London: Signet Classics.

—— (1963b) *Macbeth*, London: Signet Classics.

Shamdasani, Sonu (1990) 'Jung, Flournoy, Myers and the mediums: somnambulist choreographies', paper read to the Analytical Psychology Society of Western New York, March 1990 (unpublished).

—— (1995) 'Memories, dreams, omissions', *Spring* 57: 113–41.

—— (1998) *Cult Fictions: C. G. Jung and the Founding of Analytical Psychology*, London: Routledge.

—— (1999) Personal communication.

Shapiro, E. (1975) 'The psychodynamics and developmental psychology of the borderline patient', *American Journal of Psychology* 135,11: 1305–14.

Shearer, Ann (ed.) (1998) *Death of a Princess*, London: Harvest Books.

Sheldrake, Rupert (1981) *A New Science of Life: the Hypothesis of Formative Causation*, London: Blond and Briggs.

Sidoli, Mara (1993) 'When the meaning gets lost in the body: psychosomatic disturbances as a failure of the transcendent function', *Journal of Analytical Psychology* 38,2: 175–91.

—— and Davies, Miranda (1988) *Jungian Child Psychotherapy*, London: Karnak Books, Library of Analytical Psychology, vol. 7.

Siegel, Daniel (1999) *The Developing Mind*, New York: The Guilford Press.

Siegelman, Ellen (1990) *Metaphor and Meaning in Psychotherapy*, New York: The Guilford Press.

Simon, Paul (1986) *Graceland*, Burbank CA: Warner Brothers Records.

Simpson, Michael (1997) 'A body with chronic fatigue syndrome as a battleground for the fight to separate from the mother', *Journal of Analytical Psychology* 42,2: 201–6.

—— Bennett, A. and Holland, P. (1997) 'Chronic fatigue syndrome/myalgic encephalomyelitis as a twentieth-century disease: analytic challenges', *Journal of Analytical Psychology* 42,2: 191–200.

Slavin, Malcolm and Kriegman, Daniel (1992) *The Adaptive Design of the Human Psyche*, New York: The Guilford Press.

Smith, Richard (1996) *The Wounded Jung*, Evanston IL: Northwestern University Press.

Solms, Mark (1997) 'What is consciousness?' *Journal of the American Psychoanalytic Association* 45,3: 681–703.

Solomon, Hester (1991) 'Archetypal psychology and object relations theory: history and commonalities', *Journal of Analytical Psychology* 36,3: 306–36.

—— (1994) 'The transcendent function and Hegel's dialectical vision', *Journal of Analytical Psychology* 39,1: 77–100.

Solomon, Hester and Christopher, Elphis (2000) *Jungian Thought in the Modern World*, London: Free Association books.

Stein, Leopold (1957) 'What is a symbol supposed to be?', *Journal of Analytical Psychology* 2,1: 73–84.

Stein, Murray (ed.) (1982) *Jungian Analysis*, London: Open Court.

—— (1996) *Practising Wholeness*, New York: Continuum.

—— and Moore, Robert L. (1987) *Jung's Challenge to Contemporary Religion*, Wilmette IL: Chiron Publications.

Stern, Daniel (1985) *The Interpersonal World of the Infant*, New York: Basic Books.

Stevens, Anthony (1982) *Archetype: a Natural History of the Self*, London: Routledge.

—— (1995) *Private Myths: Dreams and Dreaming*, London: Routledge.

Stewart, Ian (1989) *Does God play Dice? The New Mathematics of Chaos*, London: Penguin.

Suzuki, Daisetz T. (1997) *Zen and Japanese Culture*, (6th edn) Tokyo: Charles E. Tuttle Co.

Symington, Neville (1985) 'Phantasy effects that which represents', London: *International Journal of Psychoanalysis* 66: 349–57.

Taylor, Eugene (1996) 'The new Jung scholarship', *The Psychoanalytic Review* 83,4: 547–68.

Thatcher, R. W. and John, E. R. (1977) *Foundations of Cognitive Processes*, Hillsdale NJ: Hillsdale Press.

Tolkien, J. R. R. (1954) *Lord of the Rings*, London: George Allen and Unwin.

Tougas, Cecile T. (1996) 'Taking women philosophers seriously', *Harvest*, 42,2: 35–42.

Tuckett, David (1993) 'Fictions about patients', *International Journal of Psychoanalysis* 74,6: 1181–93.

Turco, Ronald (1997) *Closely Watched Shadows*, Wilsonville OR: Book Partners Inc.

Tustin, Frances (1981) *Autistic States in Children*, London: Routledge.

—— (1986) *Autistic Barriers in Neurotic Patients*, London: Karnac.

—— (1990) *The Protective Shell in Children and Adults*, London: Karnac.

Twain, Mark (1991) *The Adventures of Tom Sawyer and Huckleberry Finn*, London: Everyman.

Tyrrell, G. N. M. (1943) *Apparitions*, London: Duckworth.

Tysk, L. (1984) 'Time perception and affective disorders', *Perceptual and Motor Skills* 58: 455–64.

Ulanov, Ann (1982) 'Transference, Counter Transference: a Jungian Perspective', in Stein, Murray (ed.) *Jungian Analysis*, London: Open Court.

Ullman, Steven (1962) *Semantics: an Introduction to the Science of Meaning*, Oxford: Blackwell.

van Der Post, Laurens (1976) *Jung and the Story of our Time*, London: Penguin.

Vannoy Adams, Michael (1997) 'The Archetypal School', in Young-Eisendrath, Polly and Dawson, Terence (eds) *The Cambridge Companion to Jung*, Cambridge: Cambridge University Press.

Van Sant, Gus (1989) *My Own Private Idaho*, London: Faber and Faber.

Vesilind, Priit (2000) 'Albanians', *National Geographic* 197,2: 52–71.

Vitebsky, Piers (1995) *The Shaman*, London: Macmillan.

Voltaire (1975) *Candide, and Other Tales*, London: Everyman.

von Franz, Marie Louise (1981) 'Time and Synchronicity in Analytical Psychology', in Frazer, J. T. (ed.) *The Voices of Time*, Amherst MA: The University of Massachusetts Press.

—— (1987) *On Dreams and Death*, Boston MA: Shambhala.

Wachowsky, Andy and Wachowsky, Larry (1999) *The Matrix*, Los Angeles: Time Warner Entertainment Ltd.

Wallis Budge, E. A. (1967) *The Egyptian Book of the Dead: the Papyrus of Ani*, (translation and transliteration), New York: Dover Books.

Walsh, Kevin (1978) *Neuropsychology: a Clinical Approach*, London: Churchill Livingstone.

Wehr, Gerhard (1989) *The Illustrated Jung*, Boston MA: Shambhala.

Weiner, Norbert (1948) *Cybernetics*, New York: Academic Press.

Weiner, Yvette (1996) 'Chronos and kairos: two dimensions of time in the psychotherapeutic process', *Journal of the British Association of Psychotherapists* 30,1: 65–85.

Welles, Orson (1931) *Citizen Kane*, Los Angeles: Mercury Films.

Whitmont, Edward (1969) *The Symbolic Quest*, Princeton NJ: Princeton University Press.

—— (1982) 'Recent Influences on the Practice of Jungian Analysis', in Stein, Murray (ed.) *Jungian Analysis*, London: Open Court.

—— and Pereira, Sylvia (1989) *Dreams: a Portal to the Source*, London: Routledge.

Wilde, Oscar (1999) *The Complete Works of Oscar Wilde: Centennial Edition*, London: HarperCollins.

Williams, Donald Lee (1981) *Border Crossings: a Psychological Perspective on Carlos Castaneda's Path of Knowledge*, Toronto: Inner City Books.

Williams, Mary (1983) 'Deintegration and the transcendent function', *Journal of Analytical Psychology* 28,1: 65–6.

Winnicott, Donald (1971) *Playing and Reality*, London: Penguin.

—— (1984) *Through Paediatrics to Psychoanalysis*, London: Karnak.

—— (1989) (eds Clare Winnicott, Ray Shepherd and Madeleine Davis) *Psychoanalytic Explorations*, London: Karnak Books.

Wittgenstein, Ludwig (1961) (trans. D. F. Pears and B. F. McGuinness) *Tractatus Logico-Philosophicus*, London: Routledge and Kegan Paul.

World Health Organisation (1978) *Mental Disorders: Glossary and Guide to the Classification in Accordance with the Ninth Revision of the International Classification of Diseases*, Geneva: World Health Organisation.

Wyrick, R. A. and Wyrick, L. C. (1977) 'Time experience during depression', *Archives of General Psychiatry* 34: 1441–3.

Yorke, Vernon (1993) 'Boundaries, psychic structure and time', *Journal of Analytical Psychology*, 38,1: 57–64.

Young–Eisendrath, Polly (1996) *The Gifts of Suffering*, Reading MA: Addison Wesley.

—— (1997a) Personal communication.

—— (1997b) 'The self in analysis', *Journal of Analytical Psychology* 42,1: 157–67.

—— and Dawson, Terence (eds) (1997c) *The Cambridge Companion to Jung*, Cambridge: Cambridge University Press.

—— (1998) 'Contrasexuality and the Dialectic of Desire', in Casement, Ann (ed.) *Post Jungians Today*, London: Routledge.

—— (2000) *Women and Desire*, London: Piatkus.

Yu, Lu K'uan (1962) *Ch'an and Zen Teaching*, (series three), London: Rider.

Zabriskie, Beverley (1997) 'Thawing the "frozen accidents": the archetypal view in counter transference', *Journal of Analytical Psychology* 42,1: 25–41.

Zeller, Bernhard (1972) *Herman Hesse: the First Biography*, London: Peter Owen.

Zinkin, Louis (1987) 'The hologram as a model for analytical psychology', *Journal of Analytical Psychology*, 32,1: 1–22.

—— (1989) 'The grail and the group', *Journal of Analytical Psychology* 35,4: 371–83.

Zoja, Luigi (1989) *Drugs, Addiction and Initiation*, Boston MA: Sigo Press.

—— (1998) 'Analysis and Tragedy', in Casement, Ann (ed.) *Post Jungians Today*, London: Routledge.

# INDEX

Compiled by Judith Reading

As references to and quotations by Jung appear throughout the book, only the major references to him are indexed.